Aristocrats of the Spirit

PREVIOUS BOOKS BY EE HUNT

Sermon Struggles, the Seabury Press, 1982
Paris under Siege, 2005
Paris on Fire, 2007
A Death in Dallas, 2008
Terror on East 72nd Street, 2009
Terror on the Border, 2011
Terror in the City of Lights, 2013

Aristocrats of the Spirit

EE Hunt

(The Very Reverend Dr. Ernest E. Hunt III)

Library of Congress Control Number: 2015904626
ISBN: Hardcover   978-1-5035-5674-4
                 Softcover   978-1-5035-5675-1
                 eBook   978-1-5035-5676-8

Print information available on the last page.

Rev. date: 05/16/2015

To order additional copies of this book, contact:
Xlibris
1-888-795-4274
www.Xlibris.com
Orders@Xlibris.com
708629

CONTENTS

DEDICATION

I dedicate this book to all those whom I have known who I believe have been aristocrats of the spirit, and to my four grandchildren, who will be "aristocrats" someday: Jose, Thomas, Caroline, and Louisa.

INTRODUCTION

A M I WORTH anything? Is my life valuable in any way? Well, this book is an attempt to assure the reader that each life—no matter how long or how short—is of infinite value to God. One person who helped me with this question of worth was Merrill Hutchins and his teaching at the Episcopal Seminary of the Southwest in Austin, Texas, while I was a seminarian there from 1956 to 1959. Much older than many of us then, Hutchins was also a student himself and, at the same time, was asked to be a lecturer. That was when he introduced several of us to the thought of Nicholas Berdyaev. Earlier in his life, Hutchins had earned a doctorate in philosophy, at some point had also become an FBI agent, and then switched horses in midstream, so to speak, to become a Baptist missionary to South America. But that was not enough for this engaging, thoughtful person: he decided to become an Episcopal priest and thus entered the Episcopal Seminary of the Southwest on a course of study that would lead him to his goal. There was a problem, however. He had been diagnosed with a form of rapid-developing leukemia, and he did not know if he would graduate in time to be ordained.

As I have stated, Hutchins's professional experience before seminary prompted the faculty to invite him to teach classes in literature and philosophy. I attended his lectures, and that was where I heard him quote Nicholas Berdyaev. Who was he?

Berdyaev had been a professor of philosophy at the University of Moscow, Russia, before comrade Lenin thought him too risky as a free thinker to remain in his post so had him exiled in 1922. Berdyaev moved first to Germany, then eventually to France, consequently spending many years in the City of Lights, i.e., beautiful Paris. There he became well-known for his intellectual honesty, prolific writing, and frequent lecturing on current topics of philosophy as well as the meaning of history. However, he was also deeply religious and began an Institute of Ecumenical Studies, which continues to this day.

Through his whole life, he was a prodigious theological thinker, and in one of his books, *The Fate of Man in the Western World*, he wrote, "In a certain sense, every human soul has more meaning and value than the whole of history, with its empires, its wars and fading civilizations" (page 7).

As one can see, this kind of thought certainly placed him at odds with Lenin's belief in the dictatorship of the proletariat (the working class) and the overthrow of the bourgeois (or middle class).

Thoroughly imbued with the spirit of Berdyaev's thought, Merrill Hutchins once quoted this theological truism from Berdyaev, and I remember his words distinctly: "Neither the Proletariat of the East nor the Bourgeois of the West, but the Aristocracy of the Spirit."

I am sure that really irked Lenin and the Bolsheviks.

Included in this writing are short records of men and women of all faiths who influenced me at different times in my life. I consider each to be an aristocrat of the spirit because each was memorable in my early life, in more than fifty-five years of active ministry, and in retirement. The use of the word *aristocrat* has nothing to do, however, with the lineage of folks born to wealth or status, but just to those who influenced others in their own way for good, either the common good of society or for an enriched personal life.

These are people I have been related to or have met one way or another and in whom I admired their sense of decency or the way they endured their personal struggles. In my mind, Merrill Hutchins was himself an aristocrat of the spirit, but sadly, after he was ordained a deacon in the Episcopal Church, he soon died. He never made it to become fully ordained as a priest, which is normally six months or more or less later, but his impact has lasted on others, such as on me, without his own goal being realized. That is too often the case for many good people.

These aristocrats of the spirit are to me like uncanonized saints, similar to those who have made it by a common religious consensus into a non-Roman Catholic Church calendar, as ours is in the Episcopal Church. "Everyday" saints exist, and they don't have to be super Christians, super Jews, super Muslims, Buddhists, Hindus, or what have you. Indeed, *saints* was originally defined as all those who were simply "in Christ," regular church members and not the official ones later elevated beyond the everyday church person.

Since God is universal, there are many in whom his/her Spirit dwells, or from my perspective, the Spirit of Christ, even if they don't know it. Mahatma Gandhi would have become a Christian except for his personal encounter with apartheid in South Africa. As we know, Gandhi decided to remain Hindu to identify with his own people in India, yet he utilized the peaceful methodology of the One, who taught the beatitudes to help his country be free. In my mind, the Spirit of Christ definitely dwelt in him.

The reformer Martin Luther believed we should all be little "Christs" to each other, and in our day, theologian Marcus Borg, who had taught for years at Oregon State University, once wrote, "To belove Jesus means more than simply loving Jesus. It means to love *what* he loved." The aristocrats of the spirit in this account are those who I believe loved what Jesus loved, either in the way of their own faith background or sometimes without any reference to it.

You may ask, Can the Spirit of God dwell in those who don't acknowledge themselves as believers? Of course it can, and does. Who can limit God's influence? It is his world, and he is the Lord of history. It is said that the judgments of God are moral in time, so history has a moral timeline, even if we have to endure temporary meaninglessness or chaos, like those in the Holocaust. The madman Hitler made by World War I became the monster in World War II, a recent magazine asserted, but eventually the forces for good at high cost to themselves overcame him and his deadly influence.

Another factor in this account is the benefit of American religious pluralism, the gift the founding fathers left us through our separation of church and state. It's important to have diversity since human beings possess free choice, and at least in the United States, few will question someone who decides to change religious affiliation, except perhaps disappointed family members or friends. People of the United States are acclimated in general to a person living next door who is a member of a completely different faith or of none at all.

But one institution we retained from the English parochial system has been that all clergy in the country are entitled to marry people, and after signing the state or county license, the marriage is recorded legally. Yet I personally prefer the French law for performing marriage. The only legal marriage in France is carried out at the local mayor's office, and if one wants a blessing from a church, temple, or mosque, he or she can go there afterward for a second ceremony. It's the choice of the couple. There is a more complete separation of church and state in France since clergy have no legal right to marry anyone.

On a different but strangely similar level, many French people believe our religious pluralism is totally unnecessary and don't understand the plethora of denominations in the States. I was once asked by a Frenchman while dean of the American Cathedral in Paris, France, "Why do you have so many different churches in the US? Who needs them?" His background was defined by the fact that there were 50 million nominal Roman Catholics, 800,000 Reform Churches, 800,000 Jews, maybe 2 million Muslims, and a minor smattering of others.

I answered, "Well, there are many different church traditions in America, brought often to the States by immigrants in our last two hundred some odd years. There are also the spirit churches that rise up on the spot without a long tradition. But more or less, if you don't like your own church, you can attend another that suits you, regardless of denomination. Religious pluralism gives us a choice, while yours is more limited."

The church of the land in France is more or less the Roman Catholic Church, but while not well attended normally, many of its members are everyday saints in Paris. I came to know hundreds who helped the poor, the handicapped, or the mentally challenged. The Spirit of God has an influence through any of the varied systems of belief formed in different countries, or just in sensitive and caring souls.

For example, because his niece, a former nun, had been attending the American Cathedral with her American husband, her uncle, a devoted older Jesuit, whose ministry in India for forty years had paralleled that of Mother Teresa, asked if he could celebrate the Eucharist with us on one Sunday. I naturally agreed but was curious why he did not do so in one of many Roman Catholic Churches. I was told that he always used an Anglican church when he was not near one of his own in India, but more especially, he wanted to share the Eucharist with his niece. When I was next to him at the altar, I was humbled by him. I had a family and a nice deanery in which to live, and in contrast, he had been alone and faithful in India for the Lord. He was definitely an aristocrat of the spirit.

Even though I grew up in California, in a setting of our religious pluralism, I never took advantage of it while young by attending any church at all. I had no religious affiliation until I was baptized in the Episcopal Church while attending Stanford University.

All the people I mentioned in this book may not have been saints in the strict angelic sense, as we imagine from a statue with a halo over its head, but they practiced in their lives the saintly virtues of endurance, care for persons, and concern for the common good. I do not refer to their individual personality and its idiosyncrasies, however. I believe that Carl Jung understood that there is a dark side in us all. Remember the maxim of Queen Elizabeth I, who said, "I do not wish to open windows into men's souls," so I am an agnostic about the inner life of those I list in my account, but a believer that each one helped me or others. The totality of their inner human condition is beyond me. Only the good Lord knows their souls.

In any case, no one has ever said a "saint" would be easy to live with. My premise is that these folks in this record were important to me but not just because of some coincidental encounter. I ask, like many others, Are there any real coincidences in our short lives? Is there something deeper at work in life? I believe so. Author John Steinbeck, in his early days, was a member of St. Paul's Episcopal Church in Salinas, and sometime later in his life, he wisely wrote, "When two people meet, each one is changed by the other so you've got two new people."

Well, I believe I've been changed so much by others it isn't funny, but that is also how God's grace works. Who wants to stay the same? In any case, we don't.

Theodore Huebner Roethke, who some believe to be America's greatest poet and who was born in our Midwest and who was of German background, also wrote, "You learn by going where you have to go." I agree with this comment because I was changed through encounters with new geographical areas of the United States, as well as with other countries, different people and languages. I sometimes think I learned more from those adjustments than from formal education.

Nicholas Berdyaev also wrote in the *Dignity of Man* (quoted by Matthew Spinka, page 18, in his "Berdyaev and Origen: A Comparison") some words that apply to the people I remembered: "For everyone is responsible for everyone else (echoes of Dostoevsky): In the realm of the spirit there is no such thing as a self contained and isolated personality.

'True heavenly bliss is impossible for me if I isolate myself from the world-whole and care about myself only'"

In my opinion, these friends I have known were not solely self-centered, thinking of themselves alone. To be sure, I only got to know each of these everyday saints because I was related to them as family or because I ran across them in my own limited experience. I list them because I became aware of how much they cared or how much they endured in their own lives, and thus for me, each became a spiritual aristocrat. They prove to me how much life is worth and how much each of is needed in so many different ways.

CHAPTER ONE

Oakland and the Bay Area

EE HUNT JR.

WHEN TED HUNT was young, he liked to play baseball because he admired professional players; they were strong role models for him. He also loved model trains, and much later as an adult, as a member of the shipping department of the California Packing Corporation, he invented a system of identifying railway boxcars for the company, which was a vast improvement over the previous system. He won an award for that redesign and then other awards for similar projects. Ernest Edward Hunt Jr. was born April 17, 1908, in Oakland, California, son of Bud Hunt and Maria Augusta Dias-Mora Storch. He also had a younger sister, Maxine, both born while their father was still married to Maria. His father, Ernest Edward Hunt, was a well-known native Californian who was written up in the history of Alameda County as follows:

> [He] secured his education in the public schools of Fruitvale and when sixteen years of age, because of the death of his father, was compelled to take upon himself the support of the family consisting of his mother and seven children. For six years he worked for the water company, after which he engaged in the real estate business for two years. He then entered the office of the county assessor, where he was employed for ten years, after which he was appointed district manager for the

Woodmen of the World. For the past five years he has been district manager for the Mutual Benefit Health and Accident Association having supervision over Alameda, Contra Costa, Santa Clara, Santa Cruz, Monterey and San Benito counties. In this work he has been more than ordinarily successful and has built up the largest business in health and accident insurance in the northern part of the state, due to his energetic, persistent and progressive methods. . . . He is a member of all branches of masonry, also of the Elks, the Woodmen of the world, and the first secretary of the Native Sons of the Golden West, of which he was one of the organizers. . . . He is regarded as one of Oakland's worthy and dependable citizens.

Ted's father was born in May 1887 and died in June 1940. Ted's mother also had an interesting background. She was the granddaughter of pioneer mining expert J. B. Storch, who was born in 1834 in Bohemia, the Austrian Hungarian Empire, had graduated from the Imperial Mining Academy, and then took with him to the United States a discovery of a new leaching process that eventually interested His Honor John H. Boalt in San Francisco. He was consequently engaged as professor of mining engineering at Professor Carl Beck's Institution of Mining and Civil Engineering and became, over several years, director of many mining companies in California and Mexico. A biography of Mr. Storch can be found in the *State Resources and Mining Review* of 1893.

His wife, Julia, was Maria's grandmother, but after giving birth to her daughter, also named Julia, she died sometime before 1863. Mr. Storch consequently married Baroness Augusta von Wohsarzenitz in 1863.

Julia, JB's daughter by his first marriage, was the mother of Maria, who, after marrying Ignacio Diaz Mora in San Francisco, moved to his ranch in Copala, Sinaloa, Mexico. Born there in 1885, Maria later was confirmed in St. Joseph's Roman Catholic Church in Alameda, California, in 1901 through the influence of JB and Baroness Storch. However, in 1892, her mother, Julia, had died in Mexico, and Maria moved after the death of her mother to San Francisco, where her grandparents raised her. Her father had died in 1896.

Later, Maria lived on Storch family property in the Oakland Hills near the estate of Joaquin Miller, well-known writer, poet, and world traveler. She married Ernest Edward Hunt in May 1907, but they divorced in May 1920. She lived until December 1982.

Because of the divorce, Ted Hunt was forced to leave high school in the eleventh grade to help support his mother. He began managing personnel in various movie theaters in the general Oakland areas. Later he became a member of the shipping department of California Packing Corporation in the main office in San Francisco, remaining there until retirement. He was also a lifelong member of Masonry like his father.

Ted married Maselia Carter, born March 6, 1911, in Llwynypia, Glamorgan, Wales, who traveled from Wales with her family when she was twelve, eventually to Oakland. When Maselia finished high school, she was on her way to the University of California, but she declined to leave for Berkeley and married Ted Hunt instead. There is an extant photo of the two in the later 1920s looking happy, young, and attractive, standing next to a new touring car. Mrs. Hunt was considered a beautiful woman, resembling in her way Greer Garson, the well-known actress. Although shy from her teen years spent striving to adjust to a new culture, she had a coterie of female friends in Oakland. Unfortunately, she also had several visits to local hospitals for various operations, but the last one, a total hysterectomy, seemed to leave her lifeless and depressed most of the time. She was never the same afterward.

I was born May 23, 1934, and memories of my early days are still quite clear in my mind. One memory that was forged in me concerned a severe cough, not identified then as a virus, called the croup. It was attributed to the foggy weather of the Bay Area, which was thought to bother some children more than others. Yet it was a serious disease and brought many to the point of struggling for breath. In fact, my condition caused the doctor to visit our house often and prompted my mother to light a small burner next to my bed with some sort of dark liquid that smelled like kerosene. It was supposed to clear the throat so I could breathe, but my poor parents of this only child had to endure that strong medicinal odor in every room of the house for years. My mother was especially tolerant of the hospital-like fumes filling her home.

When I grew out of the condition, or my body adjusted to it, my dad took me to play sandlot baseball with family neighbors on weekends in empty schoolyards. Men, women, girls, and boys of all races played hardball, not in any organized Little League fashion, but with whomever showed up to play. Gradually, I became more physically capable, and in time, when an older teenager, I wound up as a catcher and outfielder at the semipro level. This was due to my father's comradeship and his helpful teaching of the sport, enhanced by a clever baseball card game he invented that we played together. He would cut out photos of ballplayers from the *Oakland Tribune* and paste them to cards, with batting averages on the back, and if I drew a good deck of players, I had a better chance to win a game. I got to know those players well.

Once, when I was a teenager, my father took me to an Oakland Oaks game in the Pacific Coast League, and I saw Casey Stengel coach, and Ernie Lombardi and Vince and Dominic DiMaggio play. I never forgot it. Much later, in the 1960s, my dad and I attended a San Francisco Giants game at Candlestick Park, and it was mind-boggling to watch Willie McCovey play first base and Willie Mays cover center field.

My dad loved music, and especially that of Ludwig van Beethoven, his symphonies and concertos we heard often on an LP or a 45 rpm player. Later in life, Ted played bridge in tournaments and won just about every time, becoming an honored master bridge player. He was also a philatelist and a professional one later in retirement. He knew by mail stamp collectors from all over the world, and he had a long list of interested and sometimes compulsive fellow philatelists. As a stamp trader, Ted would match their requests as best he could from every nation or historical period.

After my dad's stroke left him partially paralyzed, however, and unable to speak, he would often point with his good hand to the same desk where he had communicated with so many stamp-collecting friends, but he couldn't do anything other than merely point. After my mother, Maselia, died in 1957, my father remarried, but she too passed on, and then he married a wonderful woman, Georgia, who devoted her life to him. When he was well, they traveled together; and when he was ill, she nursed him. I wrote in my first published book by the Seabury Press, 1982, *Sermon Struggles*:

> My Dad had a near fatal stroke in 1974. He lost his
> ability to speak, to swallow, was incontinent, a tube in
> his stomach for most of those years, and spent his days
> in a rehabilitation center near the Bay area in California.

My devoutly Roman Catholic stepmother who almost kept a vigil by his side accompanied him when he was released to their home. He did relearn, or remember in some way, to recognize and communicate to people through facial expressions and gestures with his good left hand. He could watch television for a short time and he did learn to eat again until bouts of pneumonia, and his relatively immobile condition, began to weaken his heart. He had constant chocking spasms because of accumulation of fluid in his lungs and his inability to swallow. The end of his struggle was near, and my stepmother asked me to come to her aid, which I did for a week's visit in the midst of Lent.

The Hunt family can be traced back to pre-Revolution days in the colonies, with names like Tripp, Mott, and Fuller; some of whom arrived here in the seventhteen century, another who fought in the Revolutionary War, but this descendent, my father, died in March 1979. He was buried in a Roman Catholic cemetery in the same grave that Georgia had chosen for herself, and the two now lie together. My father enriched my life in many ways, and so I view him as an aristocrat of the spirit, a man who struggled all his life, first in the home of his mother, deciding to help support her, then in his job in San Francisco and in marriages, and finally at the very end, in his physical illness. I firmly believe that his struggles helped him prepare for that ultimate journey ahead for each of us.

WILLIAM THOMAS CARTER

In the late nineteenth century in South Wales, most labor could be found in or near a coal mine: not all, of course, but for many, it was the only opportunity. It was true for William Thomas Carter, born in Ystradyfodwg (don't try to pronounce it unless you are Welsh born), Pontypridd, Glamorgan, Wales in 1884. He began his career as a coal miner when only twelve years of age in one of those collieries, that is, in a deep dark coal pit. If you, by chance, have seen the Academy Award–winning film of 1940 *How Green Was My Valley*, then you would know something about the life most people lived in the Rhonda Valley during that time. For many, small row houses that lined up like cinder blocks with outhouses behind them or at the end of the road were standard living quarters near the entrance to a coal mine.

Yet after William Thomas married Bertha Mary Edmunds, he would live in a larger house, No. 1 Danygraig Terrace, on a hill overlooking those row houses. Bertha's father was a fireman, not a miner, a step above those who took flat, unprotected wooden platforms as elevators, down hundreds of feet into black denizens where pick and shovel were used to fill rail Dumpsters with heaps of coal. Young boys would be the ones to roll the coal-filled cars on tracks to a central pickup junction.

Mr. Edmunds's task was very important because one never knew when gas could be released by the constant probing of the walls of the pits, and fires had to be put out or managed so the miners could escape alive. William Thomas's father had died in such a disaster, and his mother had followed him in death from more natural causes. As an orphan, he was sent to live with his maternal grandmother, who, most likely, was saddened by her lonely life and took to the relief the Welsh often found in the bottle. One of the reasons Mr. Carter never drank a drop, unlike his fellow countrymen, was because of her excessive habit that led often to angry treatment of him.

Nevertheless, he did learn to play the foot-pumped organ, the piano, the oboe, the flute, and the violin like many of his countrymen who took to music and choral singing as if they were natural genetic gifts. Some also became actors, as most of us know. One contemporary actress was asked if she could sing for a part in a Hollywood musical, and she answered, "Why do you ask? I was born in Wales, where everybody can sing!" Of course, there were many who found their living in other professions, but I like to believe that most can sing, regardless.

William Thomas drove an ambulance for the priory of St. John of Jerusalem in World War 1, and after the war in 1924, he decided to leave Wales and its dirty mines. Before marriage, his wife, Bertha Mary, had decided in 1907, when she was eighteen, to leave for New York by herself and, disliking it, immediately returned to Wales. This time she agreed to travel again, along with daughter Maselia, aged twelve, and Bertha Mary's mother, Esther Morgan Edmunds, who was in her nineties. They boarded the ship *Aunsonia* from Southampton and landed in Halifax, Canada. There they stayed for a short time until immigrating to Detroit, Michigan, and then they arranged for a train trip across our rugged but often beautiful landscape, arriving on the West Coast after several days. Eventually, the four moved to the middle of California, that is, precisely Oakland, where some relatives of the surviving fourteen children of the grandmother lived. Once settled on East Twenty-Second Street, William Thomas, a devout Fabian Socialist, a true member of the proletariat, found a job at Montgomery Ward, where he worked until retirement, turning down any job advancement offered him because he did not want to be part of management.

Scotty, as he was called then by his fellow workers and neighbors because they could not distinguish a Welsh accent from a Scottish one, built a workshop next to his garage behind the house they owned and did woodworking as his hobby. His daughter, Maselia, married a local man, Ernest Edward Hunt Jr., my father. As a result of that union, I was born on May 23, 1934.

I respected my grandfather in many ways, particularly his musical and hand-tool talents. When I was boy, he built for me a small wooden pedal car from spare parts in his shop, a pool table in the empty garage (they never owned a car), and a Ping-Pong table that was fitted on its top. He and my grandmother were also hearty, tough people who had endured so much, not only in Wales, but also in the death of their only daughter. After my mother died at forty-six years of age, my dad remarried, so when times changed in Pop's neighborhood, my wife and I decided to move them to Salinas, California, near us, where I had my first job.

In Wales, my grandfather had been a member of his local chapel, either Wesleyan or Baptist, because chapels were spiritual sources of support for miners. The clergy of the chapels pressed for social change and were advocates of the miners' personal rights. William Thomas died at eighty years of age, but before that, he had agreed to be confirmed in one of the first Episcopal churches in North Salinas where I was vicar. He did it for me, I believe, overcoming his prejudice against the apparent landowning church in Wales, the Church of England. He had soon discovered that in America, that was not the case for a sister member of the Anglican Communion, the Episcopal Church. The Church of England in Wales became the native Church of Wales, but long after Pop's death.

At the age of eighty-six, my grandmother later died after we moved to Saint Louis, Missouri, in 1966. Both were interred near their daughter, Maselia, my mother, in Oakland.

My grandparents had a strong impact on me. I have never forgotten them. If anyone was an aristocrat of the spirit, it was this proletariat workingman, as well as my grandmother, who gave all they had to help my mother and father and, finally, their grandson and family.

ED TICOULAT

In Oakland, California, a young man had been stricken with polio but learned again to walk even with a limp. He was forced to give up his favorite sport, baseball. Polio was a devastating viral disease before the Salk vaccine was invented or widely used, and many men, women, and children were afflicted, crippled, or died. Some needed an iron lung in order to breathe to stay alive, while others, like Franklin Delano Roosevelt, wore heavy iron leg braces in order to walk. He would strap them on while in his wheelchair in order to stand up, giving his audience the impression that he was strong and capable enough to be president of the United States. But his case, and almost every polio victim, no matter how severe, meant a long path to rehabilitation, if at all. *In the Man He Became,* a book about the early FDR, James Tobin wrote (page 113), "And now he is a cripple—will he ever be anything else!" We know how Roosevelt overcame the limitations of polio, but I can only guess at the struggle Ed had with his paralysis. However, in his own way, he became much more than a cripple.

Polio has been literally wiped out since the introduction of the Salk vaccine, that is, until a recent outbreak occurred in war-torn Syria due to sanitation problems and malnutrition.

One reason I never learned to swim properly was because my mother, afraid of the virus, prevented me from using the high school public pool because it was supposedly a source for the spread of the disease. This was before the introduction of chlorine into the water. It was a proper fear since regular pool swimmers often came down with the disease then.

When Ed Ticoulat was a grown man and married, he often recalled those times when he enjoyed playing ball, but instead of feeling sorry for himself because he was crippled, he decided to help youngsters play ball themselves. He formed a team, which could be classified today as perhaps single A, not triple A, as in the farm system Branch Rickey, manager of the Brooklyn Dodgers, once joked was for all those players they grow in the farms like corn. This was after World War II through the early 1950s. Ed and his wife lived at that time in the Fruitvale section of Oakland (have you seen the film *Fruitvale Station*?). There were no subways then but a few remaining streetcars and many buses. He began talking to several neighborhood kids of all backgrounds about his idea of creating a team. It took quite a while, but in good time, he had a team of players.

Ed was about five feet eight inches tall, the same height as my father, whereas I had somehow reached six feet one, which made Ed seemed short. I recall that his wife was extremely attractive, or at least I thought so at my age then. She was taller than Ed, thin and shapely with raven hair and large blue eyes. Ed had an oblong face, and he wore a serious expression most of the time. His dark hair was full, and his voice had a musical element to it, not a singsong, but more of a pleasant cadence. He never got mad at us when we committed errors or mistakes in judgment, but merely insisted on showing us the right way the game should be played. I never remember his wife speaking, other than looking at us as if we were her own boys, and she seemed always to wear a smile.

Ed had somehow become acquainted with local baseball officials who managed the local Pacific Coast Baseball Team, the Oakland Oaks, and persuaded them to offer him their cast-off flannel uniforms for our use. The Oaks were the forerunners to the Big League teams that eventually moved west from the East Coast, encouraged by the same Branch Rickey, who had turned baseball on its heels by hiring the first black player, Jackie Robinson, another Californian.

Ed's wife and some mothers of the players changed the name on the uniforms from the Oaks to the Acorns, and we were proud to wear those every time we played, which were mostly on the weekends. The league we were in had often been nicknamed the Beer League because we played in city parks all over Oakland and Alameda wherever each had a regulation baseball diamond with bleachers for onlookers. I don't remember if anyone watching in the stands actually drank beer, but it was possible. Former well-known older professional players often integrated themselves into these local teams. I vividly remember my father recognized many of them, pointing them out to me. My dad loved baseball and, when I was younger, had created a card game for me using photos of player's pictures and statistics cut out from the sports sections of local newspapers.

I was so proud one time when I was in a game in Alameda and my dad and our neighbor Mr. Nick Pino, who was with him, watched me play. I had a great baseball day with three hits and a rare and difficult catch in the outfield, but that was due in many ways to my dad's support.

Ed was different in his coaching style than my former junior high baseball coach, who often got extremely angry when we made mistakes. I misjudged his pregame signals one time and hit a ball on my second swing instead of letting it go by, and he was so mad he threw me out of the game. Of course, hitting into a double play didn't help.

Yet I learned more personally from my Acorns coach, and not just baseball. Most of the time in the Bay Area, the weather included fog from the Pacific Ocean that seemingly rolled in the morning and then back again at night, hiding the last vestiges of sunlight. This day was bright and sunny, and one could see well at a distance, unlike the overhead shroud that usually routinely covered us. On this afternoon, I was in right field instead of in the role of the catcher behind the plate, which I played every other game. I recall a fellow outfielder, a Latino friend, who played next to me, who was so proud of his knife he carried. When the game slowed momentarily, he came over from center field to show me his knife—the kind with a button on the handle that made it slip in and out of its bright-blue carriage—and Ed saw him dawdling alongside me when he should have stood his position. When we ran in between innings to the dugout, the coach stopped us and challenged him, "What were you talking to Ernie about out there? Why didn't you stand your ground?"

Standing next to him, Juan muttered something I could hardly hear, trying to distract the coach from his moment of field inattention in the game. Ed already knew the kind of neighborhood the boy lived in and assumed that he was showing me something he was proud of.

"Was it that shiv you carry?"

The boy, now looking testy, didn't answer but frowned.

"Why don't you show it to me? I collect them."

Juan lightened up a bit and slowly removed it from his back pocket, handing it to Ed.

"Oh, that's a honey!" Still holding the stiletto, Ed looked into the boy's eyes and asked, "What do you need to play ball, Juan?"

"Uh, this glove, my bat, and of course, the ball—that's all."

"You don't need this, then, unless you think Ernie is a dangerous Pachuca punk, which he isn't. I'll keep it till the end of the game. It is a beauty, though. You can take it home with you then."

Juan smiled but never brought his knife to practice again. Ed didn't shame the boy, like my junior high coach did to me, but gently pointed out in his rhythmic voice that it was not needed in any game of baseball with friends. Ed Ticoulat was a diplomat who, I believe, influenced me to become like him in crises, as minor as that specific occasion was.

Ed was French in background and most likely Roman Catholic, and in my mind, he was a real representative of Berdyaev's definition of an aristocrat of the spirit. In any case, I was not a religious person in those days, unaffiliated with any denominational church, and pretty much ignorant of any faith. The only important pastime I knew aside from family and school then was baseball. Ed taught me much, especially the importance of team play.

JOAN WILDERBRANDS BACA

My parents moved from Twenty-Third Avenue in Oakland to be nearer my mother's Welsh parents, since the two, Mr. and Mrs. William Thomas Carter, never owned a car and needed transportation for everyday necessities. My own family settled on Twenty-Sixth Avenue near Foothill Boulevard, so when older, of legal age to drive, I often had an opportunity to drive my grandmother for groceries, as did my mother. When in 1948 I entered Fremont High School from Alexander Hamilton Junior High School, I would walk to the new school from Twenty-Sixth Avenue, about twenty-five blocks, or hop on the public transportation bus on Foothill Boulevard.

One person I remember at the new Fremont school was Joan Wilderbrands, even though I did not know her well. Perhaps I recall her because the two of us were chosen by our senior class to be "most likely to succeed." She won this honor because she was smart, inquisitive, friendly, attractive, and a high achiever in many ways. Yet we didn't stay in contact after graduation because both our lives headed in totally different directions.

Of late we have contacted each other by e-mail, enabling me to find out how much she has lived up to all those high Fremont expectations. It's a good thing to reconnect with one's background, especially as we grow older and reminisce. Sometimes we exclude from our conscious memory the circumstances of what happened when young because we become too involved with other struggles later in life. I had a real testing while at Stanford University and just after graduation. That dominated me for some time, but now I realize that at Fremont, my life really had its original turning point, even though I did not know it at the time.

Perhaps this was true for Joan also. She was born in Oakland a little after I was, October 1, 1934, and her brother followed seventeen months later, so she is the oldest sibling of the two. Her parents were solid role models, hardworking, and both finished high school. She wrote that they had many abilities that transcended limited economic opportunities, as so many who lived through the Great Depression did. Her maternal grandfather was a third-generation Californian whose father mined in the gold rush days with mining engineer and later US senator George Hearst, father of the famous William Randolph Hearst. She described her grandfather as a truly self-made man who began the May Transfer Company and had the means from agriculture investments to leave her mother upon his death enough funds to provide a college education at USC for both Joan and her brother, assisted by school scholarships.

In 1957, she graduated with a BA in political science after working part time in the office of the university's development office. In her last year, she took a course in Russian, which was pivotal for her in two major ways. First of all, that was when she met her husband, Albert, who already had two degrees in Latin from UCLA. Secondly, she waited to be married for a year in 1958 because studying Russian prompted her to apply for a year of intense study at the Russian Institute of Columbia University in New York City. I must confess that Joan's feat in conquering a foreign language has always been arduous for me, even though I can manage in Spanish and French.

Albert Baca completed his PhD in classics and eventually moved to the faculty of California State University at Northridge, where even today, he continues to teach when needed, and is professor emeritus. For thirty-six years, Joan has been connected with the Burbank United School District, and in her final examination to become a principal some years ago, she was asked, "What is your greatest weakness?"

She responded, "I care too much."

After leaving classroom teaching in 1969, she became an office district teacher, a math lab coordinator, an English second language coordinator and teacher, and finally the principal for a Title I school for poorer children of Burbank, which is 40 percent Hispanic, thirteen other languages, with sixty deaf and hard-of-hearing students. She worked for years with its teachers to improve the school and its buildings. Also, every four years since 1984, she and the students have celebrated the Olympics by inviting its actual medalists and athletes to speak at the Title School. Kathy Johnson, the captain of the 1984 gymnastic team, was one she remembered especially, but more so was Louis Zamperini, the youngest Olympic runner in the 1936 Olympics. A book named *Unbroken* was written about his heroic survival in World War II and a new movie, directed by actress Angelina Jolie, has been recently released. He recently died at ninety-four.

Joan and Albert have two children, Christopher and Timothy, both doing well as grown men who preferred not to be in the field of education, like the children of most clergy! Why is this often true? I suggest that the intensity demanded by these fields pushes offspring to other vocations for the sake of their own individualization.

After attending a language institute in Mexico, Joan decided, along with her husband, to expand their family by inviting a Mexican boy to live with them for two years, followed by a German boy for a year, and then his younger brother from Mexico for another year. A few years later, Joan and Albert hosted a Russian student who is now a doctor at Harvard. Other foster-type children followed, but then the two spent a year in Germany because Dr. Baca, who speaks eight languages, was a guest lecturer in classics at the University of Munster. There they met an East Indian physicist and spouse, who became longtime friends, as well as a German couple; the husband was then chair of American studies at the University of Berlin.

Joan retired in 2001 after forty-one years in the profession, but that was not the end by far. She redirected her energies to California State University at Northridge by lecturing and supervising students for the past thirteen years. She has tried to live out her life by this motto: "We pass through this life but once, so any good or kindness we can show to a fellow human being or a living creature, let me do it now as I will not pass this way again."

Joan shared that her background from both parents was Italian, Dutch, Mexican, Spanish, and Irish, fulfilling the great American pluralistic heritage that enriches us all! She also said that her parents were Roman Catholic and that she took her first communion when at USC, but she lost faith in her religious past because of its attitude toward women along with its dogma, which was too rigid for her.

Then she discovered All Saints Episcopal Church in Pasadena in 1995 with its more open views and has been attending ever since. Was it a coincidence that in 1995 she also took a trip alone to Tanzania with a group of eight on a safari that she described as a spiritual journey? She believes the trip helped her link in time to the beginnings of our common ancestry, added by her visiting Mary Leakey's excavation site in Laetoli where Plio-Pleistocene hominid footprints were discovered along with other fossils. As an aside, I am personally fascinated with our ancient human past even though I have only visited North Africa.

Her husband is the grandson of a Methodist minister in New Mexico but leans toward being agnostic, as she says, like many who had too much religion in their past. Maybe that is why this writer became an Episcopalian, and ordained, because I had no religious past to prejudice me against organized religion!

From Fremont High School in Oakland, California, our common alma mater in 1952, Joan has cared for others through education, along with her husband. Has she fulfilled the challenge of being "most likely to succeed"? It depends on how you determine success. I say that helping others is the true test, not just in accumulating personal wealth or Hollywood glamour for oneself. As René Dubos wrote, "Think globally, but act locally," these two have been international people who have spent their time and energy helping young people move forward from all backgrounds and many countries. The two embody what I consider to be aristocrats of the spirit.

KARL MORGAN BLOCK

When you met Karl Morgan Block, you never forgot him. He had a strong physical presence, that is, as a fairly large man, but he made you feel at home because an inner self that was kindly shone through him. There seemed no weak-mannered self-centeredness at his core, but rather an ability to strengthen you for yourself. And not just because he was the Episcopal bishop of California and his office was on top of Nob Hill across from Grace Cathedral. It surely was because you knew he was in charge while not dominating but encouraging you. He was there to help. And therefore he was liked, even loved, by many. Some thought he was indeed aristocratic, a clergyman of the old school, a father figure who didn't intimidate but inspired.

Young clergy looked up to him, but no more so than when he was officiating in the cathedral, which later contained a stained window honoring him. When I first met Bishop Block, I was a young Stanford student who aspired to become a seminarian. While waiting to see him for his approval, I was frightened, but after entering his office and as I talked to him, he calmed me down, asked me questions, and also gently probed my reasons for entering the church as a priest. All in all, he opened the opportunity for me to choose a profession with his guidance, especially since I had little or no experience in church life, having been raised without any denominational affiliation.

For example, he asked one time if I had been confirmed. I responded, "No, sir, but I have been baptized."

Then he replied, quite seriously but with a smile, "I think you better get that done first, before seminary!"

I certainly did that; he arranged for me to be confirmed about six months later in our church in Burlingame. To prepare, I attended classes taught by the rector of St. Matthew's, San Mateo, for six weeks and traveled from Stanford to the church so much that I burned out my 1937 Chevrolet my grandmother had given me when I entered Stanford.

Much earlier, that entrance to Stanford University began with an unforeseen letter that arrived in the mail at my Oakland home one day. It read simply that I had been accepted, which shocked me as well as my whole family. I couldn't believe it. I viewed that letter as a kind of miracle, probably now in this part of the twenty-first century, almost impossible. Somehow I had been accepted from Fremont public high school in Oakland. I guess being senior class president helped. Two of us, a boy and a girl (she far smarter than I had been), were elected "most likely to succeed," and with a high-enough scholastic average, plus recommendations, I was accepted. Perhaps even baseball helped.

Yet that path to meet Bishop Block took three long years, as I struggled at Stanford to find a vocation in life. I was assisted by my friends in Theta Xi fraternity, two of them remaining my closest friends over the years: Peter Dahl and Robert Lawrence. We three were in ROTC, although they were navy and I was army. We "bet the odds" about when the Korean War–like conflict would end, which made me think about the shortness of life and the horror of war.

Wrestling with my religionless life, I discovered a need to seek more than the obvious hope for success from graduation at Stanford. So I began taking religion classes. The first was Comparative Religions, which introduced me to Buddha, who left his riches behind as a prince when he leaped over the palace walls on his horse to find an answer to suffering under the Bo tree. Then a rabbi personally influenced me when I attended his Old Testament class, especially when he offered quotable gems like "If this be heresy, make the best of it" or "The oldest religion was not the prophets but prostitution" (referring to the ancient agricultural fertility cults).

I often chatted with him, and he inspired me, but then Presbyterian Alexander Miller's New Testament class had a similar effect. I learned that a saint, that is, Paul the apostle, had similar inner conflicts as I was experiencing about the human condition. To paraphrase him, "The good I want to do I don't do and the bad I don't want to do I do, who will deliver me from this body of death?"

Often I felt consumed by inner ethical conflicts between right and wrong, the good and the bad, and maybe even the ugly. Were those conflicts universal? I thought to myself, "My God, a saint of the church experienced them!" I started attending a local Episcopal Church and eventually was baptized. My girlfriend at the time, Mary, and the rector stood up for me. A Stanford Episcopal chaplain, Episcopal priest Robert Morse, also influenced me. He had an extroverted way of making students feel good about them.

Slowly the idea of what I desired to do with my life became clear. I wanted to be ordained. And the way for that to happen was to be interviewed by the bishop, as I have said. After he arranged confirmation, I went to see him again.

"Where do I attend seminary?" I asked.

He told me to leave the state to gain new experience. He suggested the new seminary in Austin, Texas, formed by Bishop John Hines of the Diocese of Texas, who blessed its creation and helped raise funds for it. So I eventually drove my newer 1947 Chevrolet there after my graduation from university and commissioning as an army officer.

Bishop Block was so well-known and respected in San Francisco that a popular novelist placed him in his book, naming him. I remember the scene from memory, and it was a burial site in a cemetery where the wife of a man who had dearly loved her and could not accept her loss was about to be interred. I remember reading that in the crowd of people by the grave, the man was visibly grieving.

When the bishop was about to say "Ashes to ashes, dust to dust," with his arm raised, his hand clenching dirt to cast onto the casket as the final act of her life on earth, the husband rushed up to the bishop. He attempted to grasp Bishop Block's arm to stop the final act, and the two wrestled for a brief moment, but the bishop won and the service was concluded with a blessing. The husband slid back into the crowd. Not only did the church have the last word on her human life, but also the man finally accepted closure.

Bishop Block also had a dramatic ending to his own life. He had concluded a service in the cathedral and began to falter, his heart failing, forcing him to leave by a side door to the sacristy. It was said that he asked another priest, "Would you continue, sir?" And then he died in the sacristy—that was a fitting end for a real aristocrat of the spirit.

CAROLYN MCCULLOUGH KEEN

At Stanford University in California, as noted already, I became interested in the Episcopal Church and met several lasting friends through a fellowship of Episcopal students. One such person was Carolyn McCullough, who was far more active in her church life than I was, having been already baptized and confirmed. I was the latecomer, playing catch-up and getting baptized at Holy Trinity Church, Menlo Park, where some of us were invited by the rector to gather. The other organization for Episcopal students was called the Canterbury group, and it was on campus.

Yet I wound up going on to seminary in Texas while other aspirants stayed nearer home. I remember, when contemplating a long drive to the seminary in Austin, I was invited by Carolyn to stay with her and her folks en route at her home in Riverside, California. Doing so shortened the trip considerably, since normally in those days I drove the whole distance in one fell swoop. One night of rest was indeed welcomed.

Once I was enrolled as a student in the Episcopal Seminary of the Southwest, I didn't see her again until later, although she did send me a box of cookies, which my friends and I rapidly demolished. I heard later that after Carolyn graduated from Stanford in 1958, she began teaching in her high school in Riverside for two years and then returned to Stanford for graduate school. While in graduate school, she taught freshman English on campus, and then when she finished her MA, she began teaching at De Anza College in 1962, where she has been for fifty-two years until her recent death.

In 1984, while still teaching at De Anza, Stanford invited her again to teach freshman English, and she did so for sixteen years while never leaving De Anza. Earlier she had met her husband, William David Keen, who was a teacher also and a coach, and they were married in 1962. The two had three children: Leslie Erin Keen (Runyon) was born in 1967; Christopher David Keen, born in 1969; and Stephen William Keen, born in 1970. Carolyn was proud that Leslie earned a BA at the University of California at Berkeley while Stephen earned his degree also at UC Berkeley and his teaching credential at Santa Clara University.

Carolyn joined St. Andrew's Episcopal Church, Saratoga, in 1970, where she served on the altar guild for about ten years. Her husband was confirmed there, as were all her children, both baptized and confirmed. She was also active on the board of St. Andrew's School, and she continued to attend that parish.

Into every life, there are moments of joy and, unfortunately, moments of despair, sometimes even of tragedy. While in a happy time of their lives, David and Carolyn visited us once in the summer in Onteora, New York, and we had a grand time together. David was a complement to Carolyn, a straight shooter, so to speak, an honest and a decent human being. Much later, we would see Carolyn when we attended reunions at Stanford, and on one specific occasion, Elsie and I met with her to help young Jose, my grandson, write essays. His father, who lived in California, joined us for dinner, where Carolyn committed herself to helping young Jose, who was having a difficult time understanding the analysis of a good essay in order to enter the University of California. Carolyn took on the task by e-mail, advising him, like so many others she had taught in fifty-two years.

Yet she has been bombarded by personal trials that would try the souls of many. Their son, Christopher, died at sixteen in September 1985, her husband died of a prolonged illness in April 1993, and her daughter, Leslie, who married and had a child, Molly, became depressed and attempted suicide, leaving her blind but alive. In November 1986, I quoted in a sermon for an Easter celebration of the Resurrection a few words from a letter she wrote me about her son's suicide.

It took nine months for her to write about this popular boy, who attended the high school where his father was a teacher, had fallen into a depression, taken drugs, was rejected by his girlfriend, and then after an argument with his parents, impulsively hanged himself in their suburban home two-car garage. She was able to give a homily at his funeral service, she writes, which was attended by seven hundred high school students, but she said in her letter what a waste as it was still a mystery to her. Yet she and her husband and remaining children have sought counseling help, have joined a survivor's group of parents who had similar experiences, and she describes how her church has supported them. In spite of their tragedy, they have set themselves on a path of resurrection, but not without tears or guilt.

I hoped it might help others. Widowed and living on the same street in the same house in Saratoga, Carolyn took Leslie, Molly, and her husband into her home, where she helped care for Molly and her daughter. Why do such things happen? "Bad things do happen to good people," as Rabbi Harold Kushner wrote in his popular and helpful book after the death of his son, Aaron.

I am sure that Carolyn had asked Kushner's question, "Why do bad things happen to good people?" often, and especially now that she has been informed by a team of doctors of her mostly inoperable cancer. Yet even in her home oral treatment by chemotherapy, however, she continued to teach and to care for her family.

Cancer is like evil, because it preys on weakness, especially an immune system worn down by worry or stress or genetic disposition or age, but evil, in its converse way, can also do the opposite. It can empower weak men and women who, as in Goethe's *Faust*, become subject to Mephistopheles's bargain for self-gain and control of others. Yet they lose their soul in the process.

This is not Carolyn. She was no victim of a bad bargain. In fact, she was the very opposite, resisting the temptation to downward spirals of despair, where evil can contaminate our soul and therefore ruin others near us. She persevered, but I know it was not easy.

Who is not subject to the vicissitudes of life? Suffering is universal, and everyone shares in it to some degree; but in spite of our personal suffering, as Nicholas Berdyaev wrote, "God is a God who suffers . . . God never inflicts pain: on the contrary, He suffers it." This is also the conclusion of theologian Jürgen Moltmann in his 1975 book *The Crucified God*, published in Germany after the Holocaust. He comes up with the same claim, citing the example of people like Elie Wiesel, who endured a concentration camp, to prove his point. I assume this was Carolyn's conclusion also.

On August 3, 2014, I received a notice by e-mail that Carolyn succumbed to her illness on August 2. Her oldest son, Stephen, wrote to say the following:

> Mom passed peacefully and at home this morning. She was comfortable and surrounded by good friends and family. There will be a memorial next week at St Andrew's Episcopal Church in Saratoga, California, and I will let you know all the details once the service is arranged.
>
> I would like to express my sincere gratitude to everyone who called, wrote, stopped by, offered help, ran errands, brought over a meal or even wished us well. I am humbled by the compassion and generosity of our friends and family. My mother was an excellent judge of character and this is reflected in the company she kept.

Carolyn, like many faithful people, was a child of hope, a citizen of the kingdom of God, and an aristocrat of the spirit as she endured so much to the end.

CHAPTER TWO

Texas

WILLIAM CLEBSCH

HAVE YOU EVER stripped a timing gear in a used 1947 Chevy in the middle of the Mojave Desert at night? Well, I did. It was about 10:00 PM in the fall of 1956 and pitch-black, but after a long wait, one lone station wagon stopped to pick me up. In it was a father of a sleeping family, and I asked him just to take me to the next open service station. We chatted for a bit, and not wanting to test his patience, I saw a well-lighted open garage in a town called Amboy, and he let me out. I walked over to the lighted garage, proceeded inside and noticed a large figure on a repair roller sled under a car, and asked for help. The largest woman in overalls I had ever met got up and asked, "What do you want, bud?" I told her what had happened, and she drove me in her pickup to my car.

Once there and after moving fully to the shoulder of the highway, she put the headlights on my car, since it was totally disabled and darkened, and investigated the problem, noticing that nothing worked. After poking around under the hood, she told me the verdict. I asked if she could fix it. She said no, but she would drive me to the next town that was large enough to have a garage with parts for the job. That was Needles, sixty miles ahead on Route 66, and for a dollar a mile, she took me there.

I left the car with the mechanic, who said he could repair it, and I went on a search, looking for a place to stay. It was Saturday night, and only a noisy flophouse was available. After a restless sleep, I went to claim the car. The man had just finished the repair and demanded

$150, but I only had $100 in cash. So I walked back to the heart of Needles and found an open Shell station, and after pleading with the manager for some cash from his till he could charge to my credit card, he said he would do so only after calling Los Angeles to make sure my card was valid. When he placed the receiver back in its cradle, he was still frowning, and I was worried.

But he finally looked at me in the eye, irritated still from being interrupted. Yet now I noticed a slight brightening in his brow, and he recanted, "Okay, I will give you cash on the card."

I thanked him profusely and scampered over to the repair garage, paid the repairman, returned to buy some gas on my card to placate him, and got out of town fast, hoping to reach Austin, Texas, as soon as possible.

That was the beginning to my seminary career, where, in due time, I met my wife, Elsie Beard, an undergraduate student at the University of Texas, through two dear friends, fellow seminarian Bob Tobin and Elsie's roommate, Maureen (later Tobin also), and struggled with the classes I disliked, like Greek, and enjoyed the ones like theology and history and cultural analysis of our time. Two professors stand out among the entire fine ones: William Clebsch and Paul van Buren.

When you attended Bill Clebsch's class in history or the mission of the church, you never knew what to expect. He had a caustic manner and did not suffer fools gladly. He often picked on students whom he thought had not paid enough attention to his wise words or whom he singled out for false piety, the cover-up in his mind for not doing homework.

Somehow we two got along, even to the point that Elsie and I were later asked on occasion to babysit his children. In any case, Bill was a straight shooter, in my mind, and he profoundly disliked what we would call politely B. S., particularly in the religion field. In due time, he wrote several important books, *From Sacred to Profane America* in 1964 and *American Religious Thought* in 1973, among several others. That book I read and reviewed because it dealt with American pragmatic religion from Puritan Jonathan Edwards to Ralph Waldo Emerson to William James. Bill also believed that religion professors did not have to be ordained, although he was until he decided to renounce his orders as a priest in 1969.

In 1958, he encouraged me to spend the summer under the auspices of the Overseas Mission Program, so I flew to Mexico City, and after an orientation seminar with others, Bill drove me to the end of the road at the small town of Nopala in Mexico. There I was to work with a local Episcopal priest who had four mission churches about 8,500 feet high and north of Mexico City. He dropped me off at 6:00 PM at night and, without delay, left me with my one bag, giving me instructions to greet on my own the Salinas family with whom I was to live.

Before I had a chance to do so, I was welcomed by Señora Salinas, the daughter of the first indigenous bishop of our church in Mexico. His predecessors had been temporary bishops who lived over the border in the Diocese of Texas. They succeeded the one who had died when it was formed from the Roman Catholic Church by permission of President Benito Juarez. If you do not remember, Juarez was a reformer in the middle of the nineteenth century who had defeated and then executed Maximilian, finally ridding Mexico of foreign domination.

But it was Señora Salinas's young and attractive daughter whom I vividly recall, who, after saying hello, immediately jumped bareback on a horse and paraded around, asking if I could ride as well as she. I answered that I had never been on a horse. She looked at me as if I were a dunce, which in some ways I was.

After meeting the ultimate host, an Episcopal priest, a smiling and naturally cheerful Señor Moreno, he invited me to join him on his trips to his mission churches. We first used bicycles for the task. I smoked then, and at that altitude, I really labored and could not keep up with this jovial man. He took pity on me and one day announced, "We will ride horses instead." Well, that did not work out well either. Once I awkwardly got up on a horse that he provided, it ran away at my first tug of the tough Mexican bit in his mouth and only stopped when it became tired. Señor Moreno came to the rescue again.

He smiled as always and said, "Now we will have to use a car."

A car? Really? I thought that would be stylish, except when I saw a rusty old 1936 four-door Chevrolet that appeared magically from some local barn. I was appalled at its condition, particularly the way it was not equipped. It had no muffler, only a broken exhaust pipe that leaked clouds of exhaust that invaded the cabin of the car; no battery, so it had to be primed with a hand crank under the radiator each time it started; no lights, and very bad brakes. In addition, it did not favor high altitudes and often had vapor lock, that is, too much air in the mixture of gasoline in the carburetor.

But clever Señor Moreno arranged one time for a cheerful male wearing a large sombrero to sit on the fender beside the hood cover that was left open on one side of the engine. He carefully poured gasoline from a bottle into the carburetor every time the car began to falter and stall on a hill.

Another time, when we were coming back from a long day's visit to Maravillas and rapidly descending a hill, Señor Moreno announced, "The brakes are not working."

I saw him furiously pumping the pedal without any effect. We eventually bumped our way into a shallow ditch on the side of the road and abruptly stopped, a little shaken, to say the least. I asked, "What are we going to do now?"

He laughed in his cheerful way and proclaimed, "Don't worry, the horse will pull us out!"

That was my last adventure with the irascible Mexican horse, after having been introduced to one by Señora Salinas's daughter. She, however, remained my guide. She escorted me once on a long walk to see her doctor uncle's infirmary, and since it was a long up and down climb, we stopped on the way to rest at a little store. When I entered, some men standing at the counter inside saw me and instantly invited me to join them to drink tequila. Now, I had been told by my wise church advisors before my excursion into rural Mexico not to hurt anyone's feelings, nor to upset anyone, and to obey local customs.

"Just do as they do" was the command.

So I stepped up and choked down a round with them. My guide became furious. She immediately pulled me away, and when we were outside again, as we walked together, she balled me out, saying, "Those were *borrachos*. You do not drink with them,"

How was I to know what a drunk looked like if he appeared friendly, had a sombrero on like everyone else, and was seemingly polite? But she proved me a dunce again; that was for sure.

She and her mother, Señora Salinas, ran what was called an Internado, a project sponsored by our church that housed twenty-five *muchachos* so that they could go to the new public school built by the government. We were not a parochial school, because all Roman Catholic religious schools had been banned by the government, but a simple housing arrangement. Yet the *anti*-Roman Catholic government at the time had given permission for a Sunday school class to be permitted. That was supposedly protestant and non-Roman Catholic.

While I was there, I remember that Bill Clebsch had told me that he would routinely check on me to see if I was still alive. I never saw him.

When finally on a planned break from my duties, I took a bus into the city that was overcrowded with too many people and, worse, squawking chickens and one little pig. When finally in Mexico City, I found him in his hotel holed up because he was very sick with a bad case of Montezuma's revenge. That was his reason for not traveling, and a good one. Unfortunately, the bug he contacted would last for years, but we hung out then and even saw a movie together, before I had to return to Señor Moreno's missions for the remaining summer.

At the end of the summer, I returned to Texas and, in time, met my fiancée, Elsie, and we were married. I had lost twenty pounds but quite able to appreciate all the wedding gifts laid out on a table in her parents' home. It looked to me then like Montezuma's treasure.

Bill later left the Seminary of the Southwest for the hallowed halls of Stanford University, where he became professor of religious studies in the humanities special program and also of American studies. He remained at Stanford until his death in his office of a heart attack in 1984. He had become chairman of so many organizations that I refrain from listing them, but in 1966, when asked by the vestry for a recommendation about me as the new vicar of St. Timothy's Church, Creve Coeur, West Saint Louis County, Missouri, he took time away from his busy life and unabashedly gave it to them.

Earlier in 1963 I ran into him personally again while I was earning an MA from Stanford, by taking some of his courses and being guided in my thesis by Presbyterian Robert MacAfee Brown. One day when I was in Bill's office, I never forgot a comment he made to me. I asked him about the resurrection of Jesus, which is a mystery but the overpowering cause of the birth of the Christian Church and a fundamental tenet of belief. He simply commented from his profound theological background, "*Well, something happened.*"

That comment never left me, uncluttered as it was by ecclesiastical wordage.

Like my mother, who was born in South Wales, Bill's father had been a hardworking German immigrant in Clarksville, Tennessee, where Bill was born. Later Dr. Clebsch earned many university degrees and numerous awards for teaching and administration. Edwin M. Cook wrote in Bill's Stanford obituary, "He was at his best with small groups of students, perhaps at his very best with one well prepared and eager student at a time. Eagerness of intellect made nothing so much fun for Bill as a good, hardheaded argument."

On the other hand, aside from his strong opinions, he and Betsy were very compassionate friends. For example, Elsie and I were heading back on the road from the bishop's ranch near Healdsburg, California, when Elizabeth became very ill. Nearing Palo Alto and desperate for some help, we detoured to the Clebsch home near Stanford University. We ran up to the door with little Ernest in hand, walking along with us, and Liz in my wife's arms, to ring the doorbell, unannounced. There were no cell phones then. Betsy Clebsch was surprised, of course, but answered sweetly and took us in.

Later in the day, Bill rode his familiar bicycle on campus from his university office to his home, and we were asked to stay for dinner until Liz totally recovered. Because of their help, we eventually left for our home in the Salinas Valley, encouraged that our daughter was better.

What is an aristocrat of the spirit? In my mind, it is one who takes seriously intellectual integrity, compassion one on one, and practices, as well as teaches, true, not false, religion.

PAUL VAN BUREN

Recently returned from Basil, Switzerland, Doctor of Theology Paul van Buren had received that honor under the guidance of the famous theologian Karl Barth. Almost immediately after his graduation and return to the States, Paul began teaching systematic theology in 1957 at the Seminary of the Southwest while I was a student. In van Buren's lectures, I heard and was forced to read of Karl Barth's dominating conservative viewpoint. After all, Paul had just spent several years in Basil and obviously admired him. Why? Because as I studied later, I learned that there had been a theological war going on in Germany before World War II between those who believed the primary revelation of God was through immanence versus transcendence, that is, was God revealed in nature, literature, current events, or only through

Scripture? However, it was not just Friedrich Schleiermacher's book *On Religion: Speeches to Its Cultured Despisers* that emphasized revelation from cultural sources that Barth vehemently opposed. It was also his view that Adolf Hitler had despicably demanded that loyalty to his Third Reich was more important than loyalty beyond him to God. This was the type of "immanence" Barth really opposed.

Barth was against any attempt to ally God with human dictators and their politics and had been responsible for drafting the Barmen Declaration of 1922, which became one of the founding documents of the Confessing Church of Pastor Dietrich Bonhoeffer, who was later hanged by the Nazis. The declaration opposed the accommodation of German churches to Hitler's rule later in the 1930s. So Barth was a hero in Paul van Buren's eyes, as Barth was to many of us much later.

Yet I did not personally appreciate any exclusive viewpoint that God had been only revealed to humanity through Scripture alone, and even Paul van Buren, I discovered, was to change his ideas in due time.

As students we heard lots of rumors about teachers, but one of them unfortunately proved to be true. Paul van Buren had been feeling ill, had gone to his doctor, and was told after tests that his internal organs were riddled with incurable cancer. He was extremely sick, but undaunted, Paul had driven faithfully to Houston once a week to receive Cobalt treatments, and then after the course of radiation ended, I heard no more. I had graduated, but I did know that he continued to teach regularly, until his move a few years later to Temple University.

Then his first book, *The Secular Meaning of the Gospel,* which was published in 1966, upheld in my mind a modified Barthian viewpoint. He wrote in it, "The man who says, 'Jesus is Lord,' is saying that the history of Jesus and of what happened on Easter has exercised a liberating effect on him, and that he has been so grasped by it that it has become the historical norm of his perspective on life."

Well, something happened to Paul in those days of continuous treatments in 1957 because he didn't die from inoperable cancer, as we all expected, but lived on until he was seventy-four years of age when the disease finally caught up with him. His intelligent and lovely wife, Ann, outlived him to 2008, but I am sure she would have agreed that was a long time to be in remission. Just think: that extended life allowed him to be busy, writing, teaching, and even becoming director of the Center of Ethics and Religious Pluralism at the Shalom Hartman Institute in

Jerusalem. His work on post-Holocaust Christianity became important after his modification of Barth's total reliance on revelation from the Word of God alone. He offered hope to secular men and women and enabled them to understand the faith better. In my mind, Paul became a bridge builder to the fullness of God rather than proponent of a single path to the deity for all.

We are all changed by the events that happen in our lives, as Paul van Buren proved. Perhaps his bout with cancer opened his appreciation for the diverse ways God does work in our lives. I do not know for sure. I can only speak of the grace of God I have received from the good and bad episodes of my life. They all count.

Much, much later, I was surprised to see him in church services twice in Paris, at the American Cathedral when I was dean (1992–2003). Just seeing him then, and renewing acquaintances after more than forty years, proved to me that God's grace is real, often unexpected, and can provide an opportunity for continued growth.

Paul was in my mind a true aristocrat of the spirit. Why? Because he endured hell from his untreatable cancer, overcame it in a way I do not understand, and lived long enough to accomplish much for those whom he hoped would fathom a better understanding of God's universal love.

LOUISE HUNTER BEARD

It was the custom at the time when I was a student in Austin, Texas, for a girl you dated to take you home on holidays. It was not some grand finale to a courtship, but just a nice thing to do, particularly for out-of-state students, as I was. It meant a family meal that was always welcome.

When I met this particular girl, she invited me home. I drove her to her place of residence only to encounter that her father and mother seemed to take an instant dislike to me. Why? Well, I believe they had better things in mind for their lovely only child than some poor seminarian from California, of all places, even though they were fellow Episcopalians. I remember the father taking me aside to his car and, after a long conversation, suggested that I was not good enough to date his little girl. He was probably right, but when I heard his concerns, I knew I had to break it off. I had learned the hard way in California through a broken relationship that one needed a blessing from parents for any serious relationship, so I stopped dating this Texas girl, never revealing to her the conversation I had with her dad. She was hurt, and maybe angry, but I had to do it, and I felt bad. I still do. I was young, and I didn't handle it very well, but I kept her father's confidence.

Then alone again, a friend, Robert Tobin, a seminarian as I was, introduced me to his girlfriend's best friend since childhood. Maureen's friend from Bryan, Texas, was Elsie Maryan Beard, who was also her sorority sister at the University of Texas. The campus was not far from the Episcopal seminary, so it was easy to ask Elsie out several times, getting her home faithfully before curfew, which, in those ancient days, was 11:00 PM. In due time, she also took me to her home in my old Chevy. The reception there was quite different than my prior experiences, and not just because the family was devout Methodist. Her mother, Louise Hunter Beard, literally met me at the door and welcomed me into the home. She liked seminarians, even one that was an Episcopalian.

Well, after all, John Wesley was a Church of England priest, and he and others started the reform movement in England called the Methodists, through which they rallied the urban poor, offering them something better than the gin taverns on Sundays. In the eighteenth century, rural folks had been brought in to the city factories in the early days of the bustling, but often inhuman, Industrial Revolution. They worked long shifts with their only day off a Sunday of gin to drown their sorrows.

John Wesley and his brother Charles, with John Newton, offered a more permanent hope through hymn singing and praise of God, which led to the self-empowerment of the impoverished. So our history has a common background. Yet in due time, the Methodists and the Episcopalians became separate entities in America. The Church of England continued as England's established church while the Episcopal Church in America remained a member of the Anglican Communion.

Louise had a good understanding of our common history, but she had grown up a Methodist, and that was the basis of her faith. I also met her husband, James B. Beard, since he was at home for lunch from his local business, and later he challenged me to go hunting with him. While I wanted to make a good impression, and I had fired an M1 rifle in ROTC at Stanford, I was not too confident about the .30/30-lever action rifle handed to me.

Notwithstanding, we went out into the wilds, lay on the ground in a prone position for at least an hour, waiting for a deer to show in an open glen ahead of us. None appeared. It was getting dark, so we stood and turned around to leave. There about fifty yards away was the largest buck I had ever seen. Mr. Beard told me to shoot, and I did, but of course, I missed it. Then he told me to shoot again, and the darned rifle jammed. The big-horned deer just sauntered away. I thought to myself, this was not an auspicious way to begin a friendship. Mr. Beard looked at me like the city boy I was, but said nothing. We drove home in his pickup, and when we arrived, he never said a word about my hunting inadequacies.

He was a gentleman. Jim had graduated from the same university his mother had before him, played football there, and later when he was one hundred years old, was honored for being the oldest surviving member of the 1929 team by an Austin newspaper and his University of Texas. Louise had attended Texas Christian University and TSCW, where she had been a music major.

Elsie and I were married in Austin on August 23, 1958, and her parents spent many happy times with us in the many different locations in which we lived. When Louise died at ninety-one in February 2002, I was invited to offer the homily at her burial, and I include it as follows:

On Being Welcomed

My oldest memory of Louise has always been of welcome. I met her for the first time at her front door, after her daughter Elsie, at the university, brought me home from the Episcopal Seminary in Austin over the Thanksgiving Day holidays. Louise greeted me warmly, which was not always the way seminarians were received by some families who wanted their daughters to have boyfriends with at least some potential, like business, engineering or law! Yet Louise and I talked about theology and the church, and I realized soon thereafter that I had a new friend, who appreciated what I had chosen to do with my life, and in time incorporated me into a new family.

Louise and Jim blessed us every step of the way, traveling first to rural California, then to suburban St Louis, New York City and state, back to Dallas, and finally to Paris, France. Whenever we went Louise would come, to be helpful with two new babies, Ernie and Elizabeth, and eve our grandchildren Jose and Thomas, or just to welcome a new area, church and church friends.

Louise did request that I say one thing for her at her burial, which is: "she loved the church since she was five years old." Now I know why she welcomed a wandering stranger to the family because she loved the church so much, and that commitment continued to bless us in all the many places Elsie and I had lived and served. And because she loved the church she also knew the meaning of Christ's love, its inclusive and accepting nature, its overcoming of grief, its endurance, its seeing into the heart of things, and it helping us to look for the best in others. Such love knows no boundaries as Louise knew so well. It only knows welcome, "I was a stranger and you welcomed me."

My son sent me an article concerning Halley's Comet that was from the *Wall Street Journal* of April 1986 in which she was quoted while on a trip to Australia. As she looked to the sky to see from that vast country the comet pass by, she told the reporter that while she was being delivered as a baby in Fort Worth, her brothers were sent out of the house to "go look for the comet." Then she commented: "I just hope I don't do a Mark Twain and come and go on a comet year." She didn't. She outlasted Halley, and now it's her turn to be welcomed by the greater heavenly host who will say, "Come, O blessed of thy Father, inherit the kingdom prepared for you from the foundation of the world."

Louise Hunter Beard was indeed an aristocrat of the spirit, who not only welcomed me into the family, but also welcomed ecumenicity between churches, supported churches in different areas of the country and in different lands, and embraced new life for others in general. Indeed, she out lasted Mark Twain's Halley's Comet's 75 years, perhaps because "she loved the church since she was 5 years old."

CHAPTER THREE

Salinas, California

JAMES ALBERT PIKE

I F THERE WAS one person who created conflicted opinions in others about his words and deeds, it was this Episcopal bishop: brilliant, controversial, often before his time, sometimes uncouth and seemingly off the wall, yet memorable in many ways. He graduated from Yale Law School and became a lawyer for the Securities and Exchange Commission in Washington, DC, then converted from Roman Catholicism to the Episcopal Church, and after a brief time in seminary, was ordained a priest. Professor C. F. "Molly" Molligan once publicly stated that the church became too awed with his background and his sudden desire to become ordained and suggested that he should have had a more prolonged theological grounding and introduction to our church.

However, he was very articulate and became a national figure almost overnight. While we forget so easily in this age of instant replay and thirty-second sound bites about our history, at one time, Jim Pike was one of America's most well-known personages. *Look* and *Time* magazines had him on their front cover, sometimes looking agitated, worried, misguided, while dressed in his clericals. But he made the headlines, one way or the other, when the Episcopal Church had a more positive presence in our culture.

He was not aristocratic in the traditional church sense like Bishop Block, bishop of California, before him. Yet I would not have been ordained without his help, and for that assistance, I will retell something of his story. When I was about to graduate from seminary in 1959, and Elsie, very pregnant, and I had been married for a year, I was asked by Bishop John Hines of the Diocese of Texas to stay in Austin to become the chaplain at St. Stephen's Episcopal School and start a new mission in the area. I declined because I believed I should head home to California. One reason was the flurry of news about the former dean of the Cathedral of St. John the Divine in New York being the newly elected bishop of California. It sounded exciting, since Bishop Pike had already made headlines with his modernistic views, but little did I know that there was a minor battle going on about correct theology or lack of it in the diocese.

I sold my 1947 Chevy to Shorty, the seminary caretaker, who paid me the same price of our airline tickets in those days for the flight from Dallas to San Francisco. My dad had remarried in the meantime after my mother's death in 1957, and he and Betty were very kind to have us stay with them until I knew when I would be ordained. That event would hopefully occur after taking the local examinations for ordination from the Diocesan Examining Chaplains. This was well before the nationalized GOE tests had become standard throughout the church later.

I drove to San Francisco each day for a week from my father's home near Fremont and struggled through the daily exams, fairly confident about my ability to pass them. Yet instead of finding the chaplains at ease with themselves at the offices by Grace Cathedral on Nob Hill, I sensed a tension in the air and a slight suspicion of my training in the "new" seminary in Austin. After the week was over, and the day arrived when an announcement would be made about the worthiness for ordination of those being examined, I waited anxiously for a positive word. After all, I had a very pregnant wife, little money left after travel, and needed a job with a strong desire to begin serving as an ordained person. All of us, about seven men (well before the welcome addition of women), felt the same, I am sure.

However, when my name was called, I was told that I would not be ordained for my lack of knowledge of the New Testament. Of course, this had been one of my best courses in seminary. I was more than shocked but totally deflated and without understanding.

However, I was also told the last word belonged to the bishop, so I nervously waited on a bench of a dimly lit ecclesiastical hallway, until the bishop decided what he was going to do with me. I remember being summoned to a door to the room where all the frowning chaplains sat in a row around a table facing me. I felt as if I were at a trial. I sat in a chair facing them, when the bishop behind them suddenly stood up, walked forward, and told me directly that there had been a compromise. Standing now, waiting to hear a possible positive word, Bishop Pike announced that I would be ordained as a deacon—that is what one becomes before priesthood in our church—but that I would not be allowed to preach for six months, just in case my theology of the New Testament was not up to snuff, I imagined. Then stepping to the side of the room, the bishop beckoned me over to him to tell me personally to come see him about placement in a church after the ordination of new deacons the next week. Well, I knew that deacons could not bless or absolve nor celebrate the Eucharist, and now I could not preach, but I guess I could still work at being a pastor someplace.

I was finally ordained at Grace Cathedral on the twenty-seventh of June 1959, and those of us present there were given stoles by the bishop on the occasion. That white stole has been with me for these many eons, but this last year, it had started to fall apart. The kind members of the altar guild of St. John's Church in Naples, Florida, where I have been volunteering as a priest in retirement, sent it off one day to be totally repaired. I guess they thought it looked too shabby to wear. When the job was done, it was handed to me, looking like the day it was presented about fifty-five years ago. I was very grateful to the *rector, Fr. Joe Maiocco,* who has revived that church through his deep spirituality and sincerity, along with his wife, a nurse practitioner, and the guild.

Ernest IV was born two days later, and sometime after that great event, I had my appointment with the bishop. I remember entering his office and standing before his desk. He invited me to sit, but I was so nervous I just remained standing, and then he commanded, "I told you to sit!" I hastily did. He launched into a tale about something called the "customary," and I was hardly hearing him at all. So concentrated was I on finding out where I was going to be sent; I really didn't understand the meaning of his word *customary.* I timidly asked him something like, "What is it?"

He replied, "It's my way of handling high and low church divisions in the church concerning liturgy." Then he went into more detail by saying things about wearing preaching tabs in the pulpit and a chasuble at the altar, emphasizing both the word and sacrament. It sounded like a good idea to me, so I rapidly agreed. Then he gave me some choices of yoked churches where I would become vicar. (In our system, a vicar leads non-self-supporting missions where the bishop is technically in charge, whereas a rector of a parish is more independent of the bishop because parishes are financially self-supporting. Interesting!) Finally he mentioned North Salinas and Gonzales.

As a native Californian, I had not heard of them, so I asked, "Where are they?"

He replied, "In the Salinas Valley, but you will go meet a presbytery of lay and clergy in that area first and see if they approve of you." Bishop Pike was already experimenting with ways to line up Presbyterians and Episcopalians for a scheme of short-lived ecumenicity.

I finally thanked him and left his office and afterward returned to my dad's home, told my wife, who, smiling at last with Ernest in her arms, called her mother, Louise. She had planned to come to help us. In time, after buying a small blue two-door 1959 American Rambler, we all traveled together to the vicarage in Gonzales, a small town off old Highway 101 in the middle of the Salinas Valley between Chualar and Soledad, the Santa Lucia mountains on the Monterey, the Pacific Ocean side and the Gabilan Mountains on the more or less encroaching desert side. By the way, after reading a simple ten-page tract on the New Testament in Trinity, Gonzales's track rack, I passed my reexamination to be processed for the priesthood with flying colors and congratulations on my improvement. I should have left out all the theology I had learned in seminary in the first place.

I met Bishop Pike three more times, once at a preaching mission at St. Paul's Church, Salinas, for confirmation there, and in Saint Louis after we had moved to a new church position in Creve Coeur. After giving a brilliant speech to an ecumenical group, I went up to him to say hello. He was suddenly taken aback, but he remembered me and asked, "What are you doing here?" And I told him I had moved. He was very friendly.

Yes, I know that he was controversial and that he insisted that he had a visitation with his dead son and that Esther, his lovely wife, divorced him. I am not sure why, but perhaps for his views on psychedelic drugs that she most likely believed did not help their son. I know that he was an alcoholic, fighting the disease all his life, that he married a third time without church approval, and that he was lost in the desert searching for

Jesus of Nazareth as being the Teacher of Righteousness in the Qumran community. He also made enemies of some of my dear friends, but he ordained the first woman, Phyllis Edwards, in the Episcopal Church as deacon. While writing *A Roman Catholic in the White House?* about support for JFK, he opposed the church's teachings on abortion and birth control.

He was buried in St. Peter's cemetery in Jaffa at fifty-six years of age after losing his way in the desert when his and Diane's car became stuck off the main road. I don't know if his wild driving had anything to do with that, but I remember him being terrible at the wheel, bumping over medians on Salinas's roads and taking out middle pillars in double-car garages where he had been allowed to park overnight.

Yet he was at least memorable. Maybe he was not very aristocratic spiritually, but he was kind to me. Kindness in itself is a spiritual gift. St. Paul lists it in the epistle to the Galatians as a fruit of the Spirit .We all need more of it, and without it, some of us would not ever be able to return the favor in time.

EVELYN MCPHERSON

When we arrived in Gonzales, California, we were welcomed by lay persons Dorothy and Dick Heim, two saints of Trinity Church, although they would never know that was how the clergy viewed them, as I did over the years. They were consistently supportive of new vicars, and especially the Reverend Jerome Politzer, whose vision began three missions: St. George's in Alisal, Salinas; Holy Spirit in North Salinas; and Trinity in Gonzales, under the inspiration of Bishop Karl Morgan Block in San Francisco. The first one who completed the building in Gonzales was now retired bishop of Maryland, Ted Eastman.

The Heims took us under their wing, so to speak, and introduced us to a furnished vicarage next to the newly built church. There was a garage with an open yard between it and the house and a slough twenty yards behind our home, which was a ten-foot-deep drain ditch that allowed the runoff from the eastern Gabilan (earlier known as the Gavilan, a Spanish word for sparrow hawk, which still flourishes there) Mountain Range to flow safely by the seven-hundred-member village (now the population is about eight thousand). I don't believe that it was also some kind of tributary of the Upside Down River, that is, the Salinas River, aptly labeled such by author Anne B. Fisher, because one did not often see any water flowing in its known path.

I am no expert. Yet as far as the slough was concerned, I can never remember any water in it at all while we lived there for four years, but I recall hundreds of holes on its dry earthen walls that allowed unwanted moles to dig their lairs. The holes also seemed to fill the yard alongside the church and the vicarage, and after we lived there a while, I vividly remember watching a lone flower in our small garden patch by the house being lowered from about two feet above the ground through a hole at its roots to some unknown depth, evidently a victim of one of the little creatures beneath the surface. Once my son was old enough, he loved to fill any hole he found with water from our hose and watch a mole come out at some other end, scampering away before he drowned.

At twenty-five years of age, I was quite capable of helping to install posts in the open yard with a hole digger, in time erecting a fence to contain a small yard in which our children, Ernest and then Elizabeth, born eighteen months later in Salinas, could safely play. Elsie's grandfather and her dad, Jim Beard, recovered a Texas locomotive bell and had it shipped to Gonzales. Good thing that Mr. Beard owned six United Van Lines agencies and later was a board member of the company. It didn't cost the church anything. Cliff McElrath, the senior warden at the time, and some others helped to erect a sturdy wooden frame high enough to hold the heavy bell. Young acolytes loved to ring it before services with a long rope hanging down that they pulled on, probably more often than they should.

There were great people in that parish: the Wileys, Jack and Jean, especially their son Buck (my next senior warden) and his spouse, Nancy, the Mark Clarks, the Lopeses, the Howard Handleys, the Walter Riandas, Patty Johnson, Sparky and Lenore Iverson, and a faithful organist, Peggy, Erma Lopes's daughter, and especially Evie Anderson, later known as Evie McPherson. There were others who were special in the community: Dr. James Fassett, whom we called often for our children's health, and Dr. June Dunbar. The Clarks lost a nine-year-old son, Douglas, to leukemia after trying all the medical techniques available at the time to no avail. It was a terrible loss that I also shared. I have never forgotten him, and whenever I hear the Easter hymn #208 in our hymnal that was played at his burial ("The strife is over, the battle done, the victory of life is won"), I think of him to this day.

Trinity often had a yearly fair and barbecue, but we did not have a big-enough pit to roast a sheep on. So many of the local ranchers banded together and built one that was large enough, end to end, to roast most any size of meat, mostly lamb. I remember the men gathered around it during that fair, sipping drinks from bottles of whatever, mostly while the ladies were inside by tables with their wares. I often thought maybe these gentlemen would attend church services more now that an Old Testament altar (of sorts) had been built.

There was also the other yoked church that needed a building because the congregation met in an American Legion Hall, and in time, it was replaced with a small first unit church in North Salinas. I used to drive about twenty miles back and forth for services on Sunday and often during the week for meetings. The Church of the Holy Spirit was an alter ego, because I didn't live there. You grow the most where you are planted. Then there was the army reserve obligation at Fort Ord in Seaside near Monterey as a chaplain to the 6211 Garrison Unit, and Soledad Correctional Facility, previously known as a prison, where I assisted the Protestant chaplain and celebrated the Episcopal Eucharist once a week. Busy times, but I was young.

To be an army chaplain, one had to attend the chaplain school, which was located then at Fort Hamilton in Brooklyn. By taking my first jet airplane trip across the country, I spent a month or so there. It was also my initial exposure to Manhattan, which I was curious to explore. When off duty, I took the subway to the city often and walked around, not having the slightest idea I would live there one day. On one occasion, while in uniform, a fellow Chaplain and I were caught staring at a theater billboard by a producer of *Tovarich*, starring Vivien Leigh. He told us if we wanted to attend, he would arrange tickets for us later in the week. I never forgot Abel Farbman's warm, indeed aristocratic-like invitation, and we did enjoy the award-winning production. That is New York City at its very best.

After I left Gonzales to become an assistant at St. Paul's Church in the city of Salinas itself, I eventually handed over the new mission to Lester Kinsolving, who became a full-time vicar. In Salinas, on my days off, I decided to return to Stanford, my alma mater, to earn a degree in Hispanic American studies, driving back and forth fifty or more miles to the campus to attend classes. Trinity, Gonzales, had been taken over by Irishman Dan McHugh, a former Roman Catholic priest, as a form of what we often call devolution in the church.

In spite of all the wonderful people at Trinity who taught me ministry, it was Evie who, over the years, kept up with us the most, mainly because of her thoughtful ministry of remembering each of our anniversaries and birthdays, sending us cards faithfully for about fifty years to this day. I remember when we visited her recently noting her open a tattered address book full of names and dates that she kept track of over the years. It was like a well-used Bible of sorts, with frayed leaves and turned-down edges to its handwritten pages, some with corrected addresses made necessary from keeping up with people over the years.

Evelyn McPherson was born in Arizona on October 29, 1924, but after her mother died when Evie was three years old, she was soon sent at eight years of age to Oklahoma to live with her grandparents. With her grandmother, she moved to Fresno, California, where later she assisted a woman run a dress shop. That lady moved on to Salinas to open a new store, and when she was established, she asked Evie to join her. Evie was about seventeen years of age then, so she has been a longtime resident of the Salinas Valley.

Sometime after that, she married John Anderson, whose mother ironically worked for the family of the soon-to-be-famous author John Steinbeck. By the way, not many people remember the article that John Steinbeck wrote in the *Salinas Californian* about his early life when he attended St. Paul's Episcopal Church,

One day, he reminisced in his piece of writing, he vied to carry the cross in the procession when the bishop at the time came to the church for confirmation. Steinbeck won out over another acolyte and proudly led the procession of choir members, clergy, and the bishop to the altar, where the bishop was seated nearby. He took the cross to a wall behind the bishop where it was to be latched and, being slightly nervous, failed to attach the cross properly to its holder. When he turned away, all he remembered was that out of the corner of his eye, he watched the heavy cross leaving the wall and begin to fall directly on the head of the bishop. When he saw that the bishop had been knocked out of the bishop's chair, unconscious, he was so scared that all he could think about was running out of that church quickly, vestments flying around him, and never returning. This is how he said his career in formal religion ended. A true story written by the author himself!

Back to Evie. Much later, John Anderson died, leaving Evie alone for three years, but she fell in love with Todd McPherson, and they were married. That was when she moved to what was called the cabin, as she described it, on Arroyo Seco Road, which winds from Greenfield, off Highway 101, south of Gonzales and Soledad, west into the depths of the Santa Lucia Mountains.

If and when you decide to drive that long road, you would see a partial panorama of what was once called the Salad Bowl of the nation, as the Salinas Valley was known because of all the crops grown in large sections of acreage separated by rows of windbreakers of medically odorous eucalyptus trees and thick ranks of tall brilliantly yellow sunflowers. The wind still howls in the valley every day around 4:00 PM, and if you lived there, you understood why those windbreakers were needed. Until you got used to it, it could be irritating.

The reason for this local "Mariah" wind is that the valley becomes a funnel for ocean air from the nearby coast through a break in the mountains, but otherwise for reasons I have never understood. Yet that is a minor fault of a beautiful place to live.

Now the valley is filled with vineyards because well-known and prosperous wine companies have purchased much of the open fields from lettuce growers and sheepherders. Local wine is now celebrated nationally. For example, where we lived in Gonzales, it was once nicknamed the Heart of the Salad Bowl, but now it is called the wine capital of Monterey, with Blackstone, Paul Masson, and other wine growers headquartered there.

There is also a circuitous slow road route from where Evie now lives to the Carmel Valley on the Pacific Ocean side, but I have never taken it. It always took too long anyway to reach her home from Highway 101 off where we lived in Gonzales! What she described as just a cabin is now a paneled house with a large back porch with newly built extra bedrooms and extra baths off to the side, all in natural wood. The house is set back in a small canyon and shielded by large trees. One has to drive across a low water natural bridge to reach it. Her home is very scenic and quite protected. But to reach it, one must first enter a gate from that Arroyo Seco Road and then cross the bridge to what I would call now not a cabin but more like a small estate. Its location forms a beautiful, quiet, almost serene setting, except perhaps when too much rain falls and the natural bridge is too inundated to cross, but that is rare.

After attending my last university reunion a few years ago, we drove our rented car from San Francisco through the Salinas Valley onto the Arroyo Seco Road, and after becoming slightly lost, a neighbor of Evie's kindly opened the gate for us and said, "Drive over the bridge."

All I saw was water, but after my befuddled brain started to function, I realized it was merely a water bridge, and we drove easily through six inches of clear, sparkling water flowing over a dam. When we met Evie and her daughter, they showed us to our "suite," the new bedroom. We had a great time, a second reunion for our visit to California. The next day, two events happened: one, my wife accidentally locked the keys to the car in the trunk of the car that stymied me at first. But a wonderful noon reunion occurred of Trinity folks from the past, which Evie hosted.

Alas, later I had to call AAA, and in twenty-five minutes, a truck from Greenfield rolled up; the Latino man popped the side passenger window so that I could open the car to reach the manual release lever near the steering wheel. And then we were back in business. Although the car was equipped with OnStar, we were too deep in the Santa Lucia Mountains to reach satellite reception to unlock the car.

Evie was as gracious as ever, inviting me to use her phone and assisting me to reach the proper AAA number. She will be ninety years old soon, and she is as spry and as thoughtful as ever, revealing still the former young beauty I remember when we lived in Gonzales in the early 1960s. We received a Christmas card from her, and it read, "Feeding Time for My Furry Friends" with a photo showing her feeding four or so skunks plus two wild foxes in her backyard. That is Evie.

Like so many at Trinity, she is a spiritual aristocrat. Why? Mostly because she has sustained a ministry of communicative caring for fifty years, remembering hundreds of birthdays and anniversaries and sending out greetings regularly. How many have done that in their lives?

CLIFFORD MCELRATH

In 1959, Clifford McElrath was senior warden (a chief lay position in the Episcopal Church parochial system) of Trinity Episcopal Church, Gonzales, and a stranger to us. That soon changed. His wife, Marguerite, and he invited us out to the ranch where they lived. At that time, he was the superintendent of the Jacks and Thomas interests in Monterey County and held that position for thirty years. He had horses that he encouraged us to ride and a fine house where we often had dinner with the two, or we would go over to Monterey to a restaurant with a piano bar that was his favorite.

One night, he told us one of his many stories. This one concerned his sister, Katherine, who had married James Byers Black, whose son, James Alden Black, had married the famous child actress Shirley Temple, who of late has recently died at eighty-five years of age. He said the Blacks had ancestors going back to the Plymouth Rock Aldens and that James Alden had graduated from Stanford and had served with distinction in the navy in World War II. However, since Cliff had lived such a diverse career away from San Francisco society, he had little contact with his sister, who was three years older than he was. To illustrate this point, he said he was heading back once by train to Monterey (when there still was a railroad operating) from San Francisco, when he noticed that his sister was on the same train. He tried to say hello, but she did not return his greeting, and so he said, with little remorse, that was the end of their speaking relationship.

Why was she so distant? Unlike his father, who was a prominent lawyer, Cliff chose a life quite different and perhaps perceived as being too wild. As a teenager, he liked to tend cattle in the Oakland Hills, leading them on occasion on a trail over the summit behind the Claremont Hotel near Berkeley. He also loved boxing and football. After graduating from the University of California, he joined the army when we had gotten into World War I in 1918 and was sent to Camp Kearny, where he became a machine gun sergeant and also won the light heavyweight boxing championship of the camp. But the war ended just before he was to be sent overseas, which he regretted.

He did meet Marguerite Reynolds as an army nurse, however, while there, and they were married later in 1921, but before that happy event, he spent four years as assistant and then full-time superintendent of the company that ran Santa Cruz Island. The island is twenty-four miles from the Santa Barbara coast and is the largest at sixty-four acres in the Channel Islands. Today it would take one hour and a half by modern motorboat to reach it, but in Cliff's day, a sturdy sixty-foot two-masted schooner named the *Santa Cruz,* as he described it, took much longer than that but was available when needed. That experience of his on the island was worthy of being published a year after we left the Salinas Valley in 1967, called *On Santa Cruz Island*. A review of it appeared in the University of California Press in 1967 as follows:

> This delightful little volume of regional history offers a nostalgic word picture of the California that was, nearly a century ago. It is replete with homespun accounts of the everyday chores on an island ranch running short-horn cattle and sheep; and it depicts in detail the ordeal of seasonal cattle roundups and las corridas, roundup of some wild sheep for shearing, docking, shipping, etc. Also, there are exciting accounts of brushes with ferocious wild boars and with seagoing rustlers of sheep and cattle.

Cliff told stories to us in more detail about cattle rustlers that had to be fended off by his rifle and men who saw John C. Fremont lower the Mexican flag and raise the American. One story he told us, without any bravado at all, is best described by his own hand in *On Santa Cruz Island* (page 45):

> The raid was to be in the Aquaje on a moonlight night. I was waiting for them. They landed from their skiff and started walking up from the beach toward where a group of cattle were grazing in a flat. Before they got within shooting range of the cattle I let out a whoop and fired a couple of shots in the air. They started on the run for their skiff as though the devil himself was on coattails. A couple of them stopped and fired a couple of shots wildly toward the hill where they thought I was and then ran again. That ended that raid, except for a couple of shots I fired in the air to let them know that I was still around.

He also told us a story about Joaquin Murrieta, the notorious Mexican part-Indian bandit during the California gold rush, even though Mexicans considered him a kind of Robin Hood. Since Murrieta only lived until 1853 when US soldiers killed him as a robber, Cliff relied on stories told him by El Vaquero Viejo, or Old Joe. When he was younger, Cliff heard Old Joe relate the incident when Murrieta was killed, along with an associate named Three Fingered Jack. Evidently, Murrieta's head was cut off and put on display and exists somewhere even now.

Old Joe said that Murrieta's nephew, named Procopio, continued to fight into the 1870s, but he and other descendents insisted that Murrieta, who had lost everything, including his wife, from deceitful gold miners, thieved for more than revenge. Old Joe claimed that he and his relatives wanted a part of California lost in the Treaty of Guadalupe Hidalgo returned to Mexico.

In any case, there were many other tales, but these few I remember the most. Otherwise, Cliff came to our rescue often at the vicarage, particularly as we needed help with fences, church bell frame holders, and the ever-present moles burrowing into our yard. He was wise, a churchman, and solid as a rock, a spiritual aristocrat of old California at its best.

JEROME FOUTE POLITZER

Jerry Politzer has had the reputation of being the "King of the Salinas Valley," not because he owned the largest lettuce or sheep ranch or a prominent savings and loan company, or competed with John Steinbeck for literary honors, but because he has been a faithful traditional priest of the Episcopal Church. He began three missions for our church in the area. He was and is beloved by many in the valley and in Monterey. Jerry was born in San Francisco, December 13, 1926, graduated from Stanford University, and was ordained in 1952. His father was a well-known lawyer in San Francisco.

Jerry's first church was St. George's, which he formed in what was considered a rough area of Salinas, Alisal, and although the building was destroyed in a fire started by a gang called the stompers, it was rebuilt and then later moved to North Salinas.

I knew him as soon as I arrived in the Salinas Valley, but how did I become best acquainted with him? I will tell you. When I came down with a terrible case of the flu and was in bed, struggling to rise to complete all my responsibilities as a father, husband, and priest, Jerry came by to wish me well but then asked to use the prayer book service of the laying on of hands to help me regain my health, and that act stayed with me over the years. I can't remember the exact sequence of my path back to health, but I remember that watershed act of his, and I can still visualize it as a pivot point in my early ministry. Someone cared enough to offer a rite of healing for me, when I was supposed to be up and about doing that for others! It meant a lot. But that was Jerry, always.

Aside from our ministries, while in Gonzales and Salinas, Jerry and his lovely wife, Beverly, Ernie (me) and my wife, Elsie, had many fun moments together, especially if we drove ten miles over to Carmel or to Monterey, where later he became rector of a historic church, St. John's, with a long ministry. Before he retired from that church, it had grown from a handful to over seven hundred parishioners, revealing what everyone already knew: his genuine pastoral care and leadership. Jerry and Beverly were a great support to us when we were young, but that friendship lingered on for decades.

After we moved to Saint Louis and St. Timothy's Church, Jerry watched after my grandmother, Bertha Mary Carter, whom we had moved from Oakland to Salinas. We wanted her and my grandfather to be nearby so we could be helpful to them with groceries and drugstores, hospitals, and doctor's visits. My grandfather died at eighty years of age there, while my grandmother continued to live to be eighty-six. Jerry often checked in on her until we had her moved to our new location in West Saint Louis County with us, but Jerry also took care of her house in Salinas after she left, but before that, he helped her to fly to Saint Louis to join us.

Many years later, when I became dean of the American Cathedral in Paris, one Sunday, to my surprise, I met again his youngest daughter, Mary, and discovered that she had married a Frenchman and was living in an area nearby the city of Paris. Jerry and I soon discussed the baptizing of his grandchildren. Then he asked, "May I use the 1662 English prayer book?"

I was surprised at his request. It was not so novel since two English churches in the Paris area, St. Michael's, a British embassy–designated church, and St. George's, both used them, along with the additional English liturgical series booklets, A, B, and C. Both books, one traditional, the others innovative, were side by side in their pews, unlike our American Episcopal Church usage of supplanting the deeply revered

1928 Book of Common Prayer with the versatile *1979 Book of Common Prayer*. The 1928 book was adapted from the English 1549 book, and its revision in 1552, compiled by Archbishop of Canterbury Thomas Cranmer, who had translated it directly from the Roman missal into the vernacular, English. A later revision was published after the English Civil War in 1662 with the restoration of the monarchy, and it has been the official book of the Church of England ever since.

Elsie and I attended two babies' services at the baptismal font in the back of the cathedral and celebrated the baptisms afterward at their following receptions. In any case, the Episcopal Church has always allowed the 1928 book for pastoral use on occasion, but a generation went by, and some forgot how elegant that book is. Not so Jerry. He has been the president of the Prayer Book Society in the United States, and now emeritus, in an effort to keep its historic language and theological context alive.

The historic virtue of the Episcopal Church and of the Anglican Communion in general has been that one can agree to disagree, and I hope that attitude continues, because the theme of diversity within unity is the essence of a family of Christ. We don't have to form new denominations *in our own image* and leave, although I respect American religious pluralism. It gives us choice, but too many have gone from one denomination to another, only to find the same old sins, the same devil in the details. However, the Prayer Book Society exists *within* the church and makes many traditional Episcopalians feel at home. Microbiologist and humanist René Dubos once wrote, "Trend is not destiny." Jerry understood this truth very deeply.

In my mind, we are not meant to be in lockstep, nor should we be—ever; that is false religion and only another form of domination of the human spirit. Authoritarianism does not serve the God-given liberty of the children of God. One reason I personally appreciate Anglicanism is because we are a loose federation of international churches, 70 million or so, all related to the See of Canterbury.

There is latitude and diversity. People in the Anglican Diocese of Uganda, for example, do not often agree with those in the States or with Canadian Anglicans, because we have no single magisterium, as does the Roman Catholic Church. We have simply the prayer book, the Thirty-Nine Articles of Religion, and the catechism. Yet we also have deacons, priests, and bishops, all ordained or consecrated in the historic order by bishops in good standing with the archbishop of Canterbury.

Cultural differences abound, however, but the "One Holy Catholic Church" in our Anglican expression remains. This is so whether elected lay delegates or we American clergy banter over issues in a heated national convention, or where in some countries the democratic process is not so deeply ingrained. While we American Episcopalians are not part of any established church, as in the Church of England, some wag once said of the National Cathedral (Episcopal) in Washington DC: "The National Cathedral is the only non-established church that often acts as if it is the established one."

Jerry, as I call him as a friend, or Fr. Politzer as many know him, has written several books about general Christian themes, Anglicanism in one form or another, or in his opinion, the folly of prayer book revision, but in his latest, *Night Prayers on Calvary*, I especially appreciated these words:

> French social scientist, Alexis de Tocqueville, who visited this land 181 years ago, observed that "Liberty regards religion as its companion in all its battles and triumphs." If you read the Declaration of Independence you will see that the belief, upon which our independence is founded, is faith in God who has provided inalienable rights for mankind.
>
> We know also that a great many of the people who came to this country were not looking for religious freedom at all. They were looking for the opportunity to express themselves. They wanted no master. They wanted no one to rule over them. They were ex-convicts . . . before the revolution Dr Samuel Johnson, the British scholar, said of the Americans; "They are a race of convicts and ought to be thankful for anything we allow short of hanging."

I find this section of Jerry's words refreshing, reminding me of how diverse we Americans are and why we have so many denominations in the States, yet the statement to "agree to disagree" is not just a figure of speech. It is basic to faith and to our country. We look around the world and see people who act just the opposite, with murderous results.

I admire Jerry because he was a committed, dedicated priest whose independence of thought had shown him to be an aristocrat of the spirit. His faithfulness to what he believed made him, in my mind, truly the "King of the Salinas Valley," even though I read of late, sadly, that Jerry died in the early summer of 2014, but he remains a priest, in my opinion, who joined the ranks of all the spiritual leaders that I have known.

CHAPTER FOUR

Saint Louis, Missouri

GEORGE LESLIE CADIGAN

W E HAD LIVED in the Salinas Valley for over seven years, but in 1966, we were moving on like many clergy have done for centuries. After spending a little more than three of those years at St. Paul's Church as an assistant and living in Salinas on South Riker Street, we packed up our belongings and began our eastward journey to a part of the country we had never seen before. In our new 1966 two-door Chrysler Newport sedan, we began the trek to West Saint Louis County, minus our dog, Rumor, and my grandmother. They would come later by a quick and easier airplane flight.

The road trip was challenging, however, especially as my new 1966 V8 car, which cost $3,600, equipped with power steering and air-conditioning, had an unexpected difficulty getting over the hump at Pike's Peak. The car was loaded with luggage and every little thing the large trunk could hold. Yet we slowly made it up on the high summit and more quickly down, viewing intriguing new sights along the way, especially in the Rockies before we encountered the long flat lands that reached nearly to our new suburban home. We were excited at the adventure as a total *newbies* to the Midwest and to the great historic city of Saint Louis, the Gateway to the West. We were the exact opposite to the early covered-wagon pioneers, but pioneers nonetheless.

Ninety municipalities of West Saint Louis County were very Jeffersonian, as it was described to us, because each was independent from the other, with mayors and council members. The new church and residence were located in Creve Coeur and Chesterfield. When we arrived, our furniture had beaten us there, because Elsie's dad had his United Van drivers hustle to deliver it.

Once settled in our new home, we waited for our dog, Rumor, to arrive by plane but heard that he had missed his connection and would not come into Lambert International Airport until the following Saturday night. The Dunns, who were warmhearted parishioners, had us for dinner that evening, and later Jack Dunn offered to drive me to the airport, where we waited and we waited and we waited. Finally Rumor arrived about 1:00 PM, and poor Jack, trying to stay awake, took it in stride. So did Rumor, who could not constrain himself and leapt into my arms out of the cage-like box he had been in for travel. I took services the next day, a Sunday, and our life at St. Timothy's more or less began.

The priest in charge between the Reverend William Thomas, who started the mission, and my arrival had been the Reverend John C. Danforth, who had earlier graduated from Yale Divinity School and Yale Law School at the same time. After he was ordained, he had been a Sunday associate at the Church of Epiphany, Manhattan, and a lawyer for the firm Davis, Polk and Wardwell in the city. Then he returned home to Saint Louis and helped at St. Timothy's, but when I arrived, he naturally became involved in the diocese elsewhere. But in time, he turned his attention to politics and decided to run for attorney general of the state and, after that successful campaign, in time was elected a senator from Missouri.

Besides meeting wonderful people like Vernon Montgomery, a PhD and MD, head of space medicine at McDonnell Douglas, and his wonderful wife, Jean; Ginny and George Campbell; David Metcalfe; Lee and Marylou Dudley; Harry and Mary Cuthbertson; Donna Hansen; football center for the Saint Louis team, Bob De Marco, and his spouse, Jean; Chuck and Jean Decker; Dr. and Mrs. Bones Hamilton; Dr George Benson; the Powells, the Stenicks, and the Tapleys, from England; Mr. and Mrs. Rodney Weiss, to name a few of so many great people. Our dear friends whom we were able to meet again in Dallas, Texas, were Dan and Kay Tucker.

Dick Brandt, CPA, was its faithful treasurer, and the Moenkhauses are still active, whom we met again a few years ago on a visit. Then there was the incomparable organist, Robin Russell and his wife, Carolyn, who conducted the choir. Robin liked a drink or two at night, and as a chemist at Monsanto, he suggested that to remain healthy, when you imbibe a cocktail or two, it's wise to take plenty of vitamin B.

I also remember vividly Harry Cuthbert's speeches for our annual stewardship drives. Harry, a true thither, would say, "I don't want justice from the Lord, I want and need mercy!" I don't think this was because he was the regional manager for one of the three major American car companies, but because he knew the essence of a relationship to God.

Very modern religious needlework tapestries were unique at St. Timothy's, hanging on each sidewall of the original nave and sanctuary; one depicted *Jesus carrying a black sheep on his shoulders*, which encouraged us all. When we were about to leave for New York City much later, a tapestry by designer Robert Harmon (but lovingly executed by his wife) was given us by the parish. It depicted movement lengthwise across its wide girth, ending subtlety on the left with a colorful rendering of a Eucharistic cup and the Holy Spirit. It now hangs in our current dining room.

On a serious side of the pastoral ministry, I distinctly remember calling on Germaine Cuthill in the hospital. She had developed some form of deadly cancer and was about to leave behind three children. When seeing her just before she died in her hospital bed, she asked me to bend down to hear her, since her voice was low and words were hard to discern. All she whispered was, "Make sure my children are okay," which may have been her last words. In my newsletter about her burial, I remember quoting Berdyaev about her, an aristocrat of the spirit, because she surely was.

Dr. Gorge Benson, psychiatrist, held a Lily Foundation study with the clergy of the area and enlightened all of us by helping us with our unspoken needs. He wrote a book that was very popular, and his son became a priest, who later worked with me in New York City.

One of our first distinguished guests to our home was the bishop of Missouri himself, the Right Reverend George Leslie Cadigan. I could not believe it! One day, on a Saturday afternoon, I heard a knock at the door, and there stood at our doorstep George himself, unannounced, making a courtesy call. In California, the diocese was so large that one met bishops at receptions in San Francisco or when coming to you only for confirmation, as an official church visitation, but this was quite different in a smaller diocese. The bishop was congenial, cheerful, and complimentary, wishing us both well in his gentlemanly manner as Elsie served tea.

How would I describe him? He was what most women would say handsome for his age, at that time about sixty years old, nearly six feet tall, slender, hair thinning of course, but not gray, with a partially broken nose from football, and a big smile. He had a winning way about him. He liked the ladies, but in the nicest manner. His first wife had died, and his second was a good-looking woman, as I remember, although we didn't see her very often. She later contracted Parkinson's disease, which preoccupied him at times, and he often expressed his concern for her openly. As a graduate of Amherst, he had been the captain of the football team, but he was also a conscientious objector, who did important alternative service in World War II. He was no shirker, just principled about killing people, even in wartime.

One clergy member of the diocese stands out in my mind. Claudius Miller was a feisty low churchman when rector of Good Shepherd Church not far away. He, like my friend Ed Ticoulat, had been injured by polio also when young. After he retired, he maintained a ministry, like Evie McPherson. Every anniversary and birthday, I received from Pete and his wife, Sally, a card with minted coins for my age and a handwritten hearty congratulations.

Another is the Reverend Howard Park of St. Martin's Church. The three of us had the newer churches at the time in the growing area of West Saint Louis County. All of us were involved in ACID, active clergy in the diocese, formed, I think, by Claudius Miller, a group that tried to help clergy with low stipends at the annual conventions and with the bishop and assert issues of the day.

Living in River Bend Estates in Chesterfield was interesting. On one side was the main road, and on the other, away about half a mile, was the Missouri River. Our lot was almost an acre, so neighborhood houses seemed distantly removed, compared to our small piece of property on South Riker Street in Salinas in the midst of a cluster of crowded new homes. This would prove important in four months when we were hit by a tornado, January 24, 1967.

On a warm day, indeed some would have considered it hot at seventy-two degrees for a winter in January; a tornado alert had been issued because a massive cold front was approaching. I remember hearing the TV newscaster note that the danger of a tornado would be over at 7:00 PM.

Well, guess what happened at that bewitching hour, exactly when the threat was supposed to be over? The power went off, and our roof was hit with a clattering heavy load of hailstones. The off-and-then-on-again predicted tornado passed directly over our house, but we were lucky mainly because our house had been built in a small valley below the high road level above us. The noise of the storm above and around us sounded like a thousand bees buzzing. Since Elsie was Texas-born, she knew what to do in a tornado alert: open all windows a few inches so that a vacuum was not created and the incased pressure could not blow a wooden house into splinters. The home did not have the safeguard of a basement, however, so we all crowded underneath the dining room table in the southwest corner of the house. Except our daughter, Elizabeth, sat on the dog that whimpered loudly, and there wasn't much room for someone as large as I was.

The noise of the tornado, the loud pounding of shutters and of tossed debris was over in minutes. Our house was spared, except that the next day, in the sunlight, I discovered that the metal garbage cans and the heavy play equipment had disappeared. Just swooshed away, I assumed.

I found a flashlight that night and went outside, joining my neighbor to explore damage to other houses, and after the fire trucks with bright flaring lights arrived, we saw that three houses down the curving street were pretty much demolished, splintered into little pieces. In a two-storied home across the street, the cosmetic colonial columns on the front porch were completely gone, swept away, and a dirty four-by-four beam had been forced half into the side of the second floor, a bedroom. No one luckily had been at home.

A few days later, I went around to check houses of parishioners, and while one home looked normal, the inhabitant standing outside chatted to me, "Look where the drapes are."

I did and was shocked to see that they were hanging on the outside of the eaves. The roof had been torn off but had resettled back in place again—a total loss.

As soon as the roads were clear, I went to check on my grandmother, whom we had located in a second-floor apartment complex about five miles away. Since she was nearly deaf since childhood, she hardly heard me knock. After climbing an outside stairwell to her room, I finally was let in, and all four feet eleven inches of her complained, "Last night I think I heard knocking on the door at dinner time. How impolite. Why were people disturbing me?"

I responded, "Grandma, there was a tornado!"

I explained what that was as I stared up to her ceiling to see that all the nails had popped out about two inches, and through her rear window, that her back stairwell had collapsed. Later we decided she should live with us, although she liked her own space. About three hundred homes were destroyed, but only a few were injured, but one had died.

The church was undamaged, but in time, we went on a building campaign that felt to some like another storm tearing up old familiar sights. The quaint old farmhouse was torn down. It had housed the Sunday school on the former property of Farmer Brown. Then we built a separate Sunday school building with a parish hall underneath it off to the side of the church and sold the house in River Bend. All this finally allowed St. Timothy's to become financially independent of the diocese and a parish church, not a diocesan mission. We moved to Ridgemore Subdivision, just over the hill behind the church property, with a basement and a side bedroom to the garage so that Nana could live with us. Archdeacon Charles Reckhoff helped us with these deliberations, as did the bishop.

Not too long after the tornado, there was a clergy retreat led by the bishop where new clergy and spouses were introduced. Our turn came, and we both had to say a few words. He asked Elsie to speak, and she described the results of the tornado, describing it as going "swoosh." From that time on, George always called her by her new nickname, Swoosh.

We endured several ice storms. Once, anticipating a routine army reserve meeting and dressed in full army chaplain uniform, I went out to fetch the morning newspaper at the bottom of our driveway, and not noticing the thick sheet of ice that covered it, I slid all the way down on my derriere.

Another time I was in the newly built parish hall that was an undercroft underneath the street level where we had roundtable adult classes and debates about all the issues of the '60s, from Vietnam to civil rights, when the floor trembled and a crack began appearing in the wall and the ceiling.

"What is this?" a fellow parishioner asked, and I replied, "I think it is an earthquake."

"What do we do?"

I replied, "Stand in a doorway or an arch."

This was my best answer from my California days when we had these quakes often, but in Saint Louis? Yes, indeed the largest earthquake in the United States occurred in the nineteenth century in New Madrid, Missouri, where the Mississippi River changed course. We remained calm, and it passed.

George Cadigan was also a calm man for different reasons, and I will illustrate this quality of his. At one diocesan convention held at our downtown Christ Church Cathedral, where Tom Blair was then dean, the bishop was presiding before two hundred lay and clergy delegates. His chair faced from the altar in the east to each of them in the large nave in the west. I was sitting off to the side of the chancel near the altar behind him. In the midst of the proceedings, two hippy-style young ladies, dressed in an outfit that belonged to a radical protest group demanding reparations from the diocese for the ill treatment of minority groups in the past, brought into the cathedral a long unwrapped banner. Remember this was the '60s, when protest groups abounded with marches, banners, and flags.

The two slowly and quietly approached into the open space in front of the bishop, one girl walking to the bishop's right, then the other remaining on his left, when suddenly they stretched the stiff long banner, holding it up so that it could be read by the delegates but not by the bishop.

It read simply, "Fuck you, Bishop." The delegates twitted, some hooted and howled, but the girls quietly and serenely rewrapped it and slowly left by the two-side aisles. Later the bishop was applauded for his coolness in the midst of that fuss, but he said to a few, "I couldn't see what it said."

We loved our new home across from the church, and so did our dog, Rumor, for whom I built a small pen with a doghouse next to the fence between our place and Farmer Brown's property. An old horse still roamed on his side of the fence. When I would routinely walk home over the hill through our backyard where the pen was located, the dog would usually go into a battery of barks to let me know he was protecting the place or had chased the enemy, the horse, away. Yet one time, I guess he hadn't heard my tread, and I caught him standing on his doghouse, nuzzling the horse as his old buddy. Animals surprise us often.

So do determined Welsh grandmothers. When we were going to have houseguests one summer, my grandmother, who never liked being idle, suddenly decided to use her electric lawnmower to mow the front yard. It must have been ninety-five degrees, with the humidity just as high, but there she was, a wide straw hat on her gray-haired head, at least eighty-four years of age, whirring back and forth loudly with that little electric machine. So I went outside to encourage her to stop. Not only was it steaming outside, but I also didn't want our guests to think I was a slave driver of the elderly. When I was finally standing next to her, trying to gain her attention as she mowed, she suddenly noticed me but kept on. I said, "Grandma, it's too hot!"

She looked at me with those deep blue eyes as if she couldn't hear, which she couldn't. After the third attempt to tell her the bad news, she finally stopped the mower, adjusted her hearing aide, and asked, "What do you want?"

I said again loudly so she couldn't miss my words, "Grandma, it's too hot!"

She stared at me intently then declared determinedly, "Well, if it is too hot, go inside!"

And then she continued her task. I gave up.

This was a time when Elsie had her turn at earning an advanced degree, which she did at night at the University of Missouri in Saint Louis UMSL while I off and on babysat with the children. She taught in the Parkway school district, and two friends who taught, a former Roman Catholic priest and his wife, a former nun, invited us to the "underground church" at Saint Louis University, a Jesuit-run institute. When a Jesuit priest heard that I was coming, he called me up and told me to bring my alb. This was right after Vatican II and the opening of the ecumenical gates, so to speak, by Pope John XXIII. I did carry a vestment, and when we both found the chapel, I was invited to stand with the clergy at the altar, which was an invitation to concelebrate.

I asked in surprise, "What about the cardinal?"

He looked at a fellow Jesuit beside him and said tersely, "We work for the pope!"

Another older priest came later and inquired where my church was. I told him, "Creve Coeur."

He replied, "We don't have a church there."

The two young Jesuits, looking a little sheepish, muttered, "He is an Anglican."

The older priest, who turned out to be the president of the university, said, "Oh hell, that's all right"

Those were the days when ecumenicity between our two churches was at a high, but sadly, it didn't last for very long.

After Bishop Cadigan retired, he returned to Amherst College as a chaplain, and he told a story on himself. He was given a not well-identified office, and he waited daily for students who needed a friendly ear to stop by. He had not seen anyone for days, which made him worry that he might not be needed at all. Finally, one late evening when he was about to leave and expected home to meet guests for dinner, a young man came in to talk. And talk he did. The bishop listened and listened and listened for about two hours. Finally, the boy got up, thanked him, and said he was going to leave. Just before he did, he paused, turned around, and asked, "Who the hell are you anyway?" Not only was George calm, he was humble.

Much later, when the bishop was ninety-four years old, the clergy who had known him when he was diocesan were corralled to attend a birthday party for him in Brunswick, Maine, near his retirement center. We had a great reunion the first night in a lovely old hotel, after which he said he would meet us for breakfast the next morning at 8:00 AM.

When we gathered, we waited for him, but he had not shown up for an hour. So I was delegated to go knock on his door to see if he was all right. His room was on the main floor, next to the concierge. When I failed to gain a response, I finally asked the concierge to open his door with the master hotel key, and she did. I entered slowly before her and found him still in his bed. After whispering, I finally spoke up with a voice that could raise my grandmother from deafness, and he suddenly woke up. He thanked us and told us he would be out in ten minutes. I went back to the table where the clergy were gathered, and finally George came out of his room to join us. He looked at me and offered his thanks again for waking him. Then he asked, "The staff here is wonderful, and by the way, how long have you worked here?" I felt guilty explaining to him that I had worked with him as one of his priests, and he sighed the sigh of a man who hated to forget.

Then after coffee, he launched into a story about the time when he was in seminary and believed it was his responsibility, as former captain of the Amherst team, to gather together eleven seminary football players to challenge the inmate team of a nearby prison. It was outreach. The day came and the game was played, but when it was tied, a player who was returning a kickoff threatened his side. George, playing defense, was the only man standing in the way of the prisoner's rapid advance to the goal post with ball in hand. George stood his ground and knocked him down. Then, ever polite, George extended his hand to help the inmate up, asking, "Are you all right, sir?"

The inmate replied, "If I'm not, bud, I've got twenty years to recover!"

George was not only memorable, but he was a gentleman and always "aristocratic" no matter the circumstance.

L. DAN TUCKER

One of the first families in West Saint Louis County that Elsie and I grew close to was that of Dan Tucker because his and Kay's children were the same age as our children, seven and eight years old. We lived near each other, and Dan was a vestry member, as he would be later in Dallas; in fact, while living in Texas before retirement, he was senior warden several times. One time at St. Timothy's, we invited Dan and Kay over for Bloody Marys after church, but we had ulterior motives.

Somehow our daughter, Elizabeth, had acquired a little black kitten, which we named Midnight. She hated to give him up, but then she dearly loved Rumor, our ranch dog that had adjusted to being a suburban dog in Saint Louis. He had not taken kindly to the cat. So we talked to Dan and Kay, suggesting that their daughters, Laurie and Dana, needed a kitten in their lives and that he would be no trouble at all.

Sure, we thought or as we both hoped, but sadly that did not prove to be the case. This sweet kitty grew up to become a very self-willed black cat that increasingly found and fomented trouble. First of all, one day after becoming frightened somehow, he crawled up a telephone pole in front of Dan's home but refused to come down. The girls were crying for Dad to help Midnight, as he had been named. So he did and survived. I don't know how he climbed that pole, but climb he did and rescued the wandering beast.

Then the cat formed the bad habit of sleeping on the top of the closed automatic garage door but didn't know what to do when one day the garage door opened and rose up. The cat became stuck, allowing his black felt-like body to be squeezed, but not exactly flat. That repair of Midnight cost Dan, I believe, about $300.

On another fateful day, I saw their station wagon driving happily along, but I also noticed that the stubborn cat was clinging to the roof. Even though the family had perversely become acquainted with how much the cat loved their car and its garage door, on this particular day, Dan nor Kay didn't hear me yelling and were ignorant of the cat above them. They just drove on. As soon as Dan stopped at the next light, that cat suddenly fell off and became concussed. I believe the veterinarian told them that would be another $200.

But suddenly Dan's troubles were over. The cat ran away and could not be found. The girls cried, but Dan toughed it out, not smiling in front of them, but secretly telling me he was not unhappy that old Midnight had found a better home.

Yet one year to the day, his smile vanished, and now frowning, Dan said to me, "My girls are very happy."

"Why?" I responded.

"Guess what, Midnight just walked into the house, looking satisfied with himself after his yearlong adventures." But I could tell that Dan was not nearly as pleased as Laurie and Dana, who were ecstatic.

On a totally different subject, Dan as a lawyer was very helpful to St. Timothy's Church as we negotiated a loan with a bank to build a parish hall and Sunday school and more especially to sell the vicarage, purchased by the diocese, allowing us to pay back the loan, permitting the church to become independent. Once all that was squared away with the help of the diocesan archdeacon Charles Reckhoff, we were able to apply to be a parish, which meant two major benefits: we could incorporate ourselves as a self-sufficient parish, no longer being a mission church, and I could become a rector with tenure, according to our national canons. The canons represent a check and balance system formed since our religious constitution was written after the American Revolution.

St. Timothy's continued to do well, even after Dan and Kay moved to Dallas, Texas. Our friendship continued over the years, especially when we were in Dallas ourselves. Dan became senior warden of an Episcopal church in Richardson, a suburb of Dallas, and endured several years of troubled but successful ministry, leading the church when two rectors in a row, I believe, left preemptively. Why? They ran off with ladies, not their wives.

Both daughters married, and the youngest, Dana, married the tallest former basketball star, Joe Kline. Joe is a generous man who had given much to help others after his retirement from sports. Dan and Kay visited us in Paris and stayed in the deanery with us, but unfortunately, in the extra bedroom, an old rickety bed fell apart on him. He survived that event as he did the life-and-death of Midnight as well as the crunch of being a longtime senior warden in both Saint Louis and Dallas. They have retired to the villages near Little Rock, and yet he is again a glutton for punishment by being senior warden of their church in that lovely area. To me, he is an aristocrat of the spirit for such endurance.

CLAUDIUS "PETE" MILLER III

After arriving in West Saint Louis County and settling into the new mission church in Creve Coeur and our vicarage in Chesterfield, I had a phone call welcoming me from Pete Miller, rector of the Church of the Good Shepherd nearby. After a few pleasantries, I realized that he had certain issues on his mind. He immediately laid out plans for my new job as the vicar of St. Timothy's. These were his goals, not mine, but I listened. I was young and new, so what did I know? He told me that the three churches the rector of the church in Ladue, the Reverend Dr. William Laird, had begun, including his Good Shepherd, were meant to be small islands of progressive thought for the church at large, not just another big, growing, fat parishes. I didn't know exactly what he was talking about, since my idea of a church was that it was for everyone, no matter his or her personal views. Of course, I fully knew that in America, people who attended churches could switch parishes and find one they liked, but the whole idea that they were formed for a few was way beyond my comprehension. I could understand what Pete was hoping for; eventually I determined more of a faithful remnant, a minority, committed to the best in the church than a cross-section of the majority. Yet it was not to be. I respected Pete but thought I would allow the Spirit to guide how St. Timothy's should develop.

In any case, I was too new and too young to worry about what Claudius thought was best. However, he invited us to dinner, and I accepted. Elsie, children Ernest and Elizabeth, and I went to his house about a week later and met Sally, his blond, thin, kind, and helpful wife, and their children and dogs.

Let me describe Pete. He was not tall but of average height. He had a booming voice and a kind but stubborn face, and he was very dominant, even feisty, in spite of a slight limp—which I found out later was from polio. At his home, we had pleasant drinks and dinner, but afterward Pete suggested that we have a cordial. When he went to look in his cupboard for his liquor selection, he discovered that the pantry for such drinks was empty. We heard him say just that and therefore politely declined, but he insisted that we have an after-dinner drink, ignoring us and saying that he was going to the store to buy a decent cordial.

While continuing to try to dissuade him, he left quickly, exiting to his carport to drive his sedan, but then we heard a loud crash and some cursing. We found out later that he had driven over his children's bicycles, which had been loosely left behind the vehicle, as children will do often. When he returned, angry at the way his kids had parked their bicycles, we had the after-dinner drink and soon left. Pete was forceful and often intractable, but also passionate and very pastoral, and these aspects of his personality served him well.

For example, the Guggenheim Productions of Washington, DC, made a film under the sponsorship of the Kennedy Foundation for Retarded Children, prompted by Good Shepherd parishioners' difficult decisions regarding their own retarded child. They had raised their child Becky for ten years even though doctors thought she wouldn't live more than a year because of her mental condition. When Becky was nine years old, the couple had heard of another child who needed a kidney to live, so they offered Becky for the transplant; but the doctors were in a quandary and, after much soul-searching, declined. Tragically, within a year, both children were dead. Pete was quoted as saying, "Honest, intelligent, and understanding human beings could come down on either side of the issue," and the family was on one side, the doctors on another. The family commented that the film was difficult to make, but Pete was also quoted as saying that "the reality created by the filming caused [him] to wonder if this indeed is what 'bottom line' Christianity is all about."

The family had another retarded child, who was fourteen and making good progress at a school for such children, but they didn't want anyone to think that Becky was just an organ bank.

As a result of their effort to protect the rights of retarded children, the family became the leading force behind the establishment of a school for three- to five-year-olds with mental difficulties at both Good Shepherd and St. Martin's churches in West Saint Louis County. Pete wrote to his congregation the following: "Living into unavoidable choices where there is simply no way for one to be either all right or all wrong and consciously to accept one's responsibility for one's choice by both rejoicing in our courage and forgiving ourselves our sins" is at the basis of our faith.

Claudius decided to retire after twenty-one years at Good Shepherd Episcopal Church. In 1976, he and Sally settled in Chapel Hill, North Carolina, where he was promotion coordinator for WUNC radio for five years and editor of the *New Harmony Journal* until his death at the age of eighty-three. He also continued in remembering his many friends' birthdays and anniversaries, including ours. Claudius was born June 20, 1926, and served in the US Navy in World War II, after which he graduated from Guilford College and the Virginia Theological Seminary.

I always respected Claudius in many ways, even if we had different ideas of ministry. Our backgrounds were very different, but we shared the one priesthood, and in that ministry of his, he helped many of the less fortunate people born to this earth. He was an aristocrat of the spirit in my estimation, because he understood the true meaning, like St. Paul himself, of the difficult ethical decisions we must make in hopes of serving the common good.

JOHN E. HINES

The Right Reverend John Elbridge Hines, presiding bishop of the Episcopal Church, returned to Saint Louis in the early 1970s while I was rector of Timothy's Church in Creve Coeur. He was leading a diocesan conference. While sitting in the parish hall at one of the round tables that we used for adult class discussions, he said to me, "I hear you are going to New York City. Why would you want to leave this ideal place and go there?"

This was a time when Bishop Hines had been living in Manhattan in the apartment provided for the PB on top of 815 East Second Avenue, our national headquarters. I believe he missed Texas and his native North Carolina at that moment in his life. He had been PB in a very turbulent period of the church and society. The *Christian Century,* a highly respected ecumenical magazine, wrote at the end of his term as PB in 1974 that "Hines . . . had remained astride the bucking bronco of a polarized church during one of the most controversial decades in American history."

Yet John Hines had been prepared for such crises by his first assignment in ministry in Saint Louis at the height of the Great Depression, where he discovered his direction for his own ministry under the guidance of Diocesan Bishop Will Scarlett. Scarlett was at the time the Episcopal Church's champion of the Social Gospel, a movement that sought a reformation of American society based on Christian commitment to helping the poor and disenfranchised. He and Eleanor Roosevelt, a fellow Episcopalian, were pictured together often as good friends.

When Will Scarlet was bishop of Missouri, he was also known for his open-mindedness in religion and his interfaith commitments, accepting, for example, the beautiful biblically engraved great doors to the entrance of Christ Church Cathedral as a gift from Saint Louis's main rabbi. He also invited a native of Saint Louis, Reinhold Niebuhr, an Evangelical and Reformed graduate of Saint Louis's Eden Seminary, not an Episcopalian, to be the dean of the cathedral because he was a well-known professor of social ethics. Niebuhr declined and remained at New York's Union Seminary, but it was Saint Louis's loss since he had influenced so many in, during, and after the horrific days of World War II.

For example, Niebuhr had written in one of his many books that "man's incapacity for justice makes democracy possible, but man's inclination to injustice makes democracy necessary." These were fitting theologically motivated political words to fight fascism.

Bishop Scarlet was a tireless crusader for social reform until he died at ninety years of age in 1973. During his lifetime, he influenced many lay and clergy to preach the Good News to the poor, including a young John Hines.

After Saint Louis and other places of service, such as Christ Church, Houston, Bishop Hines was elected coadjutor bishop in the Diocese of Texas. A coadjutor is elected to succeed the existing diocesan bishop, according to the canons of the Episcopal. In the meantime, while acting as an assistant bishop, John Hines was not idle. He began St. Stephen's private boarding school near Austin and the Episcopal Seminary of the Southwest in the same city.

Not only was I a student at the seminary, but for two years, I also worked as an assistant librarian each day at the school from 3:00 PM to 9:00 PM, earning my evening meal in the school's commons and $100 a month, a godsend for me at the time. After assisting Diocesan Bishop Quinn for several years, Hines took over the helm when Quinn died.

While I was a student in our seminary, I heard John Hines preach with his commanding voice and his vigorous and committed style. He also administered the prayer book rite of confirmation to my wife, a former Methodist, at All Saints Church in that city. Later he tried to persuade me after graduation to become chaplain at St. Steven's School and also to serve as vicar of a new church in the western area of the city, but Bishop James Pike had become bishop of California and expected me to return home. So Elsie and I decided to leave the capital city of Texas, flying to San Francisco upon the sale for $125 of my 1947 Chevrolet to Shorty, the groundskeeper of the seminary.

When John Hines was elected by the House of Bishops to be our "archbishop"—we never wanted archbishops as in England, so we called our leading bishop a presiding bishop—he became quite controversial. In January 1965, the youngest man ever to be elected at fifty-four years of age, he began his advocacy of social programs to help minorities, angering some by the way they were implemented and by whom they were executed. Some accused his national assistants of betraying his trust, but others did not. He retired when he was sixty-three years old, living with wife, Helen, for nearly twenty years in North Carolina, occasionally preaching and taking part in the consecration of bishops.

Before he died at the age of eighty-six in Austin, Texas, Elsie and I attended his fiftieth anniversary of ordination as a priest, hosted in the Diocese of Newark, not too far from us in Manhattan, and that was the last we saw of him. He was in good spirits and spoke with his familiar firm, convincing manner as always. A book about his life issued on that celebration of his ordination to the priesthood stated, "Those who thought that Bishop Hines is primarily interested in the church as an instrument for social reform have failed to see that his is a very Christ-oriented religion. In the sermon he preached on his installation as Presiding Bishop he said 'only when the church has been close to Christ Jesus . . . only then has the church been able to draw sufficient dynamic from the source of her comfort to effect, by God's grace the healing and renewal both at her own body and of the company of lost men.'"

I admired the man, a presiding bishop of the church, who could stay the course no matter what. In my estimation, he was a leader filled with compassion, sometimes even when not appreciated, but for me, he was truly an aristocrat of the spirit, a leading light in the national church.

CHAPTER FIVE

New York

PAUL MOORE JR.

E LSIE AND I were introduced to the Right Reverend Paul Moore Jr. after we had decided to leave Saint Louis because I had accepted the position of rector of the Church of the Epiphany in the city of New York. This meeting was expected of us since I was moving from one diocese to another, and that meant, by canon law, I needed to receive approval from the diocesan bishop to enter his domain. At six feet seven inches, a former highly decorated marine captain who had served in World War II, Paul was an impressive figure with his purple shirt and pectoral cross, sitting behind his office desk in the Diocesan Center next to the largest cathedral in the world at the time, St. John the Divine. He had a handsome yet craggy face, a full head of hair, and broad shoulders. Yet he did not try to dominate us, but was very gracious and quite pastoral, asking with a genuinely worried expression on his face in the middle of our visit, "Are you sure you want to come to this city? It is tough territory and expects a lot of people, especially of clergy. It's not an easy place."

We assured him that we had both decided that this was where we wanted to be, in Manhattan, and that we would try to do our best. I did not say that I was worried, especially when I had heard that if you made it in New York, you could anywhere, and if you didn't, forget it, which was a little intimidating. What if I screwed up? Was John Hines right in warning me away? We would find out.

In due time, we moved into 340 East Seventy-Second street. Elsie was hired as a teacher at the Hewitt School, where she would remain for seventeen years, and Ernest was accepted at St. Mark's Episcopal School, near Boston, and Elizabeth at the Town School in the city. All that I had worried about in Saint Louis while making the decision was eased into a working reality, and we settled into our new lives.

The next time I saw Paul was for confirmation at the Epiphany, and after his visitation, he came to lunch in our apartment. He looked very tired, and after we had eaten, he asked if he could take a nap in our spare room, which he did for an hour or so. This was around the time that his first wife, Jenny McKean, with whom he had nine children, had refused to join him from Washington, where he had been assisting bishop, and then there had been in a car crash, after which she had been diagnosed with colon cancer and died.

Paul was very upset, as I remember, and was so for a time until he met his future second wife, Brenda Hughes Eagle, and married her eighteen months after the death of Jenny. I remember going to their house next to the cathedral with our Kylin group, a study group for some clergy in Manhattan and Brooklyn, named Kylin, which was, by the way, the Chinese word for the "Dragon of Knowledge." Each of us noticed the difference in Paul, who seemed happier than ever with Brenda.

At a monthly Kylin meeting one time, I remember Paul and another friend of mine, also a member, Fitz Simmons Allison, then rector of Grace Church, fervently debating an issue. I can't remember the subject, but I do recall that Fitz, a theological scholar more or less, seemed to win the debate, while Paul, a pastor at heart, never doubted his stand. They were deadlocked. Later Fitz left New York and was elected bishop of Upper Carolina.

The only time I disagreed with my diocesan bishop was after the General Convention and the House of Bishops approved the ordination of women. The Church of the Epiphany had a woman waiting in the wings. Paul was in favor of such an ordination, but not for our particular candidate, so I made an appointment with his secretary, Lucilla Woodard, to see him to discuss his decision.

When I was in his office again, it was not as pleasant as the first time. In fact, we had a rousing argument, but toward the end, Paul more or less reluctantly agreed to review his decision, which he did. Lucilla and her husband, the Reverend Canon Jack Woodard, a fellow

Seminary of the Southwest classmate who at the time was at Trinity Church, Wall Street, were close friends of ours.

Lucky me; she told me on the QT that she had never heard Bishop Moore curse anyone as loud as he did me after our visit. I thought, "Oh well, that is Paul. He is a big guy and doesn't like to be countered."

Yet Paul revealed that he was a real gentleman, because two years later, he called me up to invite me to lunch. I accepted, and we met at a popular bistro across from the cathedral on Amsterdam Avenue. After we had ordered and were pleasantly talking, he said, in no uncertain terms, that he was wrong about that candidate, who since had proven herself. He said, "I want to apologize for my wrong decision."

I couldn't believe his deep sense of conscience, and I told him he didn't have to do that, but inwardly, I was moved by his sense of honor. I guess this was why he had won the Navy Cross, Silver Star, and a Purple Heart in the Battle of Guadalcanal in World War II.

Not everyone always agreed with Paul because of his commitment to minorities and their issues, but his heart was large. I know that his daughter, Honor Moore, wrote an exposé about him after his death at eighty-three years of age in the *New Yorker* magazine and then a book, but to me, that was irrelevant and too personal. I know it is a Facebook age where all is revealed, but that doesn't mean we know the true worth of persons and their inner struggles.

I admire Paul for how I knew him and not for what one child out of nine wrote about him. He had done a lot with his life, from the Pacific theater in World War II, to the streets of the city of Newark with Jenny by his side, to Indianapolis where he had been dean of its cathedral and then Washington, DC, to New York City. He may have been aristocratic by birth, being from one of the East's richest families, but he used his background for the good of others. In my estimation, he was a real New York City aristocrat of the spirit.

KATHERINE VAIL MARSTERS

We met John Beresford, Katherine Vail Marsters's grandson, in Saint Louis because he was a Washington University student at the time and had heard that I had been called to be the rector of the Church of the Epiphany in New York City, where his family worshipped. We invited him for dinner two or three times, and he filled me in on the type of church I was going to lead. He described one Christmas Eve service when before me Dr. Hugh McCandless had been rector. He said that he and his family were sitting in their pew when a latecomer arrived and sat nearby. He was different in many ways from them, actually a homeless man, whom later I heard the sexton at Epiphany label as "another weary traveler." Jimmy implied to me that it was normal routine for street people to seek relief from the winter chill in a warm place, like an open, heated church.

John described what the man did after he sat down, as well as the reaction of Beresford's family and all fellow attendees. The individual, scruffy, bearded, an old floppy and dirty hat on his head, warmly dressed in old leftover clothes, carried a well-used and wrinkled paper bag. After quietly getting comfortable, he placed the bag on the pew bench, opened it, and took out a bottle of perhaps Night Train (it will get you through the night) or some form of cheap whiskey. Then he placed next to it on the bench a well-used paper cup, poured himself a liberal slug of the stuff, downed it with a satisfying sigh, then placed it all back in the bag, stood up, and left the church. The family and others seated nearby did not bat an eye. The service never paused.

That scene was in direct contrast to anything I had experienced in my younger, more cohesive suburban congregation in upscale West Saint Louis County. When my grandmother attended services, she stood out, for no other reason than she was the lone *old* person present. I knew when she was present, because I could hear her hearing aids whistle on and off as she adjusted them. Who else normally needed hearing aids then but an elderly person? She may have interrupted others, but not like that old street guy in the Epiphany could have.

Yet there was another side to Epiphany. There were many older men and women, some probably with hearing aids, who were not poor or lacking in historic family background. Take for example John's grandmother, Mrs. Katherine Vail Marsters, the adopted daughter of Theodore Vail, the first president of AT&T, the American telegraph company. Her real father, who was Theodore's brother, died prematurely, and she was raised as his own.

Elsie and I became acquainted with her, because in her eighties, she was always inviting diverse people to her home on East Seventy-Second Street after church services for lunch. She assembled many intriguing people in order for them to become acquainted with one another: an FBI agent, an older actress, the distinguished pastor and his wife from Madison Avenue Presbyterian Church, a famous band leader, Benny Goodman, and her own older friends. We were the newly arrived young ones then, but the occasion was always entertaining.

Kate was not tall. She had gray hair and wore glasses, but she commanded attention, calling a yellow-taxi man driver, as in the old days when she had the family's own chauffeur. Her eyes seemed to bore into you, as if she were assessing your worth. I think we passed the test. She was also highly intelligent, having been a cofounder of Bennington College in Vermont.

She was not only a unique hostess but also a very intriguing person who learned new skills in later life. She taught herself to play the piano in her eighties; she was "up" on world events, au courant, so to speak, challenging some of us in her home on the finer points of foreign policy. She never talked about her father except to say that he was a "telephone man" and that they had traveled around the East in a railroad car that later I found out was their own Pullman car.

She even lectured our son, Ernest, then a budding teenager, on his need to eat borscht soup, which he declined to appreciate. Once, an older man and his wife were with us on one Sunday, and as Kate got up to leave the table, she asked the man to bring in the candy to the living room to have it with coffee. After she had gone on to the salon, he at first looked bewildered because he hadn't heard her correctly, so he made a decision by dutifully picking up the candelabra from the table and carefully carrying it, still lighted, into where she was seated. She only politely scolded him. It was obviously not just my own grandmother who needed a hearing aid.

Sometimes her daughter, lovely Kate Beresford Hurd, and her husband, Fred, would be present. At one time we also met Susan Beresford, Mrs. Hurd's other child besides John, and Catherine's granddaughter, but before she became head of the Ford Foundation. Mrs. Marsters loved the Church of the Epiphany and had made a ceramic devotional with symbols of the three kings as a gift and attended services as often as she could. She also spontaneously gave us her father's paperweight, a heavy wooden piece that I treasured, but Elsie and I believe it should go to the grandson, and eventually we will send it to him.

Kate Marsters died at ninety-five years of age, and in the years we knew her, she was a very special friend who introduced us to old New York at its best. Not only was she aristocratic, but also she was indeed an aristocrat of the spirit, improving and yet challenging so many diverse people in her own indomitable way.

HUGH DOUGLAS MCCANDLESS

While I was still in Creve Coeur, deliberating whether or not I should leave and travel to a city I knew absolutely nothing about, except in movies from the 1930s Depression years, I called Dr. Hugh McCandless for advice. He had been rector of the Epiphany in Manhattan for twenty-seven years and, I heard later, had the reputation of being the "Saint of the Eastside" for his pastoral care and for his commitment to outreach.

I reached out to Dr. McCandless, who had already committed to his retirement but was staying on until the new rector arrived, saying, "There were three finalists out of the 150 candidates for your position." I therefore thought another might be better qualified. Maybe I should drop out. After talking to Mr. Edward Wardwell, the senior warden, he told me that the search committee had called me to be rector. I thanked him, but I had had my doubts. I therefore told him, "I am sure the church could do better with one of the other candidates."

He responded, "Nonsense. You are the only one they wanted. The whole search process will have to start over again, old boy. Carry on! Take your time. We don't need an answer right away. Talk to the junior warden now, who is David Clark." I did, and he reassured me the same, so I said that I would think about it and get back to them.

In the meantime, I did some deep thinking about the transition to such a large unknown city from Saint Louis County and the familiarity of our pleasant Midwest suburb. What about schools for Ernest and Elizabeth, both just on the edge of teenage? Where will we live, since the church did not have a rectory? I talked to Elsie about all this, and she replied simply, "Don't you have any faith?"

That did it. In time I called David Clark, and we agreed that I would come again to New York to work out the details. After that meeting, it was decided that I should arrive in October in time for the

Every Member Canvass. What is that? That is the fall moment when we ask people for pledges of money to support the church. They would like to show me off, so to speak, which is common. The people understood that someone new would be in charge, and they hoped for the best! The change in leadership that time of year proved true when I moved from one place to another, even to Dallas later and then to Paris, France.

After I agreed to be the new rector, I flew to New York ahead of the family to become acquainted with the parish and to find an apartment. Mrs. Merz "Nancy" Peters, a longtime parishioner along with her parents, escorted me to various coops, and eventually one was found, 340 East Seventy-Second Street, about two blocks from the church. I was offered a housing allowance to cover costs. Dr. McCandless was still in residence in his NY apartment, and he became my mentor as I got to know people and my way around. David C. Clark, of Clark Dodge and Company, found me a fine hotel on Madison and East Seventy-Fourth, a bit old-fashioned, but in a nice neighborhood. I had to ask for a television, however.

One of the first persons I remember meeting at the church was the theater actress, elderly Marjorie Maude, daughter of Sir Cyril Maude of England. She had volunteered to be the head of the lay readers. I sat in on a rehearsal that she was conducting for several of the lay readers, advising them to project their voices. This was before the church had any microphone system.

On a trip away from New York City later to show our children historic Williamsburg, Virginia, we saw her in *The Story of a Patriot*, a film depicting a hero of the American Revolution. She played the older mother. Her main success had been when in 1913 to 1965 she was on the New York stage, but we could see her in action in this short movie.

Dr. and Mrs. Nathan Starr; Jim C. Sargent, once head of SEC, and his wife, Rebecca, president of the Cosmopolitan Club; Charles H. Erhart Jr., CEO of the Peter Grace company, and Sylvia Erhart; Mrs. Harold "Frederica" Landon, whose cousin Frederick King was an architect of the church; Mr. and Mrs. Sumner W. White Jr. and son Edgar P. E. and wife, D. J. White; Walter Birge, headmaster of the Town School, and Susan, his wife; William H. Whyte Jr., who wrote the classic *Organization Man* and an advocate for open spaces in the city in his book *City*; Merz K. and Nancy Peters and her parents, the champs Dr. Sam and Marian Yeh, who was an expert in nuclear medicine at Sloan Kettering Hospital (his father was head of the YMCA in a province of China and was imprisoned; Sam was only allowed to visit his family after his father died); Barbara Chang, who formed the Joyful Noise, a youth singing group, and her talented son, Michael; Richard C.; Emily McQuillan; Van Santvoord Bowen; Eunice Riblinger; Helen and lawyer Arthur Siegrist; Priscilla Wyeth, whose husband was another architect of Wyeth and King; Jane Nickolic, indefatigable head of clothing the poor along with Phyllis Given; Margaret "Peg" Ijams, niece of Mother Seton, a former Episcopalian, were members. Mrs. Ijams attended the canonization of Mother Seton at the Vatican, saying to friends how much she really enjoyed it. Mr. and Mrs. GE Kidder Smith (Dorothy) were regulars, and he had authored *The New Churches of Europe*, a painstaking survey of hundreds of new church buildings.

Walter and Pat Junker were always very helpful; indeed Pat was a part-time bookkeeper, and Walter gave me a box of cigars, with each label named as "Walk a Dog" because of how often at night I walked our dog, Rumor.

Then there was John F. Cartwright, MS, AAGO, FTCL, the talented yet humble organist who helped design the Aeolian-Skinner organ console; Steffi, the secretary from the neighborhood, of Czech background; and Jimmy Urso, the ever-present and knowledgeable sexton and verger (he would have been a graduate of the old Tammany Hall largesse if it had not been for the church). Judith Sayer, assistant director of New York's English-Speaking Union, and Rosemary Vananame were in the altar guild, among so many saints of the parish.

In terms of clergy, the Reverend William Tully, who later became rector of St. Bartholomew's Church on Park Avenue, was a bright, articulate seminarian whom I waited for to be ordained as curate. He and his wife, Jane, asked me to baptize their firstborn son, Adam. Hugh Hildesley, a director at Sotheby's Parke Burnett, who later became ordained and rector of the Church of the Heavenly Rest on Fifth Avenue, with his wife, Connie, was in charge of the Sunday school. Under Dr. McCandless, the Reverend Alan Houghton had become rector of Heavenly Rest earlier.

Later there was also the Reverend Constance Coles, who broke ground in 1978 as the first woman assistant at Epiphany. By her gracious manner of ministry, she patiently waited it out so that some could catch on to the idea of a female priest, especially older women who had known ministry only in terms of lay service and others not used to receiving communion from a woman. But she persevered, and in time, everyone loved her, as you will read later.

After the Reverend William Stemper, who also headed the Forum for Corporate Responsibility, the Reverend Martin Seeley became a fellow curate. Martin was born in England, a graduate of Cambridge University, and had just completed an advanced degree at Union Seminary. Martin was also an assistant at Trinity Institute, under the direction of the Reverend Dr. Dustin MacDonald, later dean of the Seminary of the Southwest in Austin, Texas.

After Epiphany, Martin became director of a popular graduate training center in Saint Louis, but he returned to England to become head of the ordination process for the House of Bishops. He then was called to be the rector of All Saints Church, London, where he married a female German-born Anglican priest, and now he and his wife and two children live in Cambridge, where he is dean of the seminary on campus. As of December 2014, however, he wrote that he has been appointed bishop of a Diocese in Suffolk, which included Ipswich, a long way from Cambridge but an honor no one would turn down. He and his wife, Jutta, will adjust well. He is the first priest from Epiphany to be become a bishop.

Epiphany had many illustrious clergy graduates. The Reverend Dr. Lee Belford was a longtime Sunday associate, as was the Reverend Dr. John Johnson, both serving long tenures.

Julian Robinson Jr., later president of the Tiger Fund, and Josie, his wife, were members, and I was asked to baptize their son. Blake Newton, who was a lawyer and a cartoonist on the side, was a vestry member; well-known Henry D. Whitney and the artist Alma Kline, who sculptured figures in the garden, were very active.

Because of that enclosed garden, the church had been given the nickname of the "Country Church in the City." Dr. Rita Morgan, a Quaker and social worker, loved the Epiphany and attended often. You can see by the diverse list of lay members that I had my job cut out for me.

Most of the others I first met were English nannies, those who had taken care of babies and children, who lived in the many walkups in that area of Manhattan. The church at that time had a reputation of being not just a social attraction, so to speak, but also where the more well-to-do families chose to worship, where their former maids lived. These nanny ladies were formidable and were not to be taken lightly.

This neighborhood south of Yorkville, where many German immigrants lived and incidentally where actor Jimmy Cagney grew up, had a Czechoslovakian background. The parish secretary at the time was of Czech background, and several Czech restaurants with delicious menus, like the Ruc or Vasata, as well as others, abounded in the immediate area.

Meanwhile, church people hoped for a seamless transition from Dr. McCandless to the new guy from Saint Louis, that is, where I would not ruin the smooth running of things by thinking I always knew best. For example, I was walking along East Seventy-Second Street with Dr. McCandless one day when the soon-to-retire Bishop Horace Donegan stepped out from a cab in front us.

Once on the sidewalk, he noticed then greeted Dr. McCandless, "Hello, Hugh. How are you?"

Then he asked who I was. Hugh told him. The bishop, attired in a black suit with his pectoral cross hanging in front of his purple shirt, firmly stated, "Now don't you ruin what Hugh has done!"

That was it. He left me standing with Dr. McCandless on the sidewalk without a further word. I felt like a schoolboy who had a lot to learn, which I found out soon enough that I did.

Hugh McCandless was rector from 1945 until 1972 when I arrived, but actually until I was instituted by the bishop a little later. Previously he had been rector of Christ Church, Suffern, New York, and before that, St. Simons in the Cove on Staten Island. His father had been a priest also. While at the Epiphany, he was busy in ecumenical affairs and had founded the East Midtown Hospital Chaplaincy, located at New York Hospital, just four or five blocks south of the parish. Carleton Sweetzer, another Episcopal priest, was the first chaplain, but it became increasingly interfaith over the years. Hugh was also a trustee of the Blind Players Lodge, the Cathedral of St. John the Divine, and the Corporation for the Relief of Widows and Orphans. In addition, he was also a chaplain to the Holland Lodge No. 8, where FDR had been a member earlier. He had graduated from Yale and the Virginia Theological Seminary and had earned an honorary doctorate from that institution, so he was most capable as rector. So capable, in fact, that he was loved by many for almost three decades! That is a feat in and of itself.

When we were together for two months in transition after I arrived, he offered a few pointers. For example, I noticed that he did a quick dress change before going out on the streets of the city. He would take off his clerical collar attached to a black dickey or rabat and, in its place, attach a Brooks Brothers white collar and tie to his white clerical shirt. Brooks Brothers in those days still sold those Victorian detached-style collars.

I asked, "Why do you change so often?"

He replied, "Are you taking the bus to a meeting?"

I told him that I was, and all he said was, "You will find out."

I walked over to Second Avenue from East Seventy-Fourth and York dressed in my clerical collar, and after waiting a few minutes, I saw the bus coming down the road. When it screeched to a noisy halt, I stepped up to get on. Almost immediately, a loud chorus of voices from some semi-inebriated passengers began.

"Hey, Father, do you think we are all going to hell now?"

"What do you think of Billy Graham?"

"How about the Ten Commandments, Father? Shouldn't more people obey them?"

Then I realized that guilt was hanging in the air, triggered by a clerical collar, and I understood what Hugh meant. Who needed such attention when it was obvious that answers were irrelevant? Any response would go nowhere. I sat down smiling and waited it out.

Another time when I was having some difficulty dealing with a parochial problem, I told Hugh about it. He replied, "Old boy, don't worry. Problems like these are just like the weather. You can't change it—you just have to endure it."

After Hugh and his wife, Dorothy, had moved from the city to their home slated for retirement outside of Yale University, I would invite him back to preach or to celebrate the Eucharist. Yet he was reluctant to step back into the fray, which was proper. It was my hand that was at the wheel now, not his, but Easter and Christmas, he often made exceptions and would return for one or more services. When he did, we would take breakfast down in the undercroft kitchen, with Margaret Wilkinson, the queen of the kitchen, a former English nanny, hovering over us. At that kitchen table, I remember seeing him line up five pills to take next to his coffee and jokingly explain about how each kept him alive. Now, later in life, I do the same.

I remember Hugh with great fondness, especially as a mentor who unselfishly helped me adjust to a new and different parish. He died at the age of eighty-one in January 1988, sixteen years after he had retired. He was truly an aristocrat of the spirit, the Saint of the Eastside.

CONSTANCE C. COLES

The first woman ordained at the Church of the Epiphany was Constance Coles, whose husband, William McKewon, also graduated from Union Seminary in New York City as she did, but then attended law school and became a nonprofit lawyer. They have two grown children, Sarah and Isaiah. Constance was one of the very first to be ordained in the whole diocese, and I asked her to become a curate on our staff after undergoing the difficult ordination process. She knew that she would find resistance to her being a priest because many of the older women were used to ministries that were not ordained and at which they had worked hard: the flower guild, the altar guild, lay reading, and service oriented toward helping the poor. However, those women often shared secrets with one another in the ladies' room, and Constance proposed to let me know if she overheard any serious squabble where no man dared to enter.

Older, famous, and seasoned Jeannette Picard had preached at the Epiphany earlier before it was fully legal for women to become ordained, and I am sure that Constance, still in seminary, was as impressed with her as I was. Jeannette and Jean Picard had set the record for the highest stratospheric balloon flying. However, when asked as a child in Belgium what she desired to be when grown up, she told her mother that she wanted to become a priest. Her mother broke out in tears, but the Reverend Jeannette Picard got her wish. It was a very, very long path, however.

Constance had the patience to quietly go about doing clergy duties without upsetting people, which was a difficult task. Some of the nannies, or English home nurses, were tough and did not accept change easily. But in time, by being low key, she won most people over. Knowing that Bible and broom go together, she rolled up her sleeves and shared the service ministries with these ladies, especially in our Every Monday Rummage Sale started by stalwart Jane Nickolic.

Also, there was an older gentleman who found it very difficult to receive communion from a woman and would not. He was old-school in many ways but also a delightful person, but at first, it was too far a reach for him. In a year or so, this same person finally gave in and accepted her as a priest, but it meant that Constance had to take the insult in stride. She believed that after people got to know her and had seen evidence of an effective ministry, that the proof was in the pudding, so to speak.

One young girl, Nicole Bingham, also joined her confirmation class by specifically changing churches to do so, seeing Constance as a role model for her in the early days of women's ordination. Later, this young lady became a lawyer, helping the poor through legal aid, not seeking the riches of Wall Street but the rewards of helping the less fortunate. Her parents, Walker and Nicolette Bingham, were faithful church people.

As an aside, I remember Constance telling a story about her father, who was a Quaker. Her mother was the Episcopalian whose brother had become a well-known priest, perhaps a model for Constance herself. Yet young Constance sometimes attended Quaker meetings in the Glen Cove area of Long Island, where she grew up. She told me that the meetinghouse had hard wooden benches for pews, and three people sat up in front of those benches on one of their own. No one spoke in the assembled congregation until an inner light moved a member to articulate his or her faith. She said she often became restless, waiting for the inner light to shine, and usually it was one woman each Sunday who broke the silence. Unfortunately, she said the same words from Scripture at each service, "For God so loved the world that He sent his only son." I believe that Constance probably became tired of that one text, but at least she had a personal story to tell in relation to it.

One of our oldest nannies, Molly Harvey, who volunteered in our Every Monday Rummage Sale as well as for the free clothing of the homeless of New York City afterward, died suddenly. A day or two later, I asked Constance to accompany me to her walkup flat. Since Molly had no relatives and lived alone, I suspected that like my Welsh grandmother, she kept cash hidden in case of emergencies. My grandmother did that in the earlier Great Depression when the banks closed.

We dared to pass under the yellow police tape of her open door to the flat and searched the tiny apartment. After an hour or so, we discovered, much to our surprise, mostly in shoeboxes here and there, not a few hundred dollars but at least three to four thousand dollars. I must say that Constance was astonished, but we knew what to do with the detected cache. Constance placed it in her discretionary fund at first and then legally had the money formed into the Molly Harvey Fund for the Needy. It served others well.

After seven years, Constance became the rector of All Saints Church in Harrison, New York, and then after a distinguished ministry reviving that parish, she was asked by the bishop to become canon for ministry, a big job in a large diocese. I only saw her once in those years, and that was for lunch on Amsterdam Avenue, next to the Cathedral of St. John the Divine. She was very happy in her position, relating that when she was given the title canon, she gained a fourth *C*, and in fact, the other canon called her 4C all the time. She has since retired, and I almost forgot that she was eleven years younger than I am, so she is entitled to be a retired aristocrat of the Episcopal Church.

WILLIAM VAN ORDEN GNICHTEL

Bill Gnichtel was not the first to introduce me to the Union Club in New York City, because vestry member Walter Birge, headmaster of the Town School, was emphasizing to me at the time that the club was a relatively short walk from the Epiphany. It had squash courts for exercise, the best dinner wine for modest prices, and a library where I could meditate on what I needed to say in a sermon. Ryland "Red" Chase sponsored my membership, for which I have always been grateful. Yet that was where I met Bill one day through Scotty, the squash trainer, who said politely that the two of us would be a good match. That is, we were not that accomplished at the sport. As a result, we hit it off as friends while working up a sweat in the small courts, where we ran and batted the little black ball, not nearly as proficiently as some. After a while, we routinely enjoyed the exercise around 5:00 PM with a discussion to follow over a drink in the pleasant surroundings of the Union Club's East Room downstairs. We would talk about life in general, foreign affairs, or the latest domestic politics.

Scotty was the squash trainer then, a man literally born in Scotland, as his nickname indicated, and he was a true gentleman. I learned from him enough of the game to play it, as I am sure Bill did to improve his, although I believe that Bill started earlier than I did. One evening, in the East Room, I mentioned that Elsie and I were looking for a place outside the city to enjoy summers while on vacation, and he suggested the Onteora Club, high up in the Catskill Mountains, about two and a half hours away by car. We had searched earlier for such a place—one, a cottage rented by us four hours away in the Adirondacks from Jack and Lucilla Woodward, a fellow classmate from the Seminary of the Southwest, another on Block Island, and third, even farther away in Maine. On Bill's urging, who actually started the reciprocal privilege around 1973 when he was on the Onteora board, we decided to give it a try. So we drove up by way of the New York Thruway, then encountered the windiest mountain road, named 23A, in the whole state, past scenic Kaaterskill Falls (painted by the Hudson Valley romantic school of artists), and finally arrived in the mountaintop village of Tannersville.

Above the village, about another five hundred feet, we found the entrance to the club and discovered there a truly hidden Shangri-La. From the Field House rooms for guests, we enjoyed a magnificent view of a valley between mountains that contained a small lake and a nine-hole golf course. The Field House itself also included a dining room, bar, and fireplace. Above the dining room, the guest rooms were more than adequate. Next to that building was a theater where children and adult plays were performed in the summer, and slightly above the first tee nearby was a tennis and golf shop with the tennis courts one level up again from the first golf tee.

One could see two more levels in this 2,400-foot piece of property where interesting homes existed between thick pickets of trees and bushes. A library, filled with books as well as photos of notable members in art, writing, and sport, was also on the club grounds. Just off the county road from Tannersville, next to the back entrance to the club, was a lovely turn-of-the-century church, Episcopal in background, with a cemetery across the road from it. We immediately decided that Onteora was where we would like to reside, even live part time in the future.

On our first trip, Bill invited us over to his home, named Briars, and we met vivacious Emily, his wife, and two sons, Bill Junior and Ned, the youngest. Later, when Ned was still young, we always called him Neddy, but since he has grown up to stand at least six foot five and has an adorable wife and son, we hesitate to use his nickname ever again. Bill Junior became a well-known sculpture artist. Other club members were invited to meet us, such as Macy Chamberlain and his wife, Erma, also his daughters Christina and Marsha, with Tom and Daisy Wenzel, and many others.

We discovered that Emily was very active in philanthropic organizations, such as Sheltering Arms Senior Services and the Welfare Trust Fund of the Junior League, and volunteered for educational institutions such as Smith College, her alma mater. She loved horses and international travel, especially to Paris and London, where she lived briefly as a teenager. In fact, when in London, she and other young ladies were once presented to the queen. Her mother, May Davies Martenet, was a novelist of several well-known books and articles, particularly in the *Ladies' Home Journal* and *Harpers*.

Bill and Emily's church membership was at Heavenly Rest Episcopal Church near their apartment on East Ninety-Sixth Street and Fifth Avenue, but Bill often came to the Epiphany. One day, in some conversation we had after squash, he once ironically asked, "Do you know what Oscar Wilde once said about the subject we have been discussing?" I said no. He stated, "A saint has a past but a sinner has a future!" Of course, I used that poignant phrase in a sermon—how could I do otherwise?

Bill graduated from Trinity College, Hartford, Connecticut, and the law school of Columbia University, New York City, and in time, he became a partner with Whitman and Ransom law firm in the city. In a leap of faith, he and Emily traveled abroad to Riyadh, Saudi Arabia, where Bill became a licensed Saudi Arabian lawyer. In 1983, a preface to his expertise in regard to the intricacies of performance guarantees in Saudi Arabia stated the following:

> The many U.S. banks now joining in Middle East bank loans and guarantee syndications totaling billion of dollars will be interested in the discussion of the syndicated bank guarantee facilities provided by contractors to Saudi governmental agencies. The author explains various widely misunderstood aspects of bank guaranties under Saudi law and practice, particularly

the circumstances under which performance and advance payment guaranties may continue to be binding beyond the expiration date expressively stated in the guarantee. He also describes recent developments in Saudi administrative practices.

I don't pretend to understand all this, but I get the gist, and in any case, Bill knew his stuff and paved the way for better relations with the Saudis in more ways than oil production alone. By the way, Bill must have stood out by his personal presence in Saudi Arabia, being well over six feet tall, with a shock of black hair, chiseled features, perhaps Dutch in background, a strong chin, and considered, I believe, by most women as handsome.

After we moved from the city to Dallas and then Paris, France, we saw Bill and Emily on occasion when we returned. Bill was so intelligent and popular that he was elected president of the Onteora Club. In 1972, Bill forged the way legally to incorporate all Souls Church in Onteora as nondenominational, therefore saving the church many unneeded costs and, in Bill's words, "obtain a ruling from the Internal Revenue Service that the Church was a qualified tax-exempt entity and that contributions were tax-deductible."

Much loved Bishop Brown, retired Episcopal bishop of the Diocese of Albany and local member, supported this move, along with Macy Chamberlain, who at the time was a kind of patriarch of the club. There was some debate about whether the church was nondenominational or Episcopalian, but Macy Chamberlain insisted that the church be incorporated under the nondenominational chapter of the New York religious corporation law because that had been an understanding since its beginning. Bill had been on the Onteora board for seven years, as executive vice president and then as president in 1977 for his last year.

One of the saddest events in Bill's life was that Emily died of heart failure at the early age of fifty-six after a short illness, leaving Bill alone for some time. After the two had moved earlier from New York City to Madison, New Jersey, Bill sold his home in Onteora.

After much time had passed, Bill got lonely enough like most of us to date a few ladies. One young woman evidently did not realize Bill's age as they began discussion over dinner about World War II. They started talking about Adolf Hitler. When Bill mentioned that he had heard him speak on the radio (Bill and I were both born in 1934, too young to fight but not too young to follow the news of the war), she looked at him and, with a surprised look on her face, decried, "You heard Hitler speak?" He said that after that, they did not see each other again.

Eventually, he renewed acquaintances, however, with an old family friend, Mary "Molly" Bell Gayley of Lincoln, Massachusetts. She was an accomplished artist who was administrator of the American Wing of the Metropolitan Museum of Art in the city, and they were married in 1996 at the Church of the Heavenly Rest in Manhattan. They both live in Lincoln, Massachusetts, with routine trips to the city and also back to Onteora. They joined a trip through France sponsored by the American Cathedral in Paris before Elsie and I left the City of Lights, and we were delighted to spend time together again.

Bill has been a longtime friend, a fine churchman, and an expert international lawyer, with a keen sense of humor, and I consider him to be an aristocrat of the spirit in more ways than one.

FRANCIS D. EVERETT

Fran and his lovely wife, Ellie, were some of the residents of Manhattan we first met in Onteora after Bill Gnichtel encouraged us to become guests in the Field House. While at the Field House, Ellie Everett called us by phone to invite us to a dinner party to meet several other people, including her sister Happy Davis, who at the time was married to John Davis, whose family had sponsored the Davis Cup. We had an encouraging time together with the Everetts and, in the process, became better acquainted. In fact, after we were accepted as members, we asked Ellie, who was in charge of Onteora real estate at the time, to show us cottages to purchase. We settled on an old home that was dated back to 1888, named Crowfoot (it's a flower!). Although it was not expensive to buy at the time, it needed a lot of work, and we have been at improvements and repairs for more than thirty-five years now!

Fran soon invited me to play golf with him and his favorite partner, Dr. Craig Smith. We therefore began a threesome to play on weekends, but when each of us proceeded to the first tee, we usually tried to hit off without a mulligan (that is, a failed first shot that led us to a freebie second shot), but we almost always failed.

Then I became used to hearing Dr. Smith's groans when his bell bounced off a tree on a narrow fairway and ensconced itself in deep foliage. His moans of self-degradation then turned into very loud curses after he could not find the ball and had to take a penalty. We all did the same very often, but we had fun.

It is interesting to note that Smith served in World War II as a tank commander in the Canadian army's invasion of Normandy in 1944, and in the battle, he was blown out of his tank by the superior armored shells of the German Panzer tanks. He had had back problems ever since that horrible time, but he never used that injury as an excuse for a poor golf shot!

Yet you may ask how an Episcopal rector of a parish got away from the city and returned in time for his services on Sunday. Well, most Fridays were my days off, so after retrieving the car from the bowels of a garage where English was often a second language, I drove in typical hyper New Yorker style through honking cars and cutting-in taxies to pick up Elsie after her teaching ended at the Hewitt School on Madison Avenue. We then hustled out of the city before the massive 4:00 PM weekend traffic caused by an impossible jam-up and scooted along, avoiding barging, noisy trucks on the upper deck of the George Washington Bridge to the Palisades Parkway. Then we exited to the thruway and finally reached the mountaintop of the Catskills, taking only two and a half hours when lucky. I returned to the city by car most Saturday evenings, although when activities slowed down in the summer, I would arise at 5:00 AM on Sundays and drive lickety-split back in about two hours because there was no resistance, no traffic at all.

Francis D. Everett Jr. and Eleanor Delafield Everett have been fast friends since 1976. Fran is one of the most interesting persons I have ever met. He is ninety-one years old and has now left New York City for a residence near their son John and his family in Virginia near Washington, DC. Fran was born May 17, 1923, in Milton, Massachusetts, and his sister and brother are still living at ninety-four and eighty-seven, respectively. The family moved to Rye in 1928 because his father became managing partner of Hornblower and Weeks, a Boston firm that expanded to New York. Fran attended St. Mark's Episcopal School in Southborough, Massachusetts, but contracted bronchitis that resulted in an invitation to spend the winter in a warmer climate, the Fresnal Ranch School in Tucson, Arizona. Actually, Fran really wanted to go to Arizona so badly because his brother had done so and had grown six inches as a result, or at least that was Fran's hope as well.

Since Fran was shorter and thought he would grow taller in Arizona, he had turned a hose on himself, hoping that if he caught pneumonia, he would be sent there. He was successful and consequently got very sick and attended the prized school in Tucson, but as he once stated, he was disappointed to grow very little. When he was well again, he finally returned to St. Mark's, where he graduated in 1941, starting a freshman year at Harvard in that fall. Fran wrote up what happened next:

> In December of 1941, the Japanese bombed Pearl Harbor and the US was at war. I wanted to enlist right away, but my father insisted that I finish my freshman year and apply for a leave of absence, which I did. I then tried to enlist in the army, but was turned down as 4F because of hay fever and because I had to wear glasses! Through a school friend I heard about the American Field Service that had been doing front line ambulance work for the French in France and following the fall of France, was now enlisting men to serve with the British 8th Army in North Africa. This was just the ticket for me and I enlisted in June 1942, but transport did not become available for my group until October 3rd. On that day we left Penn Station for Baltimore where we boarded a Norwegian freighter loaded with nothing but munitions bound for India, but it would stop in Durban, South Africa and let us off there. Because of our cargo we traveled alone and it was a long scary voyage of six weeks, climaxed by a close call with a German submarine off the entrance of Durban Harbor. From Durban we were transported to Suez on the New Amsterdam which had been transformed from a passenger liner to a transport.

The war years were spent in North Africa and at the end in Germany. I came home end of July 1945 and was immediately ordered to take an army physical and this time I was 1A! Shortly after I received a notice from my local draft board in Rye that I was their man for August.

The irony of Fran being their "man for August" after more than three years of being shelled and attacked while helping the wounded and dying, and even liberating a Nazi concentration camp, was more than most his age then could bear.

When he was summoned to the draft board, he confronted the man who headed it by asking what he could do to relate his previous service. The draft board head responded, "Only General Hershey himself, the head of the Selective Service Organization, and no one else."

"What's his number?"

The draft board chief reluctantly gave him the phone number, shaking his head as if it would not do Fran any good. It was a Saturday anyway, but Fran walked determinately over to the phone hanging on a wall, dialed the general's number, and after several operator delays, got him on the phone personally, pouring out to him his long story of active service. The general listened and then told Fran he wanted to speak to the head of that draft board. Fran went back to the board table, and the man behind it asked with a smirk what he wanted.

"I have someone on the line who wants to speak to you."

"And who could that be?"

"General Hershey!"

The man's face dropped, but he quickly picked up the phone extension in front of him, and listening to the rant from the general for several minutes, he kept saying "Yes, sir" four or five times. He finally hung up and then, as quickly as he could, stamped Fran's selective service card "Already served" and with a frown told him to leave.

Do you think today we could call up a general on a Saturday and reach him directly? I doubt it. I remembered General Hershey because he was still in the job in the 1950s when I received my SSO card with his name authorizing my service. This card prompted me to join ROTC in 1952 at Stanford, where I was commissioned in 1956.

After Fran finally graduated from Harvard, he decided to earn an MBA from Harvard Business School and then was hired by Morgan

Stanley and Co. Later, in the summer of 1952, he met his bride to be, Eleanor, on a train ride to Martha's Vineyard, and they were married in 1953 and, after two years at Madison and Ninety-Fifth Street, moved to 125 East Eighty-Fourth Street, where they lived for fifty-six years.

Fran is one of the best storytellers I have known. For example, he related a fascinating account of a plane trip he and Ellie took in a four-engine propeller-driven TWA Constellation flight from Spain to New York. He said that the plane took off just fine, but after several hours, the pilot informed the passengers that they needed to land in the Azores for more fuel due a very strong headwind. That evidently went well. And they took off again. About halfway across the Atlantic, during dinner, Fran looked out the starboard side of the plane and was frightened to see that the number 1 engine of the four was on fire. After a moment or two, the pilot came to the cabin to calm the passengers, saying, "We had a fire in the first engine due to the terrible winds, but not to worry, we have feathered it, and this plane can fly on three engines."

Fran and Ellie settled back to relax as the plane droned on for several hours more until another shocking event occurred. Fran could see that the far engine on the port side had lighted up with flames. Again, the pilot came on to say, "Yes, we had another engine failure, but while we can't fly as high as we would like, please keep calm. The British navy has assured us that they will pour oil on the waters so we can land safely, if necessary. However, please assume the emergency posture just in case."

So Fran and Ellie did as they were told, and when Fran bent over as the pilot instructed for the emergency position, he could feel the plane flying lower to the sea. In fact, he could see out the window that the waves were way too high for oil to do any good. They were both terrified.

Suddenly, however, they felt the airplane begin to rise sharply, as if the pilot had pulled the yoke all the way back toward him. The plane kept rising until it began to flutter down again, and it landed hard and bounced but kept rolling until the remaining engines burned out as well. They had landed on an abandoned WWII army air strip in Greenland. A jeep came out to see why they were there. Then they realized they were safe and were overjoyed to be taken in several trips to a Quonset hut at the end of the long landing strip. Another TWA airplane finally arrived and took them home to New York.

The amazing thing for me was that I remember reading in *Reader's Digest* about this flight and the brave pilot who saved everyone at the last moment. I never thought I would meet face-to-face someone who had actually been on that flight.

Later, Fran related that his only son, John, was born in 1963, and consequently, Fran began working in a firm that paid higher wages and, two years later, bought his home in Onteora. He then worked for a family firm, F. S. Smithers, for twelve years, but after a Wall Street crisis, he found another job at a unit of Fiduciary Trust Company and stayed with this firm, Mengel, McCabe and Co., until it went out of business in 1988. He was sixty-five and eligible for Social Security, so he retired. Yet needing to do something, he took a course at H&R Block Co. and did a season of tax work with them. Then he joined a Manhattan church that needed bookkeeping and financial assistance, and eventually it became a full-time job. He called it quits at eighty, and that was eleven years ago.

If anyone qualifies to be an aristocrat of the spirit, it is this fascinating man and his many, many life experiences that occurred before WWII, during that horrific time and after it to today.

HELEN CLARK BERLIND

Helen Polk "Polky" Clark Berlind was born in Mississippi but was an active church member and a mother of four children at the Epiphany when I arrived as rector. She was vivacious, warmhearted, and pretty, as I remember her. Helen was also a hard worker as a volunteer and a devout supporter of community causes, as were many others at the parish. We loved her strong Southern accent, but we didn't know her husband well at the time. Her children attended different New York private schools on the Upper East Side. I soon discovered that she was married to Roger Stuart Berlind, an extremely talented theatrical producer and a director of Lehman Brothers in its heyday.

It was his Broadway productions that interested me, such as *Amadeus, Long Day's Journey into Night, Guys and Dolls, A Funny Thing Happened on the Way to the Forum, Kiss, Me Kate, Driving Miss Daisy*, and a revival of *Wonderful Town*, among many others. Even though he was not a member of the parish because he was Jewish, he attended with

Polky on occasion and especially at the baptisms of her children. They were like many other mixed-faith families at the Epiphany.

However, sad to remember, she and three children were on board Eastern flight 66, a Boeing 727 that crashed in Queens, near JFK airport, while attempting to land in the midst of a sudden wind shear, which was unknown at the time but later discovered to be the culprit. She was thirty-nine, her eldest daughter was twelve, and her two sons were aged nine and six. They were among the 113 that died on the flight, along with the Episcopal bishop of New Orleans, the Right Reverend Iverson Noland.

The news of their deaths came as a great shock since I was not immediately aware that she was on that fated plane. When I read the names in the newspaper, I suspected that they were our parishioners, but of course, I hoped, like many others, that there was some mistake. No first names were listed, and I had not known the vacation plans of the family, but then a former vestry member called me in the evening and confirmed my suspicions.

When I was absolutely sure that the family had perished, I called Mr. Berlind to see if I could make a pastoral visit at his home. I did not know what state Roger would be in since I heard that he had been at the airport, holding the baby, who was two years old, who did not go with his mother, waiting for his family like so many other tragically stricken people.

Ever gracious, he invited me to come by and was very hospitable when I did so, in spite of his grief. Yet as we talked, I remember him saying something to the effect that it was absurd. Literary Philosopher Albert Camus would have probably agreed with him, but I sensed that he was trying to put the tragedy together, and it was hard, if not impossible.

Later, when Polky's family arrived in New York along with Roger's brothers, they all slowly, ever so slowly, began to talk about the crash and finally the funeral arrangements, which Roger hoped would be a small private affair. Actually, more than three hundred people attended the services.

Roger eventually requested that the remains be placed in our columbarium downstairs, which was underneath Faith chapel in the undercroft. It had been there since Dr. McCandless was rector, when a parishioner, in memory of her husband, gave a wall of niches so that people could be buried in their church and in Manhattan—where no usable cemeteries remained.

Later, when the Berlind plaque had been made, depicting those who had died, Roger told me that he wanted to place the inscribed plaque himself in the niche. It served as the door to the small tomb. There was little emotion as he did so, and he wanted no prayers. It was a time of silence, much like what we had together in his home with the two families, that is, no theological clichés, just a time of silent sharing, although I whispered to myself prayers for the occasion.

After the crash, the Epiphany became a communication center for all the tragic news that was transmitted about Polky and their children, but it was more than just communication, because it was also deeper: it amounted to a form of communion. The church is a fellowship of Good News and should help its members absorb bad news, placing tragedy in perspective. It isn't always what we articulate but what we share together that deepens this fellowship and can help transform suffering.

Nicholas Berdyaev opposed the word *communication* in favor of *communion*, and he believed that any unity in the world would come through a "transfiguration" of human society. For our small church community, some true communion was achieved through our communication of the events to help people get the message straight, but I like to believe that perhaps this tragedy was transfigured through sharing of information rather than avoiding or repressing it.

My thoughts turned to the theology of Jürgen Moltmann in his book *The Crucified God*. As a way to express Christian comfort, Moltmann speaks of the sense of God abandonment, as in the concentration camps of World War II, and that is what I saw in the fiery crash involving innocent people—*another crucifixion*. Pascal said that Christ would be in agony until the end of the world, and here was another case of it, which I believe God shares. I know that crash could have been considered an absurdity, as Camus might describe, but Moltmann's book helps us understand that we are not alone because *human suffering is also God's suffering.*

Incidentally, Roger often came back to the church undercroft to pay his respects to his lost family, laid to rest in our columbarium, but he remarried in 1979 and went on to create wonderful, fulfilling Broadway shows to lighten people's hearts. I believe the grace of God was with him, and I hope that the Epiphany helped him to recover. He and Helen were aristocrats of the spirit, in my mind, because people of the Book share the same hope in a god who loves us all.

EDWARD R. WARDWELL

In my view, Edward Rogers Wardwell was an awesome person, not just because he was senior warden of the parish, but also because he was a philanthropist of the first order in the city of New York. He was tall and distinguished, and he reminded one of a more handsome Charles de Gaulle. He was also a partner of the well-known law firm Davis Polk and Wardwell. My first encounter with him was when he spoke to me in a phone call in Creve Coeur, saying that I had been selected to become the next rector of the Church of the Epiphany.

While our conversation was short, I do remember referring to the name of the town we lived in, Creve Coeur, the way it was pronounced locally. He couldn't refrain from correcting me by saying, "I lived in Paris, France, for two years, and that is an incorrect way to pronounce Creve Coeur." He consequently said it correctly. I thought to myself that would not go down well with all the people who lived there.

However, I came to realize that Mr. Wardwell was as precise in speech as I had heard that he was when playing the piano. When he lost the perfect touch, he quit playing. While I respected him, I was also worried that perhaps I was too provincial at that time to make a good rector in Manhattan, and so I hesitated to agree to his proposal. That changed later with more negotiation.

When I finally accepted the position, I found out much more about him. He was a supporter of classical music in New York, along with his wife, Lelia. For more than ten years, they promoted the Lincoln Center for the Performing Arts, the Chamber Music Society of Lincoln Center, the Julliard School, and the Yale Music School.

He was a constant reminder to me of the way things should be in the parish even in the midst of conflict, which suddenly came to fruition one day when we received an unexpected gift by a young couple. The gift was totally unsolicited, and it began a long turmoil with the elected vestry. A clergy friend from out of town was visiting on a Saturday, and we walked to the church because he wanted to see the Epiphany. It was a Saturday, and only faithful Jimmy Urso, the sexton, was on the premises. When I entered the York Avenue door, Jimmy, ever solicitous, saw me, and the first thing he said was, "I didn't know what to do."

I asked him about what. He said that a young man and his wife had come by and had quickly installed a blue lily Tiffany glass pane in a small four-by-three slotted window above an equally small garden on East Seventy-Fourth Street. The man had made it himself from Tiffany glass fragments.

Shocked, I replied, "You mean it is in now?"

Looking downcast, old Jimmy said that it was. My friend and I looked at it, and while it was okay, it was not the greatest piece of stained glass I had ever seen, but it was not the worst either. I was no connoisseur, of course. So I pondered the problem: the vestry technically was in charge of the physical building, as I was only in charge of the spiritual life of the parish. Yet the vestry had advocated changes to help more new people into the church, and now two new people had installed the glass. Should we let it go and thank them, or yank it out because it was not officially approved? I took some time to ponder the problem. Here I was, still new to the church, and most people seemed to be accepting me, even though I represented for some a quite different course from the past.

Meanwhile, I had an opportunity to be a fellow of the college of preachers at the National Cathedral in Washington, DC, and I took advantage of it. My time spent in the college in study gave me a little space from the conflict. While there, I consulted the Reverend Loren Mead, brother to my NY doctor, Allen Mead, about the situation. Loren was at that time in charge of the Alban Institute, a congregational consulting group.

When I spoke to Loren about Epiphany, he asked, "How long have you been at the Epiphany?"

I responded, "About a year and a half."

Looking wise, he told me, "That is usually when parishioners find out that you are who you are, and not the 'messiah' they expected, and there is usually a temporary dysfunction. Don't worry, it's normal, and it will resolve itself."

I was greatly relieved, but I thought to myself, "Well, at least the disruption was not centered on heavy issues from the pulpit or altar, but over taste of a side window!"

Back in New York City, at the next vestry meeting, we discussed the issue, and the twelve members sitting at a round table were divided about what to decide. I thought, "When in doubt, appoint a committee." Therefore, I proposed an art committee to study the issue of removing it or leaving it.

The art committee met, with Mrs. Ewan "Louise" McVeigh, a wonderful longtime older member, and Mrs. Peter "Helen" Dubois, Edward Wardwell's daughter, and two or three others. After a long deliberation, their recommendation was to leave it in place, and if the window was not appreciated, in time the vines of the garden would cover it completely.

At the following monthly vestry meeting, that recommendation was presented, and a vote was taken. The vote was divided with Mr. Wardwell firm against the motion. When the majority voted in favor of the committee's recommendation, Mr. Wardwell stated to the group, "This is the first time in our history there has not been a unanimous vestry vote."

Of course, as a gentleman, he accepted the decision but took me aside and asked me to come to his office for lunch the following week on his top-floor highrise Wall Street office.

When we met, before lunch, I sat nervously in front of his office desk while he was situated as usual behind his. He told me sternly that the blue window was in terrible taste and that it never should have happened. I stammered a defense of the process to solve the problem, but then, like the gentleman he was, he ended our conversation by saying, "I have said my piece and now let us have lunch. Please call me Eddie from now on."

That relieved the tension, and I respected him even more as we left his office.

It is interesting to note that in regard to my call to be rector, Mr. Wardwell had taken the advice of the Reverend John C. Danforth, who, among others, including a respected consulting group, had recommended me for the Epiphany position. Jack was from Saint Louis and would later become a US senator as well as ambassador to the United Nations. Davis, Polk and Wardwell had hired him as a lawyer after graduation from Yale University with both a law degree and a divinity degree. Dr. McCandless had also asked him to be a Sunday associate in the parish while he practiced law. This was an intriguing connection I discovered much later about my call from Saint Louis to New York.

I believe it must have been extremely difficult for Mr. Wardwell to reconcile the artistic quality of the church he loved and me as the new rector, and his stately response proved him to be a true aristocrat of the spirit, a bona fide gentleman.

NANCY WALKER

One person at Epiphany who stands out in my mind needed a wheelchair to enter church services, which she did regularly, and she was Miss (not Ms.) Nancy Walker. I often found her, with some attendant wheeling her, near what was nicknamed the Walker Window, a stained-glass window at the end of the walkway that ran up directly to a niche on the side of the sanctuary with its great dossal.

The window was bright and cheerful and was given by Nancy in memory of her mother, Mrs. George Herbert Walker (Lucretia Wear). Her parents sired six children: Dorothy Wear Walker, who married US senator Prescott Bush, their son being President George HW Bush; George Herbert Walker Jr., who was an original co-owner of the Mets baseball team; Dr. John Walker, CEO of Sloan Kettering Hospital; James Wear walker; and Louis Walker.

I heard from Dr. McCandless that Nancy had had a severe stroke that limited her to a wheelchair, some believed because she was overly active in so many New York volunteer service groups that she forgot to take care of her health. As a consequence, she was handicapped all her remaining life. Yet she was very welcoming to the newly arrived Hunts, having us to dinner at her apartment, sometimes with one of her brothers present, Dr. Walker or George Walker. I remember one such social engagement when Dr. John Walker was present and he had also become handicapped, I imagine, from a stroke, but I do not know, and yet not one word in the lively dinner discussion was mentioned about their limitations.

One time we were invited to visit her in her special cottage at Kennebunkport, Maine, and we did so, not only having a grand time with Nancy but also enjoying a clear, sunny day so near the water.

Another time, she invited me to say prayers at the gathering of the Walker and Bush clan in a strategic hotel near Midtown, and I did so, not knowing much about the many there, except for noticing one young but future president in the group. Nancy was very sentimental, and she often was briefly overcome by emotion when talking about her nephew US President George H. W. Bush and his wife, Barbara.

Later in life, she became so handicapped that she decided to reside in the grand retirement center of the Roman Catholic Church on the corner of York Avenue and East Seventy-Second Street, Mary Manning Walsh Home. Because I had several others in the center nearby the Epiphany, I often visited and occasionally had tea or coffee with the headmistress and director, a member of the Carmelite order for care for the aged and infirm. She was a smart and dynamic Carmelite sister, who once said to me, "Can't you send us someone who could actually pay their way, helping us with our budget, instead of those darling nannies, who depend on Medicare? We have to subsidize those whom we have accepted from your parish."

Well, I had to write a letter to support Nancy's entrance, just like the many nannies, but she was quite capable of fulfilling the sisters' financial hope. She was so happy in her new location that she came to know a retired Roman Catholic priest living at the home. He called on Nancy probably four or so times a week, and they became good friends. Consequently, she decided to be accepted into the Roman Catholic Church. The head sister called me to tell me this, and I was happy for Nancy, because it gave her peace, and in fact, I believe her father had been a devout Roman Catholic. Jonathon, President George H. W. Bush's younger brother, and his wife, Jody, lived in the city at the time, and they expressed to me that they were very pleased to have Nancy spiritually content.

Nancy Walker was a kind, sentimental, religious, and generous person whom I consider to be another aristocrat of the spirit.

FREDERICA RHINELANDER LANDON

In my first years at the Church of the Epiphany, a person, among many I encountered, stands out clearly in my mind. Perhaps this is because she knew so much about my own field of interest. She was a faithful, every-Sunday parishioner whose name was Mrs. Harold Landon, who had been widowed for some years. I arranged to make a home call where she lived in Manhattan House on East Sixty-Sixth Street, between Second and Third Avenues. After I arrived in the building and took the elevator to her floor, I knocked on her door, and when she opened it, she greeted me with a pleasant smile into her apartment. I recall that she was extremely pretty for her near eighty years of age, thin, with white hair coiffured perfectly, and with the most excellent posture and straight spine I could remember seeing for a woman her age. We sat down where she invited me to sit in the living room, and she asked me if I preferred tea or coffee. I politely said to her tea. She seemed so regal I felt a little nervous, but she put me at ease.

She soon explained that she had a pacemaker and was adjusting to it, and she helped me understand how she could make sure it was operating correctly through a phone call on her landline, although she had to be checked by the doctor in his office regularly. While such a device is routine now, it was new to me in the middle 1970s. Then she talked about her husband and his death, but she said, "Do you know that I almost died once?"

I asked the circumstances, and she related that she was playing tennis when she was eighteen years of age, and it occurred in the middle of a tennis game. She survived and only needed the implanted device a short while ago. I tried to add up the years in my mind since she said that the attack was in 1918, shortly after World War I, the "war to end all wars."

So it was nearly sixty years before, and I was amazed. As we chatted, the subject of my last sermon came up. It concerned the quote from Nicholas Berdyaev, the one that I had heard from Merrill Hutchins in seminary. It was, again, "Neither the Proletariat of the East nor the Bourgeois of the West, but Aristocracy of the Spirit," which I had assumed, in my ignorance, no one at Epiphany had heard of before. I was very wrong, really wrong.

Mrs. Landon then pointed to her large collection of books in a shelf against a dividing wall between the living and dining area. She turned to me, and her steely blue eyes looked into my own as she stated with a steady voice full of authority, "There, Dr. Hunt, is his whole collection. I have read every one of his profound books. Did you know, for example, that he died in a home that was made for him in Clamart, France, at the bequest of an English admirer? He died at his desk in March of 1948, when he was seventy-four, having completed his last work, *The Kingdom of Caesar and of the Spirit*." Then she quoted two church fathers who matched Birdie's belief in the divine humanity of man: Iraneus, who wrote that "He became like us that we might become like Him," and then Athanasius, "He became human that we might become divine."

Well, I was completely humbled, thinking I was so smart, and I never forgot her. She was not gloating, just speaking in a natural way about a subject with which she was very familiar. I made a mental note to myself to remember how intelligent this new congregation was and to make sure I was on my toes, so to speak, in the pulpit.

She went on to talk about her husband, Harold Morton Landon, and their marriage at the Cathedral of St. John the Divine by her uncle, the Right Reverend Philip Rhinelander, bishop of Pennsylvania, which led to my questioning if Philip H. Rhinelander, who was a professor at my alma mater, Stanford University, was his son. She said that was correct. The Rhinelander I had heard of and then known as an active layman in the Diocese of California was a philosophical genius, writing about good and evil, and now I know where it came from!

We also talked about her cousin Frederick King, the architect of the Church of the Epiphany, along with Mr. With, whose wife was alive then and active in the church. The two met in Paris when young and later formed a business together. The two sons of Frederick King, named Jonathon and David, became Episcopal priests. I met David's son Nicholas King at her home once later, and we had an interesting conversation.

I called on her a few more times, and she caught me up on the families associated with the Epiphany and the greater church. When she died, she was interred in our columbarium, the first in the city of New York after there were no burial sites left in Manhattan .She wanted to be close to the church, and that was the only way it could happen. Mrs. Landon was a noble and intelligent soul, a true aristocrat of the spirit who knew what I had been talking about even more than I did.

ALLEN W. MEAD

Internist and Cardiologist Allen Mead became a longtime friend after I was referred to him as a nearby New York City doctor who treated the whole family. He was a graduate of Davidson College in North Carolina, where he was a champion varsity golfer, even vying with Arnold Palmer in 1946, '47, '48, and '49. His brother Loren Mead became a well-known Episcopal priest in Washington, DC, who founded the Alban Institute in the basement of St. Alban's Parish Church on the grounds of the National Cathedral. The institute was formed to help congregational development and assist clergy in that process, but after forty years, it finally closed in the year 2014. Allen served in the navy as a medical lieutenant officer and was attached to the Marine Corps from 1950 to1954, serving in both Korea and Japan. There are also many doctors in Allen's historic family.

Although Allen lived near Gramercy Park in the East Twenties of Manhattan, his practice was located next to New York Hospital at East Sixty-Ninth and York Avenue. He had been an instructor of medicine at New York Hospital from 1954 to 2008, then a professor of medicine to the present time, along with his practice for many years. As a lifelong Episcopalian from South Carolina, he attended the Church of the Epiphany near his office but primarily St. George's / Calvary Church in the Gramercy area. Over the years, some of his many patients included Alistair Cooke of *Masterpiece Theatre*, who lived to be ninety-four, Margaret Truman, the president's daughter and an author, and Martha Graham and her whole dance troupe.

His great sense of humor was somewhat shattered for a while by the illness of his daughter, Martha, who somehow developed advance leukemia during her pregnancy, and although Mary Ann, his granddaughter, was delivered without a problem, Martha had to be treated for her disease. That was an unpleasant task at the time because she had to be sequestered in total isolation for a long period of days until a bone marrow transplant could be attempted. Everyone waited for the day that the transplant would occur. Her brother, Allen Jr., volunteered, and when the time was ripe, the procedure was implemented. But it was to no avail, and after more of an ordeal for her, she died.

It was a devastating conclusion and had its effects on the family. I called on her fairly often at the isolation wing, and I also deeply felt the loss, but more so did Allen. It took some time for him to resume his helpful bedside manner as a caring doctor for others, but he surely did. Anne, his wife, however, had a more difficult time. Parents rarely get completely over any child's death, and it leaves deep scars. Anne became ill and was bedridden at home for some time, finally needing hospice care. Allen also took care of her in that period of their lives together, and then she too, like her daughter at the hospital, passed away at home in Gramercy.

Not long ago, however, Allen told a happy story about an airplane flight they as a family took when the children were young. On this particular flight, Anne was recognized by the other flight attendants as a longtime friend and as one of their own. They invited her to sit with them in the back of the plane while Allen and kids were in first class upfront. Suddenly there was an announcement supposedly by one of the crew, and that was a kind of joking reprimand. It went something like this: "Will the father of those rowdy boys in the front of the plane please try to control them? They're making too much noise."

So Anne had her laugh on her husband in those former days when the three children were young, John, Allen Jr., and Martha.

About his time, my daughter had a bout of facial cancer that was diagnosed by Dr. Michael Jacobs after referral by Dr. Mead. Michael is our personal friend who graduated from Baylor University, and Weill Cornell for his medical degree. He is board certified and teaches at New York Presbyterian Hospital, and his diagnosis allowed my daughter, in time, after many surgeries, to be healed, even though it was a perilous journey.

He is a renowned photographer and a board member in the Whitney Museum, MoMA, and the Asia Society of New York. Recently, he forged better relations with China's art world. *Now You See* is the first exhibition of a survey of young Chinese video artists by Dr. Jacobs, who has been collecting Chinese video art in depth since 2010. It has been shown at the Whitebox Art Center, and the write-up cites, "Unlike the West, China has no tradition of video art. The works in this exhibition demonstrate a sophisticated approach to the medium that includes references to Western performance, video, body art, cinema, animation and conceptual art that has become visible in recent years, and transforms them into a fresh new language of the moving image." Michael's office is located at East Seventieth Street and First Avenue.

When it was discovered that I had a urology problem, Allen sent me to Dr. Thomas McGovern, who, in turn, introduced me to his assistant at the time, Dr. Scott David. He took control of the bladder cancer problem and, after a year or so, finally smashed bladder stones and eliminated the growths nearby. It took several surgeries, but Dr. David was persistent, and in time, I was healed, although I need to be checked routinely. Dr. David moved his office to New York Hospital and is there now. He is a Phi Beta Kappa graduate of Vanderbilt University, and his medical degree is from Weill Cornell Medical College. He is board certified and also teaches at Cornell, like Allen Mead has also. I owe him much for his expertise. I remember, when he first saw my case, he wondered if I would lose my bladder, but no problem so far.

He is married to Alison and has a young baby boy named Cameron. I would recommend him to anyone, and Allen Mead was correct to send me to the doctors he trusted when they were ill.

Yet Allen would have his turn, unexpectedly. After he was widowed, we introduced him to Mary Evelyn Dean, retired CIA assistant director, also widowed, and they hit it off famously. But after taking a trip together and in jet lag, Allen was climbing the tall staircase in his New York apartment duplex and tripped, falling down the full flight of stairs, breaking his neck, and incurring a concussion. Mary Evelyn called 911, and he was immediately taken to St. Vincent's Hospital, but because he knew so many doctors at New York Weill Cornell, he insisted on going there, where he would remain for several months.

An operation fused his neck, and he recovered from the concussion. After a period of recuperation, the two decided to be married, and that happy event occurred at the high altar of the National Cathedral in Washington, DC, on April 10, 2010, perhaps because she was head of All Hallows Guild at the cathedral and his brother, Loren, was well-known there. In any case, I had the privilege to officiate at the marriage, and now Allen is doing well.

While caring for others all his life, he also won many awards, such as the Mason Hicks Award for Distinguished Service, and he has also over the years played championship golf from the Far East to the New York City Physicians League. Yet at eighty-six years of age, he has Mary Evelyn at his side. Now he has someone to care for him. It's only fair! I admire this man who has helped so many, and in my book, he is an aristocrat of the spirit.

RENÉ DUBOS

Mrs. Jean Dubos, a microbiologist at Rockefeller University, was at one time the head of the altar guild at the Church of the Epiphany. That relationship allowed me to get to know her and respect her, along with her famous husband. Jean was rather shy, quite pretty, and emanated sincerity and devotion to whatever her task was, in the laboratory at Rockefeller or in the sacristy at the Epiphany.

She was Bacteriologist Dr. Dubos's second wife. His first wife was Marie Louise Bonnet, whom he married in 1934 and who tragically died in 1942. In 1946, he married Jean, who had been working in Rockefeller University along with him, and together they coauthored *The White Plague*, which concerned tuberculosis. I have read that his first wife, Madame Bonnet, had died of that disease. The book urged a different social treatment rather than surgical procedure or drugs, and that reform helped many at the time. Much of the disease was later eradicated in the world, although there are occurrences or outbreaks in times of war and where poverty exists.

Jean was from Ohio and worked at Harvard Medical School, and there she became acquainted with Dr. Dubos, who was born in Saint-Brice, France, in February 1901 and attended the National Institute of Agronomy in Paris. He immigrated to the United States and then received his doctorate from Rutgers University. Naturalized in 1938, he spent most of his life at Rockefeller University, working in the field of microbes that caused dysentery, pneumonia, and tuberculosis, and in the 1940s, he demonstrated the feasibility of obtaining germ-fighting drugs from microbes, paving the way for antibiotics.

Yet I had no chance to know him then. It was only when he decided to leave the laboratory and enter the world of environmental problems that he attended the Epiphany. Consequently, I had an opportunity to meet him and get to know him.

When he wrote a book with Barbara Ward named *Only One Earth*, he helped readers understand the need for saving the earth from human exploitation. In another work in 1972, *The God Within*, he wrote, "There is no chance of solving the problem of pollution—or the other threats to human life—if we accept the idea that technology is to rule our future."

He received the Pulitzer Prize for *So Human an Animal* and is credited with the phrase "Think globally, act locally," which Dr. Dubos gave me permission to use on the bulletin cover of the Sunday service leaflet, since it was good theology as well as sound advice, uniting local cultural differences and ecological and economic problems with positive global action.

Living out his own maxim, Dr. Dubos joined Dr. Nathan Pusey, former president of Harvard University and also an Epiphany church member, as supporters and guest speakers at the formation of the Yorkville Luncheon Club. The Church of the Epiphany, St. Stephen of Hungary Roman Catholic Church, Jan Hus Presbyterian Church, and the Greek Orthodox Cathedral, under the leadership of Dean Robert Stephanopoulos, on East Seventy-Fourth Street joined together to sponsor and help fund a luncheon program for the elderly located at the Jan Hus Church.

We at Epiphany initiated this work with seed money we raised. As an aside, Stephanopoulos's son, George, is seen regularly on ABC Television nightly news. I remember, Dr. Dubos's impassioned speech at Jan Hus was so memorable that I never forgot how important "acting locally" was to those who needed assistance, especially the many older folks who lived in walkups or the general Yorkville neighborhood, many our own parishioners, as was Dr. and Mrs. Dubos. I also remember his saying that the Benedictines in France always left the fields in better condition than when they first worked them. This became his local model for all of us globally.

I also have all his books in my small library and treasure them. In his final work, *Celebrations of Life*, he wrote that "wherever human beings are involved, 'trend is not destiny.'" That gives us all hope, due to our being human and therefore in possession of free will. So impressed was I with Dr. Dubos's insight about current life that I made up a Sunday service leaflet cover with his following quotes:

> Think globally. But act locally
> Trend is not Destiny
> Optimism. Despite it all

Also, while theological ethicist Reinhold Niebuhr wrote from his early experience in Detroit slums that he was a "Tamed Cynic," Dr.

Dubos claimed that he was a "Despairing Optimist," which in my mind is a very serious and deeply theological statement. Why? Because the good Lord has given this world to us, and it is our proper stewardship of it, like the Benedictines he admired, that can make the difference. But we do not always choose the right path.

He also wrote that liturgy is necessary to the human spirit: the candles, the altar, the cross, or the torah, what have you, go back in time as symbols of the necessary sacramentality of our lives in conjunction with the Divine. In a biographical memoir written by James Hirsch and Carol Moberg, offered for his death on his birthday, February 20, 1982, Dubos was described by them as such:

> His name calls to mind a tall, vigorous, rosy cheeked man, with durable white wisps on a balding head, and beautiful large hands that enthusiastically punctuated every sentence. He was a spellbinding speaker, and prolific author. His charming French accent and his perfect command of English made any contact with him memorable. Whether it was a private conversation or a public lecture, he always spoke with the knowledge of a scientist, the eloquence of a poet, and the wisdom of a philosopher.

Carol Moberg, a fellow scientist at Rockefeller University, honored Dr. Dubos in her book *Friend of the Good Earth* in 2005.

Jean carried on after him in his and her own footsteps until her death at seventy years of age in 1988. When she was diagnosed with cancer, she came to talk to me in my office, and I remember her rather shyly, even nervously, citing that she was in a quandary. Since her cancer was inoperable, she questioned whether she should undergo an experimental treatment or just wait until the end, letting nature take its course. I listened to her for some time, and eventually she came to the conclusion that as a microbiologist, she would give the new treatment a try. She seemed resolved as she left, although I have pondered about that meeting ever since.

She was an attractive person in more ways than one, very patient and especially knowledgeable about the variables of life and death since she had done so much to help others heal and live. She and Dr. Dubos more than qualify as aristocrats of the spirit.

NATHAN MARSH PUSEY

I did not know who the silver-haired, distinguished but serious-looking gentleman was who sat with his wife about five rows in front of the pulpit one Sunday. He was new to the Epiphany as far as I was concerned, and yet he seemed to know several people in the congregation, or I should say they knew him. At the door, he introduced himself and his wife, "I'm Nate Pusey, and this is my wife, Anne. We have been going to St. James since moving to New York City, but we have just about decided to come to the Epiphany."

I had a general awareness of who this man was: the former president of Harvard University, and I was very pleased that he was considering the Epiphany, of course. Yet I knew that Dr. John Coburn was the rector of St. James Church on Madison Avenue, and I didn't want John to think that I had prompted the loss of such a distinguished member of his flock. So I decided to take the initiative and made an appointment to see him in his office. We had a fine chat. John was gracious and said it was totally Dr. Pusey's decision and that he wanted him to be happy, period. End of a friendly conversation, and we shook hands and I left. John later was elected bishop of the Diocese of Massachusetts.

Dr. Pusey soon became quite active in the parish, and his wife, Anne, immediately became involved with our Every Monday Rummage Sale, chaired by the indefatigable Mrs. Jane Nickolic. Mrs. Leila Wardwell and Anne became good friends in those busy mornings on Monday, because both were committed to helping the poor. This was not a local annual church rummage sale. This was rather quite a large operation, demanding much from volunteers, and so active that I thought the church should be called "the Church of the Holy Rummage."

When I heard the York Avenue doorbell ring several times a day, I thought it might be for counseling, but most times, it was to deliver an offering of old clothes in boxes or bags left on the doorstep, which we all hauled in to the undercroft. Jane had arranged for graduates of the East Harlem Rehabilitation Clinic to sort these clothes not only to be able to help the volunteers, but also for them to earn their first salary after treatment. There was a ceiling on annual social security earnings then, which was around $300, which aided our often lively, colorful workers.

For example, among many, a former black pimp and his girlfriend, a tall blond prostitute, worked together in rummage for several years until suddenly both became mysteriously ill, and we didn't see them again. That was in the early 1980s, when AIDS was finally being made known to the public. When the rampaging virus overwhelmed them, one soon after the other, they died. Our response was to allow the two to be interred in our columbarium. We had reserved a free section for those who were not members but had been active in our programs.

Another worker was a Russian immigrant who generally helped out, but one day we heard that he had been shot, probably most likely by other Russians, perhaps a mafia group. That worried all of us, and I spoke of it in a sermon. On the more positive side, Jane told me a story about a great author. Jerzy Kosiński came to America, and he didn't have much clothing with him, so he always attended our rummage sales for everyday attire. She got to know him well. If you don't remember, he was the author of *The Painted Bird*, a story of survival in World War II, and also of *Being There*, one of the most interesting books I have ever read. I knew of it years before in Saint Louis and used it in a sermon. I was so glad that it was made into a satirical film with Peter Sellers in the title role of Chance the Gardener, or Chauncy Gardiner, who spoke profoundly using the simplest terms of seasonal garden flower growth. He was so sincere that he convinced everyone he could be president of the United States. Flowery words often have an impact even without meaning or political relevance, especially for a presidential election.

Dr. Posey was elected to the vestry, where he was always helpful, reminding us that Harvard did not invade its capital at the time, while Yale did too often. At one meeting, I remember him saying to his credit that when economic times got worse at Harvard, the first institution to be defunded would be the chapel or the divinity school—because of lack of interest in religion on campus—so he had committed himself to raising funds to make sure the chapel continued to exist.

Dr. Posey had been president of Lawrence University from 1944 to 1953 until he was asked to become president of Harvard University, which he was for nearly twenty years until1971. Then he accepted the presidency of the Andrew W. Mellon Foundation for four years, followed by being named president of the Board for Higher Christian

Education in Asia. He also assisted Foundation House, a place for mentally limited persons.

When St. John's Anglican/Episcopal University in Shanghai was broken up by China in 1952, the board refocused its energies to develop grants to be given to similar institutions in Taiwan and Hong Kong. China later offered some reparation money, I understand, for the closing of St. John's, which Dr. Pusey said would be redirected to libraries in Mainland China, supporting inclusion of theological and religious books.

Dr. Pusey was well-known for his opposition to Senator Joseph McCarthy's scare tactics, calling McCarthy a "damned fool." Since Lawrence College was in Appleton, Wisconsin, McCarthy's hometown, Pusey's opinion carried weight that led to McCarthy's downfall. In contrast to his opposition to McCarthy, Dr. Pusey strongly supported the civil rights movement in the 1960s, and he met Martin Luther King several times.

However, he was appalled at the student protests against ROTC in 1969, which led to the takeover of Harvard's University Hall. When militant students occupied the hall and ejected all university deans, finally after seventeen hours of fruitless negotiations, Dr. Pusey called in the police and was widely criticized for it. In his mind, he was defending the institution against students who should have been more concerned with an education.

When Pusey was ninety-three years of age, he told Joshua E. Gewolb in an interview for the *Harvard Crimson* that he takes full responsibility for his decision to call the police. He believed that "learning had almost ceased." As a classical Greek scholar, he lamented that schooled faculty members, whose job, he believed, was to teach instead of provoke dissent, did not guide the students through such a difficult and troubling time. He understood the tensions brought on by the Vietnam War, but he still believed that Harvard was a place for learning, not violence.

Aside from his own interesting career, well-known friends of Dr. Pusey often attended the Epiphany. One such was August Hecksher II, who served as John F. Kennedy's special consultant on the arts, the first White House cultural advisor, and Mayor John Lindsay's parks commissioner. I remember playing softball with a cadre of folks from the Epiphany, some young and some not as agile as I was becoming, on a field named for him in Central Park.

I also became reacquainted with the Right Reverend Leslie Newbigin. I had heard him preach on church unity at Grace Cathedral in San Francisco in 1960, asserting that the Holy Eucharist represented the highest symbol of unity for all churches. Bishop James Pike had invited him since Newbigin was a bishop in the newly formed ecumenical Church of South India. That church comprised Anglicans, Presbyterians, Methodists, and Congregationalists. Newbigin had been a Presbyterian minister before being consecrated by Anglicans as a bishop in the recently formed mission church. Why Anglicans? Because we claim our church has the apostolic order of bishops, priests, and deacons.

One day, Dr. Pusey invited me to come to his Manhattan House apartment on East Sixty-Sixth Street for coffee to meet Newbigin, and I did. We had a pleasant conversation while he had tea and Dr. Pusey and I had coffee. He mentioned that it had been difficult for him to find a proper place back in England after his retirement. Was he Anglican or Presbyterian, both church sides kept asking him. He settled for teaching again, in Manchester, avoiding the conflict of what he considered to be old-fashioned denominations. He mentioned that it was disappointing to travel back in time after his exhilarating ecumenical experience for the sake of the kingdom of God in the mission field.

After more discussion, I also reminded him that I read his book in seminary, *The Reunion of the Church,* and also heard him preach about the unity implied in the sacrament of the Eucharist in San Francisco. The pleasant scholar and bishop brightened for a minute, smiling and placing his cup of tea on a nearby table, then asking, "Do you still have a copy of that sermon?"

I replied, "I certainly do. I have saved it because it was so special."

He said, "Mail it to me, will you? I haven't one."

I replied that after searching my files, I would immediately do so. What a wonderful opportunity to meet one of my own church heroes and to be able to assist him!

Dr. Pusey was also kind enough to listen patiently to my Sunday sermons for my doctoral thesis at Princeton Seminary and allow his comments to be written up. He, along with those of Walter Birge, warden and headmaster of the Town School; his wife, Susan; Janet Nelson, vestry member; Jimmye Kimmey, a seminarian who acted as clerk and kept meticulous notes; Tom Tull, director of the National

Institute for Lay Training and also a vestry member, were on the listening committee. Eventually I obtained my degree, and the thesis of such was published by the Seabury Press, called *Sermon struggles* in 1982.

Consequently, I was invited to teach homiletics twice a week with Dr. James Forbes, whose class it was at Union Theological Seminary in the city. What a privilege it was for a manuscript preacher like me to be in the same room as Forbes, who could preach for forty-five minutes without notes, stirring all of us. Since he was an African American, his preaching came from those who originally sang gospel songs, yet doing so with brilliant understanding not only of the Bible but also of sound theology and with knowledge of the world. He later became pastor of Riverside Church when, long before him, Harry Emerson Fosdick, another manuscript-type preacher, dominated the pulpit, mesmerizing his congregation.

To me, Nate and Anne were dedicated servants of higher education, civil rights, the Christian faith, the church, and its outreach to the poor, and I was fortunate to be rector when they were members of the Epiphany. They both were aristocrats of the spirit in so many unique ways.

ROBERT C. HUBBARD

Bob Hubbard loved his wife, Patty, his dogs, his church, his job as a law partner of Satterlee and Stephens, his classical music collection, his grand library of books, most having to so with World War II and world affairs, and his house in the Catskill Mountains, that is, in Onteora Park. He also appreciated his work on the Board of the American Farm School in Sophia, Bulgaria, and also the Board of the American Farm School in Greece. He was able to travel often as a board member to Sophia, to meetings in those dark days before the Berlin Wall fell and the monolithic Soviet Union had crumbled into individual and often struggling states. Today, Vladimir Putin may be trying to put the pieces of a red Humpty Dumpty together again, but if his handiwork is anything like what is happening on the ground and in the skies of Ukraine recently, his attempt is more like old KGB blind sighting and empty bravado than any real message of unity for the modern Russian Federation.

We first met Bob and Patty Hubbard when they decided to rent a house in Onteora, which is two and a half hours by car on the New York Thruway from New York City. We had already done so in 1977, an 1888 old house we worked on for years.

After we became acquainted, we discovered that they lived in the city on East Sixty-Sixth Street, not far from our place on East Seventy-Second Street. When they decided that Onteora was a Shangri-La for them in the Catskill Mountains, they purchased a large home of their own with a grand front porch that had a view of much of his four acres of property as well as of those mountains. We saw them there often on weekends, or at least on Saturday afternoons before I scooted back to the city for Sunday services, or very early sometimes in the summer, like 5:00 AM on Sunday.

Once, I remember Patty telling me that when they were first dating, they danced one night many years ago at the Rainbow Room when Patty's knee gave out, but that did not deter them. Absolutely not, because they continued the long dance of their marriage twenty-nine years later than the age when Bob thought his life was limited, about fifty, as he would remind us that most of his family did not have as long a life as he was given.

And it was an extremely interesting life. One time, Bob and Patty invited us over to their New York apartment, probably when he was senior warden of the Church of the Epiphany while I was rector, and he led me to this vast collection of books and said, "Ernie, you have got to read this book. It's fascinating. This scholar really knows his stuff. He gets to the bottom of things. For example, on page 97, the author writes about St. Paul feeling inferior to the other apostles. Here, let me show you." Bob turned to that page and read, "'At the outset his sudden conversion was not understood: in the end he was suspected of having given too much of his Jewish heritage away in order to win over Gentiles. Bouts of ill health combined with petty irritation at such things as the ability of Peter and the other apostles to travel with their wives (1 Cor. 9:1) made him more difficult. Hence he was always struggling.'"

Bob said, "Isn't that the kind of truth we need to hear about the humanity of those early leaders of the church! No pietistic cover up!"

The name of the book was *The Rise of Christianity* by W. H. C. Frend, a leading Anglican scholar in England and Scotland, that was over one thousand pages long.

Bob made me feel like I was a religious illiterate after that reading from Frend, but I appreciated Bob's deep quest for knowledge and for getting history right, which most of us usually forget and then are forced to repeat. Not Bob. His mind was like a steel trap, and he loved his Anglican heritage and the Church of the Epiphany.

In appearance, Bob was disarming. He was, I guess one could say, of average height, stout, not fat, with a jolly round sometimes red-cheeked face, and no matter his age, his thinning white hair remained all through the time I knew him. Aside from his love for his wife, Patty, one must state that he also loved his dogs, which were mostly small, white, and fluffy. He often said to Patty, "We may not have children, Patty, but we have these wonderful little dogs."

He loved them all including the *dreadful* Lancelot, who was not white but gray, and appeared always to sneer, if dogs can do that. I will tell you why. Once, several years ago when Lancelot was still alive and actively biting, Bob asked me to feed him, and of course, as I reached down to pour food into his bowl, he bit me, which was totally against the rule that one never bites the hand that feeds you. Yet I remember that our mutual friend, Fred Parker, had Lancelot's number. So did another friend, Red Chase, who bet some friends that one of them could pick up Lancelot to take him outside without being wounded, and everyone said, "No, no, only Bob can pick him up. Don't dare try it."

Red just smiled as Fred raised Lancelot up and carried him successfully, but of course, the dog was sound asleep on the pillow Fred had carefully grasped and raised without waking the dog.

We used to have drinks with Bob and Patty on that grand front porch of Bob's in Onteora. As we arrived, Patty would be attempting to control the dogs on their long leashes as they barked away, then as soon as we were finally seated, they would treat us properly as guests. Sometimes while we were both chatting with Patty and waiting for Bob to join us, I can recall vividly the vision of Bob endlessly cutting the grass on his seated power mower and loving the challenge of keeping his home, his yard, and his flower beds in tip-top shape.

Bob once wrote that the solitary nature of tending to the dozen flower beds on his four-acre property outside Albany isles is stressful than country-club sports.

As president of the New York Horticultural Society, he was also quoted as saying, "If you go out on a golf course or a tennis court and you don't play well, you end up frustrated . . . but when you battle trees and shrubs, you almost always win."

As general information about Bob, he was a graduate of Princeton, but after high school, he went directly into the army for two years, and while serving in Japan, he knew General Douglas MacArthur quite well. Then he attended Princeton and was politics editor of the *Nassau Literary Review*, director of the Speakers Bureau, and vice president of Whig-Clio, majoring in SPIA. He graduated in 1949 and spent more than fifty years with his law firm, involved primarily in acquisitions, disposition, and financing. I never knew much about his practice, but I definitely witnessed those sides of him that I valued personally, his family and his church life. In all, I considered him an intellectual and a very religious aristocrat of the spirit.

P. L. TRAVERS

One Wednesday night in winter, I was asked by Dr. Lee Belford, a Sunday associate at Epiphany but a full-time chair of the religion department at New York University, to take a service of the Eucharist that was usually his to do. He had several consultations that night at work. When I entered Faith Chapel, where small services were conducted, I noticed a few participants seated for the Eucharist. As soon as the service concluded, I walked to the front door on York Avenue to greet or say good-bye to the few who had attended. Most had left to beat the heavy rain pour that was occurring outside, except one lady I did not recognize.

She was still standing in the small vestibule between nave and door with an umbrella ready to open. Since I did not know her, I introduced myself, saying that I was the rector. The response from the friendly yet determined-looking older lady was pleasant enough, but short and to the point. She responded simply, "I know who you are. I am P. L. Travers."

I shook hands and thanked her for coming, as we clergy do; then she went out into the rain while I turned toward the sacristy to divest myself of cassock, surplice, and stole. Soon afterward, when I saw Lee again for Sunday services, I asked who she was, since her stance with feet together yet pointing outward, a large brimmed dark rain hat on her head, and a sturdy black umbrella beside her haunted me. It was not that she was dressed like our many English nannies in the congregation but somehow she reminded me of one.

Lee said, "Don't you know?"

I replied that I did not.

"That is the author of the Mary Poppins books."

I can't remember my response because I was too astonished momentarily to speak. I kept thinking about the Walt Disney movie *Mary Poppins,* starring Julie Andrews and Dick Van Dyke. Our family had seen the movie at least on three different locations. How many times had we sung "Supercalifragilisticexpialidocious."

We sang that ditty while not knowing what it meant (atoning for educability through delicate beauty), and even now our granddaughters sing the song.

Pamela Travers became an attendee of the church while living next door in a new high-rise that had been built just before I arrived. I called on her not long after meeting her, and I remember a very sparse living room furnished with a lone bookshelf of her books. We sat on a couch across from it. Obviously, those books were her life!

In the 2013 film *Saving Mr. Banks*, Ms. Travers, played by the seasoned English actress Emma Thompson, portrayed her pretty much as I knew her about ten years later in her life. She was in her seventies at the Epiphany but in her sixties in the movie. The film in flashbacks described her early life in Australia, while the title referred both to the Mr. Banks character in the movie Walt Disney had produced and also to her real father. The film *Saving Mr. Banks* began when she was a fantasying child in Australia. Her father was represented as a failure at his bank jobs due partly to his alcoholism, yet still a joyous person squelched by limited life circumstances. In the movie, young Travers as a child survived the death of her father with the help of a real-life nanny who most likely became a heroine in her mind.

Later in her life, after writing her popular books for children, Walt Disney approached her about making a movie. Real-life tape recordings of her voice offering suggestions about the making of *Mary Poppins* were revealed toward the end of the film. They sounded just like the P. L. Travers I knew.

She wrote two poems while at the Epiphany, which she offered to me. One day, in the season of the Epiphany after Christmas, she sat down on a Sunday at a round table used for forum discussions in the undercroft parish hall and wrote this ode. It hangs framed on my wall still:

A Christmas Song for a Child
"Child of the bright head, Take now your myrrh and gold and incense,
as we kneel, with the three kings of old. Child, on this winter night,
do you know that we mean to crucify you when the leaves are green?"
Pamela Travers
Mr. Hunt, a thought for you at this time

Another letter came to me from the Cosmopolitan Club on the fourteenth of January 1979:

Dear Mr. Hunt

> *Pray for my sister, of whose death I learned on the morning of my lecture—Her name is Barbara Moriarty-I thought you might like the enclosed, a sudden thought!*

Yours ever—
P.L. Travers

No Room at the Inn

The foxes in me have holes
The bird its woven bed
Lover and child pitch their tents
In my pastures by waters fed,
But where in me is the place
Where you can lay your head?

Pamela Travers
January 1979

It seemed to me that she had a profound quest for the spiritual life, yet it had evidently been a long personal struggle since it took Carl Jung's theory of archetypes to prompt a renewal of belief. At least that is what she said at the time. I do not know exactly how Jung's thought helped Ms. Travers, but perhaps it was understanding that Jung's "collective unconscious was expressed through archetypes, universal thought forms or mental images that influenced a person feelings or actions . . . a newborn baby is not a blank slate but comes wired ready to receive certain archetypal patterns and symbols. This is why children fantasize so much . . . archetypes are expressed as myths and fairytales and at a personal level in dreams and visions."

Was this how Pamela as a child overcame her personal problems and translated them later into the imaginary characters of those in the series of books about the mystical and magical English nanny Mary Poppins? I do not know, but there is a certain mysticism in Jung's thought that allows for religious expressions beyond the here and now, unlike Freud.

She also had been a Zen enthusiast, believing that meditation might help her digestive discomfort. She kept a statue of the Buddha on her Terrace in Chelsea, London, and also studied Sufism. One of her life teachers (gurus), George Ivanovitch Gurdjieff, urged her to combine Christianity with her Buddhism. One day, when she took Holy Communion at Christ Church near her Chelsea home, she said she knelt and emptied herself before God.

She was also active at the Cathedral of St. John the Divine, and thus I believe that Dean James Morton had complemented her knowledge of Zen and psychiatrist Carl Jung's theory of archetypes with his preaching and adult discussions. She also gave several talks at the cathedral on myth and the importance of fairy tales.

P. L. Travers was a baptized member of the Church of England in her native land of Australia. Later in England, she attended Christ Church, Chelsea, and I can only hope that her time at Epiphany helped her with her spiritual struggle.

Pamela Lyndon Travers's name was originally Helen Lyndon Goff, but in her teen years, she published poems and began an acting career. She changed her name to Pamela Lyndon Travers while touring Australia with a Shakespearean touring company before leaving for England in 1924. It is said that there she became deeply influenced by J. M. Barrie, the author of the Peter Pan novels. Later in 1943, she came to America to spend two years taking seriously the spirit life of Navajo, Hopi, and Pueblo peoples, studying their mythology and folklore.

Earlier, she was also a writer in residence in Radcliffe and Smith Colleges but returned to England, where she published the first *Mary Poppins* in 1934, continuing the series until 1988. She died at the age of ninety-six in London in 1996. In 1999, a complete and important biography of her was written by Australian Valerie Lawson, entitled *Mary Poppins, She Wrote: The Life of P. L. Travers.*

As I remember her at the Church of the Epiphany, I consider P. L. Travers to be an aristocrat of the spirit who contributed so much to the literary and spiritual life of adults and children as well as to fellow members of the church.

RICHARD MINER

One day in the 1970s in New York City, when I was in my early forties, I woke up with a terrific toothache and left the apartment immediately to see my local dentist nearby. After waiting in his office, he finally placed me in his dentist's chair and tested the tooth in question. He applied something to it that made it hurt more. I cringed. It was really painful. All he said was, "That is a real hot tooth. You need a root canal."

To tell you the truth, I had no idea what a root canal was. I thought you just pulled the troubled thing out of your mouth. But no, the good dentist said I should go to a specialist who did root canals on West Fifty-Seventh Street, which I did.

I arrived in the afternoon and was ushered in after a short wait by a stern-looking older female dental assistant and secretary, who seemed to treat me as if I were lucky to be in the presence of the great doctor. Before the ever-bent-back dental chair, the man who did these miracle tooth saves greeted me, saying that it wouldn't take long. He had dark hair, looked about fifty years of age and had an air of detached competency about him. My impression of him was that I was just another human being with a tooth that could make him richer.

Leaning over me like a white-coated predator, he told me to open wide and gave my gums the first shot of Novocain to begin the drilling process. After the first shot, he began to open the tooth, but I said "Ow" and squirmed, saying that it really hurt. He looked at me as if I were a poor specimen of a man and gave me another and another and another, and I still said "Ow." Meanwhile, he answered his telephone and talked about something I barely remember. I think it concerned investments.

When he was finished, he resumed his stance above me and began the process again, but I still said "Ow," and by this time, I was more or less writhing in pain.

He complained, "Sir, I have given you at least six doses of Novocain!" No anesthetic had reached the now-stubborn but still-wicked tooth, and I waited. Outside his open window, I clearly heard a jackhammer loudly being used on the street below. He gave me one more shot, and I still winced when he tried to extract the rotted root from the tooth. Seeing my body squirming around in his chair, he looked disgusted but said in exasperation, "Well, I guess I will put chloroform directly into the tooth itself."

Finally, the evil thorn calmed down, and he went to work and, after a long siege of time, sealed the tooth and declared that I could go home. Wiping my brow after that hour or more of torture, I did so.

That night, Elsie and I went to see a play called the *Runner Stumbles,* written by playwright Milan Stitt, which was about a priest who was accused of raping a nun. In the middle of the most provocative action, my tooth acted up horrifically with a repeated painful pounding. It was as if some mean earthworm inside the sealed tooth wanted to get out but couldn't. That infernal pounding went on when I went home and lasted all night. Of course, as soon as my Fifty-Seventh Street doctor's office was opened, I called the so-called specialist and told him what was happening. He said coolly that I had "a flare up," but he was prepared to relieve it when I returned to see him.

I did so as soon as I could, and when back in his dental chair, the dentist opened the sealed tooth so the little throbbing monster inside could escape. I was still in pain and very upset, even when he told me that I had an infection and that the pain now would soon pass. Since I had an inflammation of some kind, he wrote out a prescription for oral penicillin, in the capacity of 500,000 units for each dose. As I was leaving with his prescription in hand, his secretary-assistant looked at me if she were disappointed in me for being another sissy.

When I returned home after having filled the remedy from the local pharmacy across East Seventy-Second Street, I took the first antibiotic pill while standing in the living room. It was evidently too strong for me, or I had some sort of allergic reaction to it, because in about a half hour, I became very ill, then I fell to the floor, passed out temporarily in that living room. My daughter and my wife were so frightened at my reaction that they decided to take me right to the hospital emergency room. After they slowly struggled to get me up, one on each side to hold me, they did their best to rush me into a cab to the hospital, I stammered, "No, no, take me to my doctor two blocks away!"

The taxi zoomed to 401 East Sixty-Ninth Street where Dr. Allen Mead's office was located. Once inside, I waited a few moments and then stumbled into my dear doctor's inner office.

On the wall behind and above his desk were hanging several severe-looking surgical instruments of former doctors in his family, mementos from time past that looked to me like a hammer, a saw, and other primitive-appearing medical tools. Each reminded me of the jackhammer I kept hearing outside Dr. So and So's Fifty-Seventh Street office. I thought to myself, "What men and women went through in former days! I thought pain like that was over."

Dr. Mead calmed me down, but first comforted my daughter standing behind my chair, saying, "Don't worry, Elizabeth. Your dad just thinks he's going to die, but he isn't."

Holding my jaw while rubbing my stomach, I inquired, "What do I do?"

He replied in his smooth South Carolina drawl, "Stop taking the pills! See a different dentist!"

Which I did the next day; I was more than pleased by the way Dr. Richard Miner, whose office was on street level in the same building where we lived then on the sixth floor—340 East Seventy-Second Street—attended immediately to my dental problem. After he greeted me and once in the dental chair, I told him my story. He sympathized but said nothing derogatory about Mr. Root Canal Specialist's techniques. Dr. Miner peered at my open tooth and told me that I should leave it that way for some time in order to let the infection slowly dissipate. I was relieved.

I recall that Dr. Miner was tall, strong-appearing like an athlete, but not heavy as most football players, but thin and trim like a tennis player, which I found out later he was. He had a pleasant smile and ruddy cheeks and did not seem focused on his work per se, but on his patient's comfort. He described to me exactly what he was going to do, which was more information by far than Dr. Root Canal had given me. I liked him, as I would a new friend.

He said that he would place some gauze into the tooth and then confirmed that the tooth would be okay. He predicted that in due time the infection would go away, so I did not need to take strong doses of penicillin, actually nothing. It would heal itself.

I also told him that I had a jaw problem, that is, when opening my jaw wide, it hurt so much that I could go just so far. Dr. Miner told me he knew all about TMJ and offered to give me gas (nitrous oxide) whenever I needed some work done.

Gas? That was the first time I had heard of that remedy in my life, believing that it had gone out of fashion because of Novocain. Yet I was wrong, because he said, "No, I use it all the time. Just enough, however, to relax a patient. Even as a professional, I tense up in doctors' offices and especially in a dental chair. So let me know when and if you would like to try it."

I left his office feeling relaxed and on the path to recovery. About six months later, he sealed the tooth with a crown he had made for it that enabled the tooth to remain in its normal place, now for more than forty years. After we moved from New York City in 1988, we still would visit his office when we were back in the city, even while living in Dallas or Paris, France.

When possible, we relied on his expertise in his new office on East End Avenue. After his colleague and partner at 340 East Seventy-Second Street died, he moved to a different location not far away. After my retirement in 2003, we saw him more often for some years.

However, during that time, Dr. Miner had developed colon cancer. He quietly mentioned that fact on one visit, but he also said that he has a positive outlook. Yet the time before our last meeting, however, he showed me his chemotherapy shunt by lifting his loose shirt from his stomach and revealing the tube attached to his tummy, saying, "This will keep the cancer at bay."

I wondered. It evidently did for some time, but on the last visit we had with him, he looked pale; his normally ruddy cheeks now were sunken gray pockets, and his reddish hair had turned to gray. To commiserate, I described some of the surgeries I had had recently, but he reminded me by commenting, "Well, there are worse things."

I held that thought for a long time until about a month later, I called the office and heard that he had suddenly died. His secretary was in shock and did not know what to do. Bemoaning his death, I managed to ask, "Is there a service or some obituary written about him?"

She responded that his wife was so shaken that she had not done anything at all, and I thought that was a shame. It prompted me much later in the future to remember him. My son, also his patient, somehow found out that he was born on April 15, 1938, and that this death was May 20, 2011.

Ever since that dreadful time, I have looked in vain for any information in the *New York Times* or on the Internet about him or his life and death, finding only the same address for his office, as if although dead and gone, he were still there, helping his patients. I don't know where he was buried nor do I know his faith background. Yet my son said whenever he told Dick that he had a child, the good dentist said mazel tov as a blessing, so I will assume he was of the chosen race. Yet I only knew him as a decent human being, a capable and kind professional, and one who cared deeply for his patients. He is, in my book, an aristocrat of the spirit, because he truly spent much time helping me when the chips were down. I honor him now and hope this will serve as a proper farewell.

CHAPTER SIX

Dallas, Texas

ROMA KING

SOMETIME AROUND THE beginning of my sixteen years at Epiphany, I began to think about the question, "Do I stay here as Rector like my predecessor for twenty-seven years, or become like Jack Suter, who left after the new building at York and East Seventy-Fourth Street was completed, to become dean of the National Cathedral in Washington, DC? The Epiphany had not sired any bishops in its past, but deans had been. I had urban experience, and most cathedrals were in such city locations, having been "mother" churches in the early days where towns grew up. So I talked to a friend in the clergy deployment office in the Episcopal Church Center, and he put my name in for being a dean of a cathedral somewhere.

The first to approach me was the cathedral in Seattle. Three representatives arrived, asking to talk to my leading laity at the time, and they did so, including Dr. Nathan Pusey. Another was Patricia Lothrop, who, at the time, was head of the adult education committee, a young widow with a PhD who was left with two children to raise. The result of that inquiry was that they asked another priest to be dean, but then a few weeks later, three members of the calling committee of St. Matthew's Cathedral in Dallas, Texas, arrived. I remember them vividly: Bill Morris, senior warden of the cathedral vestry; Thomas Cantrell, a lawyer; and Bill Greiner—all longtime members of the cathedral. Again they met our lay leaders at the time, Dr. Pusey, Dr. Lothrop, and others.

Each member of the search committee grilled me, especially Tom Cantrell, because he was a lawyer and wanted to make sure. They probed to assess that I would fit in as their new dean. They had had a leader at St. Matthew's for twenty-three years, not quite as long as my predecessor at the Epiphany, but the process went well. Eventually, Elsie and I were asked to fly to Dallas to meet the vestry and also the bishop, Donis Dean Patterson.

On the first day when we visited the cathedral, after being located in a hotel on the corner of Mockingbird and Central Expressway, I noticed that the cathedral itself had a large plant, the church building, a large parish hall next to it, and a three-floor Sunday school and office area akin to that edifice. Then there was Cathedral Gardens, a retirement center, to the right of all the main units, and behind it was Garret Park, a rather unkempt open area that looked like it was frequented by drug users, homeless folks, and perhaps prostitutes. The verger had a small house behind the Sunday school wing, but on the left near the main thoroughfare, Ross Avenue, the bishop's newly built and modern office stood as an independent building.

All in all the cathedral buildings represented a large piece of property along with a large parking lot, all situated in a rather rundown urban area. I also noticed that the many doors around the oval parking area that allowed entrance to various areas of the cluster of buildings were painted in barracks green: thoroughly depressing!

Walking into the ground floor office area, we were welcomed by Betsy Wiles, who ran the diocesan bookstore there and who was vestry member Dick Wiles's spouse. Betsy was a lively spirit who, with a big smile and a former teacher's mastery of the classroom, directed us to others who worked there. The first one we met was Dolores Bradford, a small wiry but savvy church secretary, who was instantly likeable, and an older distinguished-looking priest with gray hair, dressed in a black suit and clerical collar, who I found out was the priest in charge. He was also a well-known scholar and former professor; indeed, his many intellectual qualifications influenced me positively to accept the position in time if it was offered.

I also met the Hispanic missioner Uriel Osnaya Jimenez, a third-generation Episcopal priest from Mexico, whom everyone seemed to love and appreciate. He was young and had a dazzling way about him—jet-black hair, sharp black eyes, and a smiling satirical face. He was not tall but stood with much confidence, even appearing cocksure of himself, or so I thought, and he was smart as a whip. He also spoke flawless English with a slight accent. His secretary, Nancy, was also present in an office on the right side of the entrance, as we had entered. A long hall divided offices on one side and the bookstore leading to the church nave and sanctuary on the other. Betsy Wiles told me that Uriel led the largest Latino congregation at the cathedral of the entire Episcopal Church. Sometimes on Sunday, way over five hundred parishioners gathered at 12:30 PM after the 10:30 AM English service, which then had much fewer in the pews. Every person I met, including the vestry, was outstanding, and Elsie and I were very impressed.

So when we flew back to New York City and talked about the cathedral in comparison to the Epiphany, our first thought was that we both hated to leave Manhattan with its interesting life and long-term friendships. On the other hand, Elsie was a Texan and had parents alive at the time in Bryan, not far from Dallas. I also worried that I was losing some of the steam, so to speak, to forge ahead effectively where I had been for sixteen years. Maybe Epiphany needed more.

St. Matthew's required a new dean for the next period of its common life, and it was primed for renewal, so when offered the position, I took it, in hopes of accomplishing the necessary task. By chance, my son was working in Dallas after obtaining his MBA from Harvard and had just been offered a new position in New York City, so we traded. Do you believe in serendipity? I do. So I moved into his apartment in the Oak Lawn area off Lemon Avenue while Elsie finished out her term under contract, teaching at New York's Hewitt School.

At the end of the school term, we joined each other and soon found an apartment of our own at Park Towers, off Fairmount Street. Things began to change at the cathedral. With Roma's help, who continued as canon, we painted the doors red, planted trees to hide ugly machinery near the buildings in the parking lot, and added a new lighted sign in that location. Peggy Patterson, head of religious studies at the Episcopal School of Dallas, where Elsie was soon hired and became head of the history department, was ordained the first woman for the cathedral and became a canon on our team. She was very popular and shepherded many new families to join from the gentrified area of Lakewood near the cathedral. That is where she lived.

There were so many faithful people at the cathedral, especially Mike and Helen Cline. Mike was a policeman, and I used to ride with him in his cruiser as often as possible. The Jones family, Joan Hodges, who was head of the Episcopal School of Dallas and a vestry member, were long time members, along with Jim and Elva Hardwick. Jim had been in the navy at Pearl Harbor when it was bombed, but he survived. Stormy and Holly Greef, the Havemacks, the Grays, Steve Crews and his wife, Patricia Shriver, and Henry Bollman were regular attendees. Mr. Bollman, who nicknamed me Deanie, would greet people at the 8:00 AM service and would offer to drive those visitors back who taxied from the train station to attend church on a Sunday. The Bacas, Dr. Philip Armour, Roger Allspaugh, Ken Rogers and his wife, Diane Pitts, Joe and Margaret Pittinger, Norwood "Polly" Parrott, Darrel and Kathleen Murphy, Dr. Percy Lueke and his wife, Marion, Juan Cordero and his talented wife, Jana, and so many, many more were very active. Then there was the intelligent and dependable Dixon "Dick" Wiles, who became chancellor of the cathedral and who entertained the archbishop of Canterbury and his wife at their home when they came to the States and to the cathedral.

We began to bless animals on the great lawn and started a history project in the parish hall to remind people of the origins of the cathedral, which went back to the early days of Dallas. Roma enhanced the education classes and the pursuit of "the arts" at the cathedral, and I believed we all were having fun in renewal. I couldn't have had a better clergy friend than Dr. King. Let me share some of the outstanding features of his life.

Born on a farm in rural Texas in 1914, he attended Baylor University in Waco and obtained a doctorate in English literature from the University of Michigan. He married Lucile Bailey in 1942, who also became a professor as he did after World War II finally ended. Roma was in the Signal Corps and promoted to captain before his discharge.

Then Dr. King taught at Ohio University for many years, finally earning the Distinguished Professor Emeritus of English Literature award at the university, probably for *being the leading Robert Browning Scholar of the United States, as well as internationally, writing many books about the famed English author and poet.* It was said of him, "The range of his critical intelligence included the secular and the sacred, the academy and the church. He had the rare ability to recognize that the most profound questions of existence and spirituality find important expression in both realms—the critical arts and ecclesiastical inquiry. In this regard, he was a unique voice among his peers."

I remember vividly his facial expression when he thought something said by clergy was outright absurd, or when even this seasoned priest wrote something not worthy enough. His frown could sink a thousand ships. I dreaded that look because I trusted his judgment and respected him.

Roma was ordained later in life in 1969, and before he died, he had served at St. Matthew's for more than three decades, dying in 2009 at the age of ninety-five.

A bit of Roma's perception of people was written up in my book *A Death in Dallas*. Lucille and Roma are at dinner in a parishioner's house, and they are discussing the antagonists I portrayed in the book (I changed their name from King to Sovereign).

> Dr Sovereign said in his striking voice, "Dolores, it's just a travesty that the Milton Company has gotten away with murder for ages and ages, and that Andrew (the son aiming to be a congressman), who would vote for such a nincompoop? He is just plain stupid. Well, I guess that is standard for office these days."

Otherwise, his smile meant that he was excited about what was happening at the cathedral and would help me in every way. He was loyal to our attempt to revive the cathedral on Ross Avenue, because like Epiphany in New York, once discovered, it was a gem, which more and more people did. I always said that its multicultural congregation was a vision of the kingdom of God in all its glory, and Canon King agreed.

After I left St. Matthew's to accept the invitation to become dean of the American Cathedral in Paris, France, as a "double dean," guess what happened? Who became priest in charge again? None other than Roma King, who was once more St. Matthew's leader—he did a splendid job as usual.

Roma and Lucille raised three adopted children, and the two were such unique people that they were, in my judgment, true aristocrats of the spirit.

WILLIAM EUGENE MORRIS

As I have already noted, Bill Morris, off and on again senior warden of St. Matthew's Cathedral (elected terms are limited in years) and outright supporter of the cathedral parish, was one of the men who had been on the search committee. He had visited me in New York City, and I remember him as tall, fair, well mannered, and extremely gentle. He and his wife had been longtime members of the cathedral, although he was originally from the Midwest. I didn't get to know his spouse very well because she died about one and half years after I arrived. When that sad event happened, Bill was the first to understand the need for a columbarium, which Epiphany had in its lower undercroft floor. No one could be buried any longer in Manhattan. There was no room on the island. But cremated remains were permitted on private grounds, such as church property.

That was not exactly true in Dallas, because there were cemeteries, but being buried where you had worshipped was an ancient tradition going back to the early days of the church's existence. When the floor of the early buildings was not large enough for those in the congregation who had died, they were then buried outside the church, as in England. Most times one sees a cemetery there by each old village church.

Thus a columbarium was begun at St. Matthew's, in one chapel wall. Once there was only one, Ruth Morris, and now there are legion, walls full. Bill was open to new ideas, and he was diplomatic and helpful on the vestry when decisions had to be made. Yet he kept his eye on the books, the endowment, and capital expenditures.

He met his second wife in time, widowed and extremely pretty Margaret, whose daughter Molly had married a popular diocesan priest, Tom Blackwell. He was part of a group called the Via Media, that is, clergy and lay not opposed to the ordination of women then, and other forward-looking acts.

At one time we had a vestry discussion about making the former dean, Preston Wiles, an emeritus dean. He had served for twenty-three years, but there was difference of opinion, including some resistance from the diocesan office. I did not know the details, but in the long run, two men specifically spoke up for the former dean. One was the stately Dick Wiles, and the other was Bill Morris, who commented, "Dean Wiles has served in this cathedral for twenty-three years. He also led the way in prayer book revision for the whole Episcopal Church in-group sessions of clergy and laity in this cathedral, and we can't forget his long and fruitful tenure. He should be honored, and that is that."

The two gentlemen carried the day, and the dean was honored. The bishop complied.

On several occasions, Elsie and I had dinner with the Morrises, that is, with Bill and Margaret, and they were grand hosts. Bill was always a perfect gentleman, and as a committed churchman, he took the high road in any dispute the cathedral encountered. I never heard him speak badly of anyone, including past clergy.

The last time I saw Bill was a few years ago after I had retired from Paris and had been given an office on the third floor of the old school building. That building in its heyday was once St. Mary's School, and Lady Bird Johnson was a graduate.

He was seated in an old chair by the office entrance, handing out food to the homeless on Thursdays, a weekly volunteer cathedral ministry. He sat there all morning, waiting for the poor to arrive, and they did in droves. That was what was special about St. Matthew's. The down-and-out were on our doorsteps, not in some partially abandoned ghetto far away from the grand homes elsewhere in the city or in the suburbs.

I found out that Bill was born in 1919 and that he died in 2010. I was not there for the burial at the time, but in Florida. William Eugene Morris lived a long and helpful life and was an aristocrat of the spirit, a devoted and faithful member of St. Matthew's.

THOMAS LEE CANTRELL

One of the other search committee members who came to see me in New York City was Tom Cantrell, then a patent lawyer, a literal tither, and a lay leader at St. Matthew's Cathedral. When I first met him, I heard rumors that he was studying on the side for the ordained ministry, but I knew him in the beginning when I arrived in Dallas in 1988 only as a well-known patent lawyer. Dan and Kay Tucker, who had moved to Dallas after we had become friends in Saint Louis, knew him by reputation. Dan was also a patent lawyer and claimed that Tom was often a very competent adversary.

Tom was happily married to Alice, a diminutive, pretty lady who possessed a very pleasing personality. The two were a very compatible couple. Tom had also been in the army. I know because I was at his internment after he had died at eighty years of age, and I remember vividly the two soldiers who presented Alice with that precisely folded American flag. He would have appreciated that gesture.

In my estimation, Tom was very intelligent, confident, and on-target in his assessment of problems to face, and in spite of his often-brusque lawyers' manner in which he appeared girded to win a case in court, he was a very kind man. He loved the church, and that pursuit led him eventually to leave practicing law to become a member of the ordained clergy. Why do men and women do that? Why do they leave a profitable profession for a poor one, even if for some its meaning is its own reward?

St. Matthew's, like many religious institutions, inspired that move in many diverse people. The Reverend Dr. Canon Roma King had done the same earlier in his life. Indeed, when I was in seminary in 1956, I was a very young student studying in the midst of many older gentlemen who had fought in World War II and felt compelled to change their initial workplace to that of the priesthood. Maybe there is truth in the saying, "There are no atheists in foxholes," while witnessing around you the instant mortality of so many leaves its scars, or at the very least many questions about the significance of human life. One question many ask is, Why am I here and they are gone? What is my purpose in life?

For Tom, I believe it was not combat experience but the same questions, distilled in his own unique life, that lead one to ponder the meaning of life. He sought a profession where he could witness to that greater meaning we all seek but often suppress for the sake of the fortunes of this world.

Albert Camus, a French Algerian literary philosopher, once wrote of a king who had flaxen fires burned regularly before him to remind him how fleeting human life is—like the smoke the fires generated. Maybe this is what motivates some of us, but of course, one does not have to be ordained to understand the contrast between eternity and human existence.

Whether as a layman or later when ordained, Tom made his presence known, not because he dominated others, but because of his natural and often whimsical sincerity. His wry sense of humor could disarm the less sophisticated thinkers, in a vestry meeting, a law court, and then from the pulpit. I remember in New York, when I sat with him in my office and we were discussing my compatibility for the cathedral, he asked, "Are you sure you want to leave this fine New York church and come to us? Why would you do that? We don't want someone who will mess up but will provide us a new future. Are you spiritually strong enough to make the adjustment?"

When I struggled to respond in some enlightened, positive way, he smiled and said something to the effect, "You can tell I am a lawyer, backing you into a corner like this. But I have a lot of respect for St. Matthew's and just want the best for it. I really believe you are okay."

Relieved that he thought I could do the job, I accepted the "call," as we clergy refer to it, and moved to Dallas. When I was later instituted as dean, Elsie and I soon found a new place to live in the city.

When Tom was finally ordained, he was given the opportunity to shepherd small outlying parishes, and one, if I remember accurately, was in Kaufman, a small but interesting community outside of the city of Dallas. I recall Tom talking about the wonderful people he had met and the pastoral ministry he had with them, as if he had finally found a small paradise. He was happy at last in his new vocation.

In my way of thinking, Tom was an aristocrat, not because of background or riches or his fine reputation as a patent lawyer, but because he loved the church and gave up much to serve through it.

JAY JACKS

One day, I was sitting at my desk in St. Matthew's Cathedral, and the secretary buzzed to say that I had a phone call. I asked who it was, and then she said, "A man named Jay Jacks."

I was puzzled since I did not know the name, but I told her to put him on.

We spoke, and he announced that he was a member of the Board of Foreign Parishes that met twice a year in New York City and that he was representing one of the church properties that the board owned overseas.

Then he added specifically, "The American Cathedral of the Holy Trinity in Paris, France, and you are being considered as a candidate for the position of dean."

I had heard by the grapevine—every church has one—that my name was on a long list, but I did not know the specifics. Jay filled me in by saying, "Since the cathedral cannot afford to fly all the candidates into Paris, its vestry has asked me to contact you as one of ten being considered, and also preapproved by the presiding bishop, whose lone cathedral in the Episcopal Church is his. So if you allow, I need to make a visit with you and bring a professional who knows how to do video to interview you in your office. I will then send the tape to that group overseas so they can consider the aptness of your candidacy."

Ironically, I had been a candidate years before while at the Epiphany, but it was at the wrong time for us, and now I was delighted to be considered. I was fifty-eight years old, and an election for a new bishop was imminent, and I thought that if I were to leave, this was the time. St. Matthew's was a special urban cathedral, the mother church of the diocese and its spiritual center, and I enjoyed being its dean, but was there one more challenge in our lives for the two of us?

After Jay's video method of communication and his personal support, I did become one of three final candidates. Elsie and I flew to Paris in the summer of 1992, and while staying at the Franklin Roosevelt Hotel near the cathedral, we were interviewed for a few days, and after I returned to Dallas, I heard from Jay and others that I had been selected by the vestry to be the new dean in Paris. I accepted the "call," and while I had had Spanish language in my background, I got moving to learn French immediately by attending Berlitz classes. This began my foray into nonphonetic French.

Jay and Marla had been supporters of St. James, Florence, Italy, since 1965 when they had moved overseas to open a design and production company for the Halston dress label. Being devout church people, both became involved in the American parish there. Jay indeed soon became senior warden of its vestry while attending the University of Florence for his graduate degree. They remained residents of Florence for nearly ten years before returning to Dallas, where Jay began his own fashion firm; one of his many private clients included the television series *Dallas*.

His experience abroad helped him understand that expatriates living overseas often needed the communal support provided by European English-speaking churches. He also learned how necessary it was for former members who returned to the States to continue their financial support of the Convocation of Episcopal Churches in Europe. Because he had known this fact personally, he was asked to become a member of the Board of Foreign Parishes that owned those properties. He became the lone Texan on the board at the time while most members were easterners.

In Dallas, Jay and Marla became very active at St. Michael's and All Angels Church and were involved in its many service-oriented organizations, especially as captain of the Lay Eucharist Ministers (that assisted in services and also formed a lay ministry to the ill and infirm). I knew of this ministry personally, because after I retired and returned to Dallas, he and others visited me at Park Towers after I had an operation. His ministry meant much to me.

In return, while serving as a retired dean at St. Matthew's Cathedral in Dallas after retirement from Paris in 2003, I called on him at Baylor Hospital when he became ill. His lovely daughters, Lydia and Alessandra, along with Marla (his wife of forty-three years), were by his side on that visit, and not much later, Jay succumbed to his illness in February 2004. It was sad for everyone who knew or loved him, but Jay was a man of faith and believed in eternal life.

During that time when I retired, St. Matthew's Cathedral offered me an office in the former school building attached to the parish hall, where I began writing six novels about human slavery, whether from radical Muslims who treat women as second-class human beings or from horrific crimes committed on our Mexican borders by cartels.

At that time, I also had surgery under the direction of a terrific doctor (nicknamed "a doctor to doctors" for his expertise), *R. Elwood Jones*, who is a professor of internal medicine at Southwestern Medical Center, Dallas. One urologist he recommended was from Israel, who reattached a kidney to the bladder blocked by scar tissue, and at the same time another from Iran removed a precancerous polyp from the colon. I was hoping the team might help the Middle East crisis, but no such luck! Yet that combination goes on in hospitals all the time, which I am sure Jay was aware of in his hospital care.

Jay had been a member of one of Dallas's and Texas's oldest families, going back to the days of a Texas navy under the direction of General Sam Houston. Yet I remember him for his solid support of the churches in Europe, especially St. James, and for his devout service to the Episcopal Church. I was also grateful to him for his advocacy when I was considered as the dean of the American Cathedral in Paris, France. He was indeed, in my estimation, an aristocrat of the spirit.

CHAPTER SEVEN

Paris, France

SOPHIE B. M. BELOUET

UPON OUR ARRIVAL in Paris in October 1992, we were met and then escorted by the senior warden, Sophie Benson MacKenzie Belouet, spouse of Christian Belouet, a native of France whom she met while a student abroad at Sweet Briar College from the States. Wayne Reich was junior warden at the time, and the two of them together were most helpful in showing us around. Earlier in New York City, I had met the presiding bishop of the Episcopal Church—who, by tradition, held the bishop's chair of the American Cathedral in Paris—and he shared with me that there had been a recent heated controversy in the Paris church. Bishop John Krum, a retired bishop who was in charge of the cathedral at the time, had told Ed Browning, the presiding bishop, that the annual meeting of the parish church had been the worse in behavior that he had ever attended in his life. People, it was said, screamed at each other. The presiding bishop asked me if I would need a consultant to sort things out, and I answered something to the affect, "Let's wait and see."

Later, I discovered that the issue causing the problem seemed to be that some expats wanted the priest in charge between deans, former business professional Henry C. "Jack" Child, whose wife worked at the embassy, to be the new dean, while the senior warden and other vestry members remained loyal to the selection process where one of the 150 candidates from the States, and especially a member of the final ten the PB had approved, would become the resident dean. This was the normal process. Assistants rarely have been allowed to be permanently in charge of any church by canon law, so the hullabaloo was more about local control and an unawareness of our tradition versus proper procedure.

We gradually settled more or less into the deanery, a building situated next to the dean's garden. At one time, the whole structure belonged to the dean and his spouse, but it was later divided, with the lower half becoming a residence for the canon and family while the upper stories were saved for the dean. It was an exercise to learn to climb three flights of stairs each day. That deanery was adjacent to the tower that loomed above the main church building. The access to all buildings was behind a locked gate in front of the large vestibule.

While waiting for our furniture to arrive from the States, I began my three quests. The first was to calm the church members down, the second was to become moderately proficient in French, and the third was to gain a driver's license so that I could insure the small car that fit in the large furniture travel container.

On the first challenge, I received help from the gracious gesture of Sophie Belouet, who, citing fatigue from the long, tiresome calling process and knowing that some resented her firm stand, resigned voluntarily. This she did, paving the way for a veteran lawyer and vestry member, David McGovern—actually the patriarch of the parish—to replace her temporarily until the next election. That move seemed to help our parish conflicts, and Sophie understood that it would, or at least she hoped. Newspaperman Bob McCabe was elected by the vote of the vestry in time to be senior warden and he, like David, represented a bridge to most of the older expats of the cathedral. This move seemed to help acceptance of my new presence. Sophie became briefly the head of the friends of the cathedral back home, who were groups of our alumni who had returned to the States after their stint in Paris.

But her life has been devoted to the cathedral while working at the Organization for Economic Co-operation and Development. The OECD's main office is located in the city of Parris, and it has a membership of thirty-four countries and a budget of more that 357 million Euros. It was established in 1961 and employs more than 2,500 persons. Sophie has held several positions from 1989 to 2010, primarily head of administrative unit of IT services. The United States appoints an ambassador routinely, and one such that we know is Dennis Lamb, whose wife, Karen, was very active at the cathedral and now is on the board of the priory of St. John of Jerusalem, which supports the largest Emergency Ambulance Service of the UK and an eye hospital in East Jerusalem and two eye clinics, which are open to all faiths.

Both Amy L. Bondurant, ambassador appointed to OECD in 1997, and Jeanne L. Phillips, appointed in 2001, were Episcopalians from different political parties, and in spite of divergent political views, they were seen sitting next to each other in services with their families at the cathedral, which was very satisfying. Religion does not have to divide people, because it can overcome lesser loyalties. Secretary of state James Baker came to services also when in France, causing me to remember what a strong diplomatic role he had in helping unite the two Germanys after the Berlin Wall fell.

The former chaplain to St. Stephen's School in Austin, Texas, where I worked while in seminary, showed up one Sunday. Seeing him helped me recall those trips from 1957 to 1959 in my 1947 Chevrolet that I made out to semirural Austin, where the school began, arriving by 3:00 PM, to be an assistant to the librarian and a monitor for classes held in the library. I returned each day to the seminary by 9:00 PM, earning $100 a month and my evening meal with the students.

Yet one time as I drove on the dirt road to the new school, I remember vividly coming across a car accident. A jeep driven by hunters had rammed into the chaplain's car, and the only hurt person was the chaplain's wife, who was in the passenger side, hit by the fast-rolling jeep. There were no cell phones then, no nearby farmhouses from which to communicate, and the school was too far away, so I decided to help place her into the backseat of my Chevy and drive her to St. David's Hospital in the city. She had broken bones, but she recovered. So the first thing that came to mind when I saw him in Paris, France, *after at least forty years,* was to ask, "How is your wife?"

He simply answered that she was just fine. Other former parishioners or clergy showed up who were from my first church in the Salinas Valley or from Epiphany in New York City, revealing what a small world the church is, no matter where one serves. Sophie understood this universal aspect of church life, because she was from the States and found a church home in Paris, as many others before her had done.

Sophie was educated at Sweet Briar College in Virginia, and after meeting her husband, Christian G. Belouet, on a year abroad after her graduation, they were married in 1968. They have two children,

Caroline and Anne Lauri, and three grandchildren, Basile, Elliott, and Casimir. She was financial controller of the cathedral for seven years and has held positions from head of the Sunday school to associate treasurer at this time.

She is also active in the Convocation of Churches in Europe, our small Episcopal Diocese, which stands aside and works in union with the two hundred chaplainries of the Church of England Diocese in Europe. It has a council of advice to our bishop, and she has been a member of that helpful organization, as well as a deputy to our Episcopal Church National Convention in the States, and she too has been a member of the Board of Foreign Parishes like Jay Jacks from Dallas. There is more! Yet all of it attests to her involvement and reveals her deep dedication to her church.

Backing up a moment to our arrival at the cathedral and the challenge it represented, a few days after our settling in the deanery, I remember vividly that the power to the whole cathedral complex suddenly was shut off because a crane operator working on a new building across from the George V Hotel, which was north of us, ran over the main power cable on Avenue George V. After it was reported to the Paris authorities, a portable power truck drove up in a day's time and parked in front of the cathedral, restoring electricity and heat to the deanery, tower, church, and parish hall. I can't remember if the Spanish and Chinese embassies to the south of us were affected, but maybe that was why we had such a quick power assist from the mayor of Paris.

On the second quest, Elsie and I took an immersion course in French, after which I hired a tutor, who was patient but challenging and helped me very much for at least two years.

Considering the third problem, Harriet Riviere, a longtime member of the cathedral and participant in its many lay ministries, who was an insurance expert, told me that I had to have an accepted driver's license in order to the insure my car. Only five US states at the time had a reciprocal arrangement with France, so I was encouraged to enter a long and tedious course to pass the French visual and driver's tests in order to obtain a valid license.

It was not to be. I failed the first tests for reasons I thought were beyond my control, but finally, after taking both the visual and driving tests again, I finally passed, and now I possess a driver's license that does not expire and is good in all European countries.

Getting to know the parish was next on my agenda. I slowly got to understand the dynamic history of the junior guild for women and what it had done to help so many from World War I to the present time—that is, helping wounded soldiers, white Russian escapees from Communist Russia, and local French people in need.

Then I attended St. Anne's Guild, the altar guild and flower Guild meetings, of which many members were highly respected professionals in their private fields. One of the member's of St. Anne's is Mary Blake, an accomplished artist whom I had gotten to know in New York City when she helped in our homeless ministry. She had moved to Paris and was one of the persons who were asked about me by the vestry, and she had given the search committee in Paris evidently a thumbs-up account when queried about my sixteen years at Epiphany.

Bob McCabe had also attended Epiphany when in New York and had recommended me. Sophie's sister in Dallas, Clara Smiley, an Episcopalian at Incarnation Church, was another. She knew of St. Matthew's Cathedral history and of my ministry there.

Special contributors to the cathedral were Mr. and Mrs. Ted "Patti" Cummings, who entertained many of us and members of guilds at their spacious home on Rue Saint-Dominique. Ted was a relative of Francis D. Everett, whom I knew well in New York.

There is some serendipity about friends in the calling process when search committees, along with careful background checks, feel confident enough to call a new pastor. George and Rosalie Hook, who lived in Normandy, invited us to stay with them often. He was wounded in World War II as an army tank commander but recovered, although he had some physical problems later in life. Every July 4, he had a fireworks display and dinner at his home, and we attended, as did Olivia de Havilland and Sophie Belouet.

Patty also introduced me to Dennis Mananay and his family, along with other friends from the Philippines. Citizens of that country have been very popular in France because of their congenial personalities and strong work ethic, but it took me five years to have Dennis and others made legal in France, even though so many work as the backbone of help in Paris families. In time, Dennis became verger and sacristan and is now, as then, the hands-on backbone of the cathedral.

The head of the Sunday school was attractive, intelligent Ingrid Leygonie, who, in time, built up the Sunday school to more than two hundred children, which was probably the largest in Paris aside from the American Church on the other side of the quay. Norwegian in background but a New Yorker otherwise, she had a gift for persuading members become volunteer teachers.

The altar guild was also a busy place with so many members, but two stand out in my mind: Lois Kumpers (she and her husband, Axel, are continuing dear friends) and its dynamic head, Francis Bomart. Others are mentioned elsewhere. Wise Sylvette was the French parish secretary who, when the staff was confronted by new parochial problems, would reply with a chuckle, "Oh, don't forget, Dean, in France, one day does not necessarily follow another!"

She and others, like Sarah Johnson, who worked for both dean and bishop, and Marianique, who replaced Sylvette upon her retirement, and Margaret Harrison, who managed the cathedral for years, would hold down the fort, so to speak.

The canon at the cathedral at the time was called by the previous dean Jim Leo, the talented and highly respected Ben Shambaugh, who later became dean of the St. Luke's Cathedral, Maine, and whom we often see along with his wife, Shari, at the annual North American Dean's Conference in the States. Others were George Hobson, Nick Porter, son of the revered Rev. Dr. Boone Porter, Sharon Gracen, and others from time to time, especially Rosalie Heffelfinger Hall, who was in General Seminary when I taught with Jim Forbes at Union Seminary for a semester. I had written a book *Sermon Struggles,* published by the Seabury Press, which was used widely in seminaries, and Rody Hall remembered me as a part-time teacher.

She had a deep commitment to helping others with AIDS, as did Canon Theologian George and Victoria Hobson, along with lay person then later ordained Tom Myers, forming a feeding group for the homeless. At that time, Alcoholics Anonymous met in the crypt, and I induced the French Coca-Cola franchise to place a Coke machine at its entrance, since those inside could not imbibe red wine as the ladies at their several guild meetings normally did. This red and chilled soft-drink machine was what was popular with arrested alcoholics, but one member of the guilds thought that I had impinged on the turf of the wine sommeliers of Paris with another symbol American betrayal.

We also hosted a historical Medieval Mystery Musical at the cathedral, *Le Jeu De Daniel,* through the good graces of our organist,

Ned Tipton, and also its producer, Michael Sisk. It was a great innovative artistic success, attended by Mrs. Jacques Chirac, the president of the republic's wife, but cost overruns almost did us in, until Mr. Sisk found additional monies to pay for our losses. But that idea of the cathedral sponsoring the arts under its roof started the Les Arts George V organization that backed countless concerts and grand orchestra productions for the city of Paris, as well as creating in time the Paris Community Chorus. Don Johnson, along with Mary Adair, his spouse, who did so much for the junior guild, has supervised that organization for many years. The last time I was there in 2013, he was signing in a concert while in his eighties.

Sophie was also most helpful when we were told by the mayor's office that we had to clean our facade, called a ravalement in French, which meant raising more than a million dollars, and before that year-long project occurred, we applied to become a Monument Historique in Paris, which meant that not only did the vestry in Paris have to approve that move, but so did the Board of the Foreign Parishes in the States, the Council of Advice of the Convocation in Paris, the bishop in charge, and the presiding bishop in NYC had to also approve.

The issue of any conflict about this move concerned ownership and how much control the French government would have over our buildings. Thus a question was heard at the board in the States, "Are you trying to hand over the Battleship of the Fleet to the French?" That was proven in time to be untrue. The French offered expert architectural advice, helped us daily, and even gave us about $150,000 toward the project. They did not control us. Yet I cannot remember how many trips I made as the communicator to various boards and councils.

Along with lighting the tower, which I thought essential since in the dark days of winter, one could not see the tallest tower in Paris, only the lights off the Seine that lit up, passing Bateau Mouche, or dining river boats.

Since World War II was a personal issue for me since I was born in 1934 and while too young to be drafted, I recall all the radio announcements from the aggression in the Sudetenland to V-E Day in Europe. How could the people of the cathedral go through such a war and not have it remembered, as it had been for those who lived through World War I? The Battle Memorial Cloister for the "War to end all wars" was dedicated in 1922.

After the fall of France in 1940, Dean Beekman traveled to the USA at the request of FDR to speak about the evil of Nazism while the organist Laurence Whipp was left to run the cathedral in his absence. When war was declared against the Axis after Pearl Harbor, Whipp was arrested and placed in a French internment camp that affected him deeply. Luckily, he was released after a time to return to play the organ when the German army chaplaincy occupied the cathedral.

After the war, we were the official church for an American memorial service in remembrance of all who had given their lives for freedom.

The fiftieth anniversary of the landing in Normandy was about to happen in June 1994, and I firmly believed that it should be publicly honored by us as World War I was. So we found donors to raise enough money to have plaques made to honor the dead in our cemeteries of Europe. We did not have another wall, so we used the pillars facing the garden. When they were completed, the Battle Memorial Cloister was rededicated for both wars and to all who died: military, civilians, and concentration camp victims. Ambassador Pamela Harriman participated in the dedication services and gave a moving talk, perhaps remembering the struggle England had in the war. I also vividly remember the many World War II veterans who returned for the fiftieth anniversary of D-day, some in tears yet proud to have their photo taken in the cloister.

On another occasion of trepidation, Diana, princess of Wales, in the late summer of 1997, August 31 to be exact, about half a long block down from the cathedral, died suddenly in a car crash in the tunnel underneath the approach to the Pont de L'Alma bridge. There was, for years, an impromptu shrine for Muslims and Christians and all who admired her and her friend, Dodi Fayed.

The shrine incorporated the bicentennial golden torch given by the *International Herald Tribune* to mark the anniversary of "our special relationship" of the United States historically with France. It stood more or less over the exact spot where Diana had died. Yet I remember photos and pasted-on notes of adoration and loss for years after her death. That following Sunday, the cathedral was full of shocked admirers. I worked hard to preach to them on September 7, so much so that the written sermon was literally lifted from the pulpit by some reporter for the *New York Daily News*. I only knew this in Paris because my son faxed me a copy of the newspaper form New York, and it was an entire insert about her. The text was biblical, but it was not mentioned, but this just this part:

> The dwarves . . . helped Snow White, unlike those (the paparazzi) who surrounded Princess Diana in her last minutes. All of them underestimated the powers of destruction, the mystery of iniquity. All of them did her in. For a beauty to die so tragically shakes us to the core. . . . Princess Diana has become overnight a tragic heroine who will not be forgotten. In this case a beauty, and a real princess, was not rescued in the nick of time by a handsome prince; and it all seems all wrong to us, shattering our dreams of an ideal life on earth. . . . But England's Princess, adored and venerated for her charm, her dignity under pressure, her youth, her motherhood, and her ability to communicate with, and also identify with the disenfranchised in life; is not rescued. She dies, and the prince merely retrieves her body."

As ever, Sophie was behind the scenes in the cathedral, helping to celebrate her life for all those who were filled with sorrow. She knew that at times like these the cathedral fulfills its purpose.

As a dedicated church person, Sophie Belouet was supportive through all the changes and additions during the time I was the dean and before that during the days when Jim Leo was dean. She has had a gift for listening, which results in her offering straightforward and honest feedback. Because she had the best interests at heart to serve the common good of the cathedral and not just herself, she is a true aristocrat of the spirit.

ROBERT MCCABE

Elsie and I met Bob McCabe in church services and then were invited for drinks to his unique apartment overlooking the tomb at Les Invalides. He was a longtime member of the American Cathedral. We really got to know him more personally when I had the privilege to marry the two at the cathedral in July 1995. Susan Meek Stocker was a widow who lived in London and Greenwich, Connecticut, and had three children. Her nephew, the Reverend Nicholas Porter, son of revered Episcopal priest and professor at General Seminary and later editor of the *Living Church* Boone Porter, attended the wedding, along with his wife, Dorothy Meek. They had been living in Jerusalem, where Nick was canon of St. George's Cathedral. After getting to know Nick through attending the McCabe wedding, I hoped that he might be interested in becoming a canon of the cathedral. After they decided to come to Paris, they were very popular, and after his tour of duty with us at the American Cathedral, he became rector of the church in Geneva.

Besides interesting new relatives, Bob himself had many, many remarkable friends, being the corporate editor of the *International Herald Tribune.* Take science fiction writer Ray Bradbury, for example, author of many well-known books like *Fahrenheit 411.* One evening, Bob invited me to meet Mr. Bradbury over drinks, and we talked about many international events. During the stimulating conversation, I brought up a short story he had written some years, called "Drag foot." The storyline was about a prehistoric man who was born crippled and was forced to stay behind in the cave due to his physical ailment instead of out hunting mammoths like the rest of the men. Even though he remained with the women and children, he found a vocation by becoming a creative artist who painted cave walls, depicting men out hunting or their common prehistoric life inside the cave.

I had used this story to describe Jesus as a "drag foot," because Jesus was also different and creative by depicting in his teaching the essence of scripture. However, my sermon had been criticized in my former New York parish by an older professional woman who thought I was being antifeminist, I suppose because it seemed to make the women weak and unable to compete like the men, I guess. I remember after hearing that story that Mr. Bradbury laughed and said cheerfully, "She got it wrong!" Then he explained why, which was simply his creative way of telling how art was born in primitive caves. I was relieved.

Bob brought many similar intriguing people together as we overlooked the grand tomb of Napoleon in Paris, and Elsie and I enjoyed Bob and Susan's company there and in their Normandy home.

Let me describe Bob's gifts as senior warden. He was always the observer and mediator, and I could count on him to take the long view on controversial matters, along with David McGovern, and neither became so caught up in an immediate conflict that they could not also see the big picture. "Think globally, but act locally," as René Dubos wrote, and Bob lived out that type of leadership.

The *International Herald Tribune* was once a combination of the *Washington Post* and the *New York Times*. Before that, it was originally the *Paris Herald*, so well described recently in James Oliver Goldsborough's novel of the same name.

As an aside, former consul general to France *Larry Colbert* and his intriguing wife, Christina, of Chinese background, sent that book to us recently because we shared a Paris background. Larry, a Midwesterner, was an outstanding CG. Indeed, when he first arrived for a four-year tour, he called me up, saying he wanted to meet me. My first reaction was, "What have I done now?"

Yet when we met in my office, he said he simply had a custom of getting to know people involved in the community, which we certainly were. Larry did not just stay behind his desk but got out and met the people whom he was charged with caring for through the consulate. He was "hands-on." Elsie also at that time was heavily involved with the American Aid Society, led by Adele Annis, which was located at the consulate. The Colberts and the Hunts have been good friends ever since.

After the name *Paris Herald*, derived from the *New York Herald* in Manhattan, it became in time the *International Herald Tribune*. Now it is the *International New York Times*. David Ignatius and his wife were active at the cathedral while the *International Herald Tribune* was of both genres, and he was the managing editor. Then he returned to the Capitol and to the *Washington Post* as well as to writing books made into films, like *Body of Lies*. David once spoke at an adult forum about the crisis in Bosnia, which was attended by well-known actor Sam Waterston, who was on location for a film when attending the cathedral for a short time. Before Ignatius, at one time, was capable Lee Huebner, and his talented wife, Berna, was a friend of Elsie's.

Bob McCabe's unique history provided his leadership both at the *International Herald Tribune* and at the cathedral. He covered the Vietnam War during his years as Southeast Asia correspondent for *Newsweek* in Hong Kong from 1962 to 1966, as well as China and Southeast Asia, then writing a book called *Storm Over Asia* in 1967 and later *Asia*, published in 1987. He was also an editor for *Time* magazine in New York and Paris (1968–1073) and earlier was foreign editor for a show that was a precursor to CBS's *60 Minutes*.

I especially remember Bob's saving the day in a church service when his nephew-in-law Nick Porter was canon. A former editor of a very popular international news magazine in Paris had decided to leave his French wife, who was at the time head of the flower guild, while he too had a top lay job. One Sunday, he and his new lady friend, who was a lay reader, were seated in a front row of the cathedral while his wife was also in the service, only seated anonymously in the back of our large cathedral. Few people noticed what she had in her hand, but it was lethally red.

Unseen by the oblivious clergy at the altar busy with the liturgy in offering the Eucharist, she walked very slowly up the left side aisle behind the large pillars where Bob happened to be seated. As she furtively flitted behind the pillars on her way to where the happy couple was blatantly seated, he was curious about her stealth full approach and became suspicious. Suddenly her intent dawned on him when he saw in shock what she held in her hand. It was a can of red spray paint, which she intended to shower all over her husband and his friend.

But big Bob rose to the occasion, stopped her in her tracks, and grappled the weapon from her, escorting her back and giving it to our canon, who at that time was seated in the rear. Later he offered it to a well-known lay person to keep and, in turn, when the service was over, brought it to me for safekeeping. That token of *unused* resistance to the French wife's pain stayed put in my office for some time.

Yet the drama of the day was not over. After the service, the husband and his lady friend left the church and were walking up hand in hand on Avenue George V to the Champs Élysées. While the Frenchwoman was getting into her nearby parked car, she saw the two strolling along, and totally pissed—not only at his leaving her, after she had raised his three children when his first wife, but how candidly they had embarrassed her—she ran up to them, and even as they smiled at her, she punched the lady friend in the eye. "Viva La France."

Later the gentleman friend of the injured party called the church, and Nick Porter caught the call. The injured duo asked for pastoral assistance, and after Nick told me what they wanted, he asked my advice, and I said, "Of course, go to them." He did so and found them seated at the only open coffee shop on the Champs Élysées that Sunday morning. After his pastoral visit, he later informed his uncle, Bob McCabe the hero, when he and Dorothy were visiting his apartment later that she had a very black eye.

Bob and young Nancy Janin, who was the junior warden, an excellent choir singer, along with being a champion of fundraising, were a great team. Together they united younger and older expats, helping them to get better acquainted, especially if newly arrived. They worked together for several years, at least two three-year terms, which vestry members by canon law could have. Bob was also our lay leader as crises occurred.

When the World Trade Centers were hit on September 11, 2001, my daughter called me from Dallas in shock and said, "Go home and turn on CNN. Something terrible happened in New York City."

I did so and saw on television the second building fall, and then we at the cathedral went into a protective mode, not knowing how extensive the attack was. I called the embassy and was informed, "Given these tragic events, the United States embassy is taking precautionary measures. The embassy and its constituent posts remain in operation but are temporarily suspending routine access. . . . US citizens are urged to maintain a high level of vigilance and to take appropriate steps to increase their security awareness."

We immediately began security inspections for people entering the cathedral but kept it open for those who mourned. We had visitors that day and many, many more in the days to follow. Flowers showered our many front steps and our entrance, while votive candles were lit by hundreds of teary-eyed French people who saw us as they had been so often, a victim. One American overseas at the time wrote in our book of remembrance and condolence. It was out on a stand in our foyer for the public to sign.

> The day the world changed! My daughter of New York
> City has been missing since the attack. I believe I shall
> discover her alive, if not I will grieve, as a father of a lost
> child. And I will harbor no reckless actions; lend myself
> to no support of unnecessary violence against fellow
> citizens of the world. In this God I trust.

What a remarkable comment and one that went unheeded in many ways in the years to follow, as we sadly know today. I spoke the day after September 11, 2001, at a hastily arranged service of cathedral remembrance, quoting General Douglas MacArthur when he was aboard the battleship *Missouri* on September 2, 1945, for the official surrender (of Japan in World war II) ceremony in Tokyo. He said, "If we will not devise some greater and more equitable system [than war] Armageddon will be at our door. The problem basically is theological, and involves a spiritual recrudescence and improvement in human character that will synchronize with the almost matchless advances in science, art, literature, and all material and cultural developments of the past 200 years, it must be of the spirit if we are to save the flesh."

Only the word *Armageddon*—taken from MacArthur's speech—was highlighted by the CNN Paris correspondent on international TV. The rest of the homily had to do with faith and not fear, as another day of infamy.

On St. Francis Day in October, when we celebrate annually a service for blessing of the animals, some exotic and others family pets, the first service ever ironically held for the city of Paris, we had special guests. The French corps of recovery dogs that immediately flew to New York City to help in finding victims in the downed rubbish of the World Trade Center had returned to France. They joined the New York City emergency recovery team of the mayor's office for the service, and it was memorable seeing being in the presence of all those who had tried to save lives after that tragic disaster.

A year later, there was a memorial remembrance at the cathedral attended by the prime minister of France, the mayor of Paris, and the US ambassador to France, along with marching police singing the national anthems of both countries. We reminded everyone that people over eighty countries died in the horrific event, and we read the list of nations. It was also when a police sniper entered the sacristy, apologizing politely but asking how to climb to the roof to protect the dignitaries.

Bob was born and raised in Minneapolis, Minnesota. After graduating from Dartmouth, he had written many foreign news magazine and newspaper articles and learned and studied Mandarin Chinese at both Harvard and Yale. From his first wife, he has three children and five grandchildren, and then his marriage to Susan expanded his family to her three children.

He is a member of the Anglo-American Press Association of Paris, where he has lived since the early 1970s, but his most recent writing has been what he calls *Day Book*, which is full of personal remembrances and biographies of stimulating friends and famous actors, with pithy comments on the nature of humanity and the repeated failure of so many attempts to settle wars and conflicts. Yet in each copy, delivered to those interested free of charge, there is a profound Christian hope along with a sense of humor about the human condition. The cover is inscribed with a quote from Angus Wilson:

> Child: Look, Mummy! There's an old man writing!
> Mother: Yes, darling. It does them so much good.

One quote inside *Day Book* from the Spring 2013 issue is from the famous foreign diplomat and international commentator George F. Kenyon:

> We are toward the end of our lives such different people, so far removed from the child figures with whom our identity links us, that the bond to these figures, like that of nations to their obscure prehistoric, is almost irrelevant.

I don't know what Bob was like as a child or when in his early years he wrote prolifically and worked with so many worldwide magazines and newspapers, but I do know that he is one of finest human beings I have met. Was he like what he is today as a child? Who knows? St. Paul wrote in Corinthians, "When I was a child I spoke as a child, thought as a child, reasoned as a child, but when I grew up I finished with childish things. . . . At present we see only puzzling reflections in a mirror, but one day we shall see face to face."

That is our hope, and I believe that Bob knows this religious truth. He has bravely fought the puzzling effects of emphysema for some years. I would call that a newspaperman's disease, but not exclusively yet probably from smoking. I see him now as true to himself, a real aristocrat of the spirit, not only from knowing what good our short lives can do, but more so about the lasting power of the well-written word.

CHARLES TRUEHEART

In the video of the American Cathedral that was sponsored by Olivia de Havilland, Charlie Trueheart was interviewed as a parishioner who told viewers that he was baptized at the American Cathedral because he was born into US Foreign Service family that traveled to Paris, Ankara, London, and Saigon. Consequently, Charles has been associated with the cathedral for many years, not just as a visitor but also as a member of long standing. Charles also lived in Washington, DC, when young and completed his education at Phillips Exeter Academy and Amherst College. Before that, he had been director of the Institute of Politics at Harvard University and then director of the John F. Kennedy School of Government's Public Affairs Forum.

Elsie and I became acquainted with Charlie and his wife, Ann Swardson, when the two were in Paris as individual foreign correspondents for the *Washington Post*. His wife, Ann, then taught Sunday school at the cathedral before moving on to other lay ministries. One time, when Charles was traveling, their son, Henry, became ill on Sunday at a class session, and I remember walking up the long staircase to the school in a location we had for it in those days to investigate the condition of the boy and to stand by his mother until Henry recovered. This set in motion getting to know Charles and Ann better. When grandsons Jose and Tommy visited us from London, where each was born, the four children became friends.

One time we took all four kids with us in our car to Parc de Thoiry safari zoo not far from the city of Paris, where more than eight hundred animals roamed free: antelopes, bears, monkeys, and more. One had to drive through the park in a vehicle for protection. It could be a little scary on occasion, not like Jurassic Park of course, because these were contemporary, not prehistoric, animals, but it was fun, and the kids loved it. So did Elsie's dad from Texas when we took him with the grandchildren once.

In any case, the four children were often together whenever our grandsons visited. Our boys could be a challenge in the sense that while Tommy was an acolyte at the cathedral and liked to join in on activities, Jose preferred to rest from his active studies in London by watching television. One time he viewed our videotape of Charlton Heston playing Moses in the film *The Ten Commandments*. He was at an age when repetition helped him understand the film, and in this case, it was four times in a row! As a consequence, sometime later, he asked me, "Who is stronger? Moses or Spiderman?"

We got a kick out of Jose's *sincere* but immature question. We naturally replied, "Moses."

Referring to *sincerity*, that word defines friendly, intelligent, engaging but modest Charles Trueheart. He may not be a Moses, but he certainly has been active at the cathedral. No wonder he has been selected senior warden of the parish church and a member of the Board of Foreign Parishes that owns all convocation church property overseas in Europe. He also became a lay deputy to our general conventions in the States. He sings as well in the Paris Choral Society located at the cathedral.

As background information, Charles and Ann were married at St. John's Episcopal Church, Lafayette Square, in Washington, DC, where many of our nation's presidents have worshipped. Attractive, articulate, superintelligent Ann was financial news editor at the *Post* at the time, and Charles was a reporter and magazine columnist. She graduated from Cornell University and received a master's in journalism from Ohio University. From a family of high-powered academics, her father was a professor of English, and her mother, a professor of mathematics in the same institution.

Ann is the senior editor now for *Bloomberg News* in Paris. Charles became the director of the American Library in 2007, with its membership growing 25 percent in the last few years. This library has the largest collection of English books in all of Continental Europe, outside of England of course. It is obvious that both Charlie and Ann are committed church persons, both being outstanding lay readers at the cathedral and often serving at the altar as lay ministers.

Charles has also been active in the Convocation of American (Episcopal) Churches in Europe even before Bishop Pierre Whalen became the first elected suffragan bishop, or bishop in charge of the convocation. Our bishop in Europe is the assistant to the presiding bishop of the Episcopal Church because the convocation is, by an anomaly, his or her only diocese.

The first full-time bishop had been *Jeffrey W. Rowthorn*, who is English born and a graduate of Cambridge University, who speaks several languages. He had been a professor of liturgics and formerly was elected suffragan of the Diocese of Connecticut. He and his gracious wife, Anne, who had met in San Francisco at one of the outreach meetings held in the time of Bishop James Pike, were very popular in all our convocation churches and were our dear friends. Jeffrey, with Anne's help, began new programs that highlighted the appreciation of Anglicanism in Europe. She has also authored several books and has taught as a professor in seminaries. The two helped begin new missions, and they honored clergy and laity alike in Bishop Rowthorn's special Bishop's Award, given each year at an annual convention of the convocation. In December 2002, the convention meeting was held at Emmanuel American Church in Geneva, Switzerland, where former canon Nicholas Porter had become rector. This was the first time after his election that Bishop Whalen presided at a convention. I was given a Bishop's Award because I was retiring at the turn of the year, and I hope not because I was finally leaving at last after more than ten years!

Charlie Trueheart was invited to give the "eulogy" that he composed, revealing his true gift as a writer. This is what he conjured up for me:

> When I think of our next honoree, I have to go back to the first lethal encounter with him. I was a brand-new member of the parish, and pretty big for my britches. He was the seasoned rector, who'd seen them come and seen 'em go. Not long after I arrived, for reasons I will never understand, he decided to punish me. He seduced me into running for the vestry. I lost, of course. My pride and dignity were properly savaged by the experience, and I thought my rector was a cruel teacher. Lashing back—as I see it now—I wrote him to complain about a friend and fellow parishioner who had been turned away at the polling place in the vestry elections because she hadn't pledged. I was outraged, I told my rector, by an apparent system of two tiers of Christians, pledgers and nonpledgers, and by what struck me as a kind of poll tax, property-based voting that democracy had stamped out a long time ago even if my church had not. And so on.
>
> He called me up and very sweetly invited me to lunch— in the heart of Paris, our honoree's restaurant of choice

is not in any guidebook—and gave me his considered response to my complaint. He said simply, "I'd like you to run the stewardship campaign next year," and then he just grinned. The man is far wilier than he lets on. He turns whiners into workers.

The rector is moving on now, and he will be missed. That shambling gait. That broad crocodile smile. Those enormous shoes. That astonishing head of hair. Those broad shoulders—now hunched in concern, now thrown back in laughter, now shrugged in a way that says priests are human too. We will miss his references in the pulpit to his favorite scriptures—the Book of Camus, the Book of Sartre, the Good News of *Time* and *Newsweek*. We will miss his rare singing, which has convinced one parishioner that he is the long-lost brother of Willie Nelson. We will miss him on the softball mound, where he and the Holy Spirit are a fearsome combination. We will miss the almost daily visits of the Coca-Cola man to replenish the supply of decaf Diet Coke. And of course, we will miss his alter ego, a spouse who has been a friend and pastor herself to many in her husband's flock and been an asset to his ministry in many ways she is too modest to acknowledge.

Mostly we will miss our honoree as a pastor of remarkable accessibility and extraordinary compassion. Another parishioner who knows him well told me they had concluded that "what he does is pastor. That is his thing." It is true. He wants everyone he meets to feel better and be closer to God. And with a conviction that ran deep, and with a stubbornness that is sometimes breathtaking, even when wiser heads are attempting to prevail, he chooses the path of love and reconciliation.

Our honoree tonight has pastured to his church in another important sense that flows from the first. A recent visitor, a former parishioner, marveled at coffee hour the other day about the energy in the place, the sense of community and fellowship, the unmistakable impression of God's work busting out all over. A former canon told me, "He makes the grass grow." That is a good image—quiet, slow, but very real and very rooted and inspiring to behold. By his ineffable combination of acceptance and encouragement and openness and risk taking and empowerment, he has changed lives. He has transformed the place where we worship, and he has blessed our common life with God.

Ernest Hunt, rector and dean of the Cathedral of the Holy Trinity in Paris—and Elsie—this Bishop's Award is an inadequate tribute to all that you have given this church family, but rest assured it is not the last.

Interesting and perhaps embarrassing words, but they derived from Charlie, who is a creative writer par excellence and who has recently sired a book called *Letters to a Friend, Kyrie* while being a contributing author to Paris Stories. These two committed church people, Ann and Charles, have done much for the American Cathedral and have caught the spirit of the place, "a home away from home" and a haven for those who wish a "common life" in worship and fellowship with God. This was true for Charles since his baptism long ago. Thus, in my estimation, the two are indeed aristocrats of the spirit.

OLIVIA DE HAVILLAND

When Elsie and I arrived in Paris, we did not expect to meet and eventually become friends with a famous classical actress like Olivia de Havilland, but that happened to the Hunt family in more ways than one. The setting was of course the American Cathedral in Paris, where Ms. de Havilland was once head of the flower guild, remaining a lay reader. She was mostly invited to read on special occasions, such as Easter and Christmas, and also when special dignitaries were making a visit to the cathedral, such as President George H. W. Bush.

I had heard after arriving that Ms. de Havilland had, a year before, lost her son, Benjamin, in 1991. He had been a statistical analyst at the University of Texas in Austin. He died of complications from advanced Hodgkin's disease in his early forties but had been treated aggressively when a teenager at nineteen in Paris. While the intense radiation program finally caught up with him, he had some time to live a fruitful and intellectually helpful life. Many do not survive more than five years. He was named after his direct descendant Benjamin Briggs Goodrich, who signed the Texas Declaration of Independence. Nevertheless, the word around the cathedral was that Ms. de Havilland was deeply saddened, as one would expect, so I took the initiative to call on her at her townhouse on Rue Benouville, one door down from the retired home of former President Valéry Giscard d'Estaing.

When I got out of the taxi in front of her gated home, I noticed two policemen watching me closely from down the street, who were standing guard in front of the former president's home, just in case I was an interloper. A smiling maid, who probably originated from the Philippines, let me into the townhouse, and she showed me to the living room, where a fire was lit in the fireplace. By the way, many from the Philippines like her form the substructure of French Parisian families because they are industrious and cheerful.

In a few minutes, Ms. de Havilland appeared in the doorway to the living room from upstairs, radiant as I remembered photos of her, and smiling, greeting me in a most friendly way while inviting me to be seated across from her. I did not notice any trace of fatigue from the loss of her son, but that is usually well hidden emotionally. I have known too many people who have lost children but who never lose the embedded scars, even years later.

Nervous at first in meeting someone whom I had admired for a long time from afar, she made me feel relaxed as we chatted. I decided to ask her about the actor Leslie Howard in the unforgettable film *Gone with the Wind*, in which she played Melanie, and she told me that he had been preoccupied with the World War that again confronted his country, England. He also worked for MI16. She said that everyone— Vivian Leigh, Clark Gable, Ann Rutherford, Evelyn Keyes, Hattie McDaniel, and all others in the film—felt dominated to a degree by what was happening in Europe in 1939. Yet I believe the motion picture helped many deal with war in its total grotesqueness, because the movie, from the book by Margaret Mitchell, was centered on our own horrific Civil War. Our conversation ended on a most pleasant note, but I believe I asked her to read a lesson in the coming days, hoping for the best.

Eventually she did, and I was happy for her to be active again and for the cathedral to have such a proficient reader. After she had agreed, she always asked for a decent translation of the text, one that people could understand while in a version where the language excelled, not some "pop" adaptation. She would come to the cathedral at least a half hour or more ahead of time to rehearse, making sure she had the right inflexions of her voice for the seriousness of the scripture.

She has been an Anglican since birth, even after having been born in Tokyo, Japan, along with her sister. Her mother had sung in the choir of St. Andrew's Anglican Church in Tokyo and later encouraged her young daughter to sing in church pageants. Ms. de Havilland is a cousin to Sir Geoffrey de Havilland, the aviation pioneer, who is remembered for the popular Mosquito airplane in World War II. Her ancestors reach back to the ancient and noble family of de Havilland from the channel island of Guernsey, so she is no recent addition to church rolls.

When she read the lessons while I was dean, I admired the way those in the pews would hear her distinctive voice and ask, "Who is that?" Others would answer, "That is Olivia de Havilland!" To me, it was not because she was so famous that counted, but because of the way she read lessons with her full heart in the text, striving to make it as real an interpretation as possible for her listeners.

The more active she became, the more we would see her at the deanery, having champagne together, her favorite elixir. We had her for dinner on occasion, or more likely go across Avenue George V in front of the cathedral to the restaurant Marius and Janette, not far from the Crazy Horse Saloon, or she reciprocated in her home. We also got to know her daughter, Gisele Gallant, who is married and lives in Malibu, California, with her husband, Andy. She has been a correspondent for *Paris Match*, where her father Pierre Gallant, Olivia's second husband, was editor. Even though divorced for many years, Olivia took him into her home when he became very ill and nursed him until he passed on.

Because she was a member of the motion picture academy—from her two awards and many nominations—she would receive free samples of new films that were nominated in the current year for the Academy

Awards. Alas, she could not play the tapes at home because she was without a video player (before DVD), so sometimes she allowed us to see them with her in our upstairs TV room, really a bedroom used as a den.

On these occasions, she soon met our grandchildren, who were born in London because my daughter married a man born in Spain and educated with my son at Harvard, who had worked there for several years. Mostly the trio—Elizabeth, Jose, and Thomas—would visit us routinely. When Jose was about six years old, he flew by himself to Paris on British Midland, and I met him escorted by a flight attendant in Charles de Gaulle Airport. Once, after I waited for him to arrive in the baggage-claim area, I noticed that he was dressed in his Wetherby school uniform: a small cricket-type gray hat, gray shorts, and a red-and-gray blazer. I asked him why he was dressed so.

He replied, "I wanted to make sure you recognized me!"

That was an endearing response, but the one who seemed to resonate the most with Ms. de Havilland was the younger son, Tommy. Once, when Olivia was about to climb two flights up to our living area in the deanery, Thomas had come forward and reached out to help her politely while she began to ascend the curved stairway. He said something to the effect, "Madame, may I help you?"

He was only about four years of age. She never forgot that gesture of his and marveled at it often. Another time, when Ms. de Havilland and we were sitting together in the living room, Tommy came in, blond hair flying, small round face smiling, and robustly leapt onto her lap and hugged her. He stayed there with her for a long time, and she never forgot that gesture also.

It was about this time that Elsie, a retired public and private school teacher, was invited to be part of an OECD team to visit the recently emancipated Eastern European countries from Soviet domination. The Organization for Economic Co-operation and Development was formed from the association that helped minister the Marshall Plan after World War II but then in 1961 became an independent entity supported by American and most European countries. Elsie's task force in 1996, for example, was to assess and then recommend changes to the educational curriculums to include a more democratic outlook. She visited all the Eastern European countries at different times, including Bosnia.

Once, when we had dinner with Olivia, Elsie's travels were discussed. My wife told of the time when in a hotel in Montenegro. Elsie opened the door of her bathroom to face a waterspout aiming its way at her from a broken pipe. She quickly closed the door and called for help. Eventually, an employee of the hotel came to her rescue, dressed in a full wetsuit, and attempted to enter the bathroom but quickly gave up. She received a new room. I can still remember the roar of happy laughter from Ms. de Havilland as Elsie described the frustrated employee dressed for a plunge in a river.

Ms. de Havilland generously sponsored a video of the cathedral expertly done by a director named Milbank from England, who had done an excellent portrayal of the ministry of Ely Cathedral in England, showing a fully vested canon chasing a llama on St. Francis Day's celebration of the animals. She loved the sample he showed and commissioned him to do our film. Once finished over a year's time, I was able to show it at all the friends' meetings I visited annually in the States and even now have offered to the English-Speaking Union and Alliance Francaise meetings in Naples, Florida.

Our friendship continued even after I was to retire, and on the last Sunday before I did so as dean, she was asked by the good-bye committee to give an impression of my time in Paris. She responded that she would, and when the time came, she rose up on the chancel steps to tell a story about my ministry that was most laudatory. It was embarrassing, but I appreciated it. And we have remained friends over the years; in fact, she entertained college student Jose and his friend with champagne in her garden when he visited Paris. Much later, she did the same, as well as Tommy when he was in Paris on a trip visiting his father's family in Spain.

Over the years, Ms. de Havilland and I have had a pact that she would read a lesson when I was invited by the current dean to preach in Paris. She is ninety-eight now and going strong, and we miss her. She is not only a great lady, a classic actress honored by so many for her authenticity and humanity, but also a devoted church person. I attended the American University in Paris when it honored her especially for being a classic actress, who expressed a deep understanding of human values in her craft, but in my mind, and I am sure that in so many hearts around the world, she is the epitome of an aristocrat of the spirit.

PAMELA HARRIMAN

Madame Pamela Harriman, the American ambassador to France, came to services at the American Cathedral routinely until she died in 1997, much like I imagine her husband, Averill Harriman, had done earlier while in Paris. Yet when I greeted her at the church door, she was never alone. Either bodyguards were shadowing her or she was escorting her former daughter-in-law and grandchildren. Her divorced son, Winston Churchill, who was named not after his father Randolph but rather his famous grandfather, the former prime minister of England.

During the terrors of the horrific bombing of London during World War II, she resolutely stayed near the man she and many most admired, not the son of Winston Churchill, who was away at war, but by his resolute father. It has been stated that she almost sat at the feet of Churchill—so admiring was she of him—as he labored in the underground war room to fend off the Nazis and to end the war in Europe.

I recall seeing her each year in the 1990s as I was asked to say prayers by tradition at Suresnes American Cemetery on Boulevard Washington just outside the city of Paris. The burial ground was built in 1937 on 7.5 acres, for the resting place of 1,541 American dead of World War I, with twenty-four unknown dead later buried from World War II. The distinctive chapel at the height of the hill holds another 974 unknown deceased from World War II. Rosettes are placed on each plaque when someone once missing had been identified.

Before her death, Mrs. Harriman would faithfully arrive, dressed to the nines, and would offer condolences in a near-perfect French speech for those who had died. One rainy year, I still remember watching from my seat near the chapel her walking from the lower front gate to the place of ceremonies at the summit of the graveyard. To protect her, she was wearing a fashionable broad pink chapeau and a rain-glistened pink dress and raincoat outfit, all in chic Parisian style. The blistering rain did not mar her elegance or her elocution.

Another time, parishioner Marie Villon Beneviste, a remarkable artist who painted our grandchildren—the boys in the dean's garden and the girls later in Onteora Park, New York—had discussed with the ambassador doing her portrait. She at first declined but then, realizing Mary's reputation, relented. When it was finished, I called the ambassador and asked if we could bring it by her office in the embassy. Parishioner Harriet Riviere joined us, and after going through heavy security, which one would suspect, we were escorted to meet her. Mary had brought a portable wooden easel, and when the portrait was in place, the three of us were watching for a reaction. We were relieved when we noticed that she was very pleased, and she immediately asked me to say prayers for her.

Mary was a member of the cathedral's St. Anne's guild, which would regularly be invited to the grand residence of the ambassador for some of the guild's special meetings, and whenever that group or any official cathedral organization was to have a special gathering, it would also have an invitation. This grand residence was built in the tradition of the great houses of France in 1710 and was similar in many ways to the Élysée Palace, home to the French president nearby. The United States purchased the large residence in 1966, but Madame Harriman never kept it to herself alone but used it two or three days a week for others, and she would always make a personal appearance.

For example, on July 4, a special party was always held to celebrate our national independence, and many interesting guests were present from both countries. On one July 4, Elsie and I escorted a longtime resident of Paris, the classic film actress Olivia de Havilland, to the fete. Outside in the large garden in beautiful weather, we were sipping champagne when next to me suddenly stood actress Lauren Bacall, a personal friend visiting Mrs. Harriman. We chatted a bit, and she asked, "What do you do here in Paris?"

I stuttered something dumb, being a little enthralled, "Well, I run a cathedral."

And Olivia, standing next to me, who was deeply involved in the cathedral for years, added, "And very well too!" Then I briefly explained more exactly which cathedral, but the conversation drifted soon after Ms. de Havilland's comment.

Besides Olivia de Havilland, we had many memorable parishioners. When Craig and Heidi Whitney were to return to the States, the ambassador gave them a personal good-bye dinner in her personal apartment section of the large residence, and my wife and I were invited to attend. Craig was the *New York Times* correspondent in Paris for several years, and he and Heidi became personal friends of ours. Craig was also a devoted organist and, on one occasion, gave a full recital. He was quite good.

When we finally had our tower on Avenue George V lighted so that it could be seen in darkest winter, we saw two young men at our front gate as I was escorting Craig and Heidi home after dinner from the deanery. The youths looked a little lost, so the Whitneys chatted with them, only to discover that they were German tourists who said, "We were on the Eiffel Tower, and we saw this other lighted tower and we walked here to find out what it was."

Since Heidi was German born, she readily talked to them easily in their language and explained to each of the two the nature of our cathedral. When she turned to me and I had heard the translation, I was ecstatic. It had taken me a long time to convince the vestry that the lighting was necessary, and several finally donated to the project. It was a commemorative memorial, and one donor was the chief pilot for American Airlines who joined a flight attendant after my wife, on a flight from Dallas, had invited her for drinks. Whiling the time away, the two talked and discovered they were both Texans. The female flight attendant she had talked to on the flight also told my wife that when in Paris, she attended cathedral services. So Elsie invited her to come to the deanery for drinks that night on their layover.

Later, when they talked on the phone about details, the attendant asked if she could bring the crew! Elsie said sure, and three pilots and three other flight attendants showed up at our front gate, and we had a great time. Later, I offered a tour of the cathedral nave and sanctuary. Somehow I mentioned about the lighting of the tower project, and the chief pilot said he would like to give something in memory of his Vietnam fighter squad members who had died in combat. That sealed it, along with Diana Nouri, an American Episcopalian friend who also donated in memory of her deceased daughter, and also Jim Thomas for his daughter, Susan, who died prematurely. It was just a coincidence that the pilot's last name was Hunt.

Mrs. Harriman also responded to many special occasions we had at the cathedral. Our Memorial Battle Cloister was finally updated to include World War II, with help of Judith Bingham and art chairman Rudi Bass, husband of one our newly established Pastoral Counseling Center members; Sculptor Philippe Andre, the ambassador; along with Bishop Jeffery Rowthorn, the first full-time bishop for the Convocation of

Churches in Europe; Wayne Blair (speaking for his infirm mother, Mrs. Donald Shattuck Blair), president for the Daughters of the American Revolution; Philippe Mestre, Ministre des Anciens Combattants of Victimes de Guerre.

Ambassador Harriman said in brief, "While we gratefully salute our military we must not forget the millions of other victims of that terrible war. In London during the Blitz I saw destruction and death come to innocent civilians."

I remember so clearly a week after D-day that there was poem published by an army lieutenant who had seen his friends die on that day. He dedicated it to their memory:

> Went the day well
> We died and never knew
> But well or ill,
> Freedom we died for you.

Before flight TWA 800 was blown out of the sky on July 17, 1996, not far from JFK, where all on board were lost, we were looking forward to the church composer David Hogan performing a concert of his music at the cathedral. But he and many others perished in the sudden explosion resembling a flaming comet falling from the sky. Consequently, in due time, we had a public funeral Mass written by David Hogan, one of the world's leading liturgical composers and who sang in the cathedral choir. I was quoted in the *New York Daily News* as urging mourners "to remember all the victims for whom the bell tolled unnaturally and before it should have." Earlier that week, the ambassador called me up and asked if she could come to the service and if there was anything she could do. I replied that naturally her presence would add balm to the seriousness of the loss of so many, French and American. I commended her for reaching out.

Elsie and I happened to be on a trip to Egypt sponsored by the American Club of Paris when Mrs. Harriman died after a stroke in her regular swim at the Ritz Hotel. She was taken to the American Hospital at Neuilly but succumbed the next day. Everyone on the trip was devastated because Mrs. Harriman was extremely popular.

Mario Casuto, owner of Travel USA in Paris, who organized and partially led the trip for us, also thought the world of our ambassador.

Mario was a prince of a man who secured a beautiful new Coptic-owned boat for us to sail the Nile. I did not know Mario through the cathedral but the American Club, whose secretary at the time was a parishioner, Helene Sullivan. After arriving in Cairo, we had lunch one day in the city before our river trip, and I was seated next to Mario. I asked if he was American by birth since he sounded like one. He answered, to my surprise, "No, I'm from Egypt. I was born here. I went to a British school here and served in the US Signal Corps in World War II. Then I married an American, and we worked at TWA for years until she died. Now I have a Paris travel agency, as you know, where we lived last."

I asked how he or his family wound up in Egypt. He answered simply, "Ever hear of the Inquisition?"

That answer will stay with me for the rest of my life. It was later when we were on the riverboat that a fellow passenger, Fred Bondi, was the first to tell me one evening that he heard the news that the ambassador had died. He suggested that the next day we have an interfaith memorial service on the ship for her. All of us from Paris attended and participated—so respected was she by all. Fred asked me to lead that service for her because he thought she had done such a great job.

After we returned to Paris, I met her son, Winston Churchill, after he came over from London to discuss details of a memorial in Paris. When he arrived, he came straight to my office, along with Mrs. Pierre Salinger, a personal friend of Mrs. Harriman, and his former wife, Minnie, whom Mrs. Harriman adored. In our discussions, he wanted the service to be at La Madeleine Church, and not at the American Cathedral, so there was not much to talk about since I had no influence over the cure who led that church.

Later after, he returned to London, he called to say he had changed his mind—he did not want a service in Paris, which severely disappointed the Americans in Paris. So much so that there was a popular request from the American Aid Society, some at the embassy, and many American groups, that we have a service in any case to honor her. We did so, and it was well attended.

When he found out what had been done, Mr. Churchill called by phone to ask why a service was held when he had not wanted such in Paris, but I explained to him that it arose not from the family but from the Americans in Paris who respected her and felt cheated that they could not honor her. Then he understood, and I sent him a leaflet bulletin as proof of all the many American organizations that were listed in support of the service.

The final service, however, was to be held at the National Cathedral in Washington, DC. Consequently, the Very Reverend Nathan Baxter, who was the dean then, called me to explore my coming over to preach at the service because I knew her, and he did not. I agreed. I therefore arranged a flight to Washington from Paris and arrived in the city. The next day of the burial, I went to the large five-thousand-seat cathedral (ours in Paris could hold only one thousand), found the sacristy, and met other clergy from many backgrounds, as well as the Harriman and Churchill families, who were waiting there as well. The dean introduced me, and as I was beginning to don vestments, a lovely blond lady entered, whom I thought at first was a member of the altar guild, since she seemed to feel right at home. It turned out that she was the vice president's wife, Mrs. Tipper Gore. Her husband strolled in later, and I had the opportunity to meet Vice President Al Gore as well. A little later, the president and Mrs. Clinton entered to pay respects to the families, and I remember that Mrs. Clinton was quite friendly, asking me where I was from.

Then the moment came for the service to begin. The families were escorted in to the front rows of the cavernous cathedral, next to the president, as the clergy and choir gathered to process in toward the sanctuary. When my turn to offer the homily arrived, I was escorted to the pulpit and then offered my piece, mentioning toward the end that the poem she remembered from World War II applied to her for her service in France. I quoted it for her.

When the service was over and as we were processing out, I noticed tall actor Gregory Peck, with his French wife next to him, seemingly staring at me with those large dark eyes as I passed by and hoped that he didn't disapprove. In any case, the Roman Catholic priest in the service had given me a heads-up when I was finished and was sitting next to him.

I read a criticism of her in the *Washington Post* after the service by columnist Maureen Dowd, now at the *New York Times*, which I thought a disservice since the writer seemed to be preoccupied with Mrs. Harriman's previous social life in the capital as opposed to that of Katherine Graham, corporate head of the *Washington Post* at the time.

However, today I read the writer zealously in the *Times* for her cogent and caustic comments on politics and world affairs.

In spite of some criticism of Mrs. Harriman's former personal life, I believe that she was placed in the right post at the right time in life when in Paris. She was experienced about France's history and its societal problems because she lived through World War II. She knew firsthand some of the reasons the French acted the way they did because of the horrific periods before, during, and after the war. Of course, she was not as historically insightful like writer Alan Furst, but nonetheless, the French loved her. She was almost considered an insider, which is not easy in that country. Many were convinced she gave her all in Paris as ambassador, and that seemingly tireless effort possibly contributed to her death. In any case, she did care deeply at that time of her life for her diplomatic mission. She also appreciated the American Cathedral. For all of which, I claim her as an aristocrat of the spirit.

S. STANLEY KREUTZER

When Cynthia and Jack Findlay were married in Paris at the mayor's office while I was dean of the American Cathedral, Elsie and I had the pleasure of being invited after the official service to the reception. As I have stated, the mayor of each French city perform the only lawful marriage while churches or other religious organizations follow suit with a blessing if the couple so wish. Both Cindy and Jack had been married before and were mature when they had met, perhaps through friends or through the American Club. At least I knew Jack through that organization even though both at various times attended cathedral services, like many Americans living abroad in Paris. Religious affiliation is never an issue for attendance at the American Cathedral, much like the National Cathedral (Episcopal) in Washington, DC.

At their reception, I had the pleasure of meeting the father of the bride. I understood that he was a retired lawyer from New York City and of Jewish heritage. Jack was of Roman Catholic background. While I was standing around and sipping champagne, the father, who, I understood later, was in his nineties at the time, came up to me, and we chatted. He introduced himself as Stanley Kreutzer, and we discussed at first how much we both loved New York City, since I had spent many years there. But then, Mr. Kreutzer became more serious and said, "Reverend, I initiated the first code of municipal civic ethics for the city of New York. My parents were immigrants, and they told me in no uncertain terms that I had the responsibility to be a *decent human being all my life*, and I never forgot that."

I was so impressed with the firmness of his conviction that I quoted him in my first book written in retirement, *Paris under Siege*. The book's chapters illustrated the attempts by a fanatic Algerian Salafist to blow up American institutions in Paris, but they were foiled in part by the four "musketeers," three Americans and one dedicated Muslim woman. I placed his comment about decency in the final chapter as a statement against what evil people do in the name of religion. After all, to be a decent human being is bottom line for all faiths, particularly when some in each are tempted to use violence to eschew their ends. A decent human being does not blow up innocent bystanders, no matter the cause.

I found out later that Mr. Kreutzer was a graduate of St. John's University Law School and took seriously that the law needed to be upheld and that corporate ethics should be enforced. Mr. Kreutzer was often accused of being a stern ethicist, but on the other hand, he also believed that "codes of ethics do not make public officials better . . . but they provide a guide for the perplexed as to what these duties are. They enable the public to judge with sharpened vision whether there are any conflicts of interest."

He was described through many articles and comments from public officials as a "tenacious reform-minded lawyer," whose draft of a code of ethics for the city of New York became a model for cities across the nation. What an accomplishment, particularly when so many today are accused of special interest! In addition, the *New York Law Journal* of February 14, 1983, stated,

> After going back as far as Daniel Webster, Henry Clay and John C. Calhoun, he recited a series of scandals (in an interview) involving politicians that brought him to the present day and a conclusion that politics brings out the best in people and the worst, just like sex and religion do.

Over his many years as a lawyer, Mr. Kreutzer was involved in several law firms as well as in private practice, and his reputation for fairness goes back as far as the 1930s and 1940s. He managed the campaign of Francis E. Rivers for the old New York City court. With Mr. Kreutzer's help, Mr. Rivers became the first black person ever elected to a judicial position in New York County.

It was rare in New York City to be such a trusted official by so many of different opinions and affiliations. For example, he mediated as the parliamentarian at a meeting of the Liberal Party state committee for which two factions were contending for power. He agreed to do so as long as both sides agreed to accept him, and then he even helped form a compromise.

In his career of nearly seventy years, he served as counsel and investigator for the State Assembly, for the New York City Council and its Board of Ethics, and for commissions on lobbying, crime, public health, charter revision, the state judiciary, and New York's bicentennial, in which we were able to see the great sailing ships of the past on the Hudson River. He must have been a busy man; maybe that is why he was blessed with living so long.

Mr. Kreutzer was known for rejecting political labels, but he called himself an independent Republican—"nine tenths independent and one-tenth Republican." He also advised many mayors, going back to Fiorello H. LaGuardia, Robert F. Wagner, and Abraham Beame. He received strong letters of commendation for his intellectual acumen and his honesty by both Mayor John Lindsay as well as Governor Nelson Rockefeller.

"After decades of influence peddling, conflicts of interest, nepotism and other largely unpunished shenanigans, much of it promoted by Tammany Hall, the powerful Manhattan Democratic organization run by Camine G. DeSapio," his official code of ethics called a halt to much of all that, according to Robert D. McFadden who gave him credit for the code of ethics that changed the political atmosphere of the city.

Not only was he a reformer, but he was also a man who made clever strategic decisions. John Cummings in *Newsday* wrote,

> He recalls an incident with LaGuardia. Once, when German-American Bund leader, Fritz Kuhn, had rented Madison Square Garden for a rally, LaGuardia

was uneasy about issuing a permit. Kreutzer told him to approve it and then assign every Jewish policeman on the city force to the Garden. The mayor said, 'Are you crazy? Do you want to start a riot?' I said 'You won't have any trouble.' And there was no trouble at all.

That quote reveals how far ahead of his time his thinking was and how much we could use S. Stanley Kreutzer, not just to advise a city or its mayors but more so to remind the entire US Congress—both the House of Representatives and the Senate, let alone all elected national officials—of their ethical responsibilities. We may not have Tammany Hall today, but we have several pseudo-Tammany's that have special interest at heart instead of the common good of all.

As an example, columnist Maureen Dowd in the *New York Times* of June 13, 2014, quoted Rick Cohen of the *National Philanthropic Quarterly* on one subject of self-interest peddling today, "It is troubling when corporate donors give to political charities with a more or less obvious expectation that softer and gentler treatment will ensue (for their corporations) in the future."

Mr. Kreutzer would have kept a sharp eye out for such "shenanigans" if he were alive today, knowing that they hold up the progress of our country, like Tammany Hall kept New York City from advancing to a more healthful civic society. Just think what it would mean to someone like Mr. Kreutzer in a global situation today, seeking to unravel shenanigans between national corporations or countries—perhaps always an impossible task at best.

S. Stanley (the *S* stood for Samuel, a name too close to another family member, so he never used it), even though in my estimation he was as "wise as Samuel," he was also a devoted family man. He married his wife, Corinne, in 1932, and she died before him in 2000, but his marriage was long and providential for them both. He has two daughters and two grandsons he adored. He lived to be ninety-eight years of age.

Mr. Kreutzer was a type of Renaissance man. He was talented in many fields. For example, he liked to write poetry for special occasions, especially this one when the American Bar Association finally admitted the first black man in the 1940s. This poem was meant to challenge the right of ABA to reject lawyers on the basis of race and was addressed to Frank Rivers, the man in question. It has a moral base.

> I see by the papers
> That some funny capers
> Were indulged in by the A.BAR'A.
> After much legal juggling
> And squirming and muddling
> They seem to have found the way.
> Now that August Grand Body
> Of educational shoddy
> Of pretense and rubbish and such
> Despite legal acumen
> They're at last human
> And did something—although not very much.
> The Bar association
> Since its creation
> Was careful to pick and choose
> For their learned Committee
> We'll have aught if not pity
> You've blasted them out of their pews.

And these less caustic words for our general celebration of Christmas:

> As the shadows of this year
> are hastened by each passing day
> to the threshold of a New Year
> It is our Hope
> That the spirit and glow
> Of this season
> With its soft candlelight
> Will usher in the dawn of a New Day
> When peace and Strength and Light
> Will be everywhere
> And Friendliness and Kindness and Brotherhood
> Will be as universal as life itself
> And there will truly be

Peace on earth and Good will.

It is my opinion that S. Stanley Kreutzer lived out what he told me in Paris his parents expected of him. I will never forget those words or his firm conviction. He was a decent and good human being who did much for his family, for his city, for individuals who needed support, and for ethics in general, and he was truly an aristocrat of the spirit.

FRED BONDI

Elsie and I have been members of American Friends of Blérancourt Museum since the early 1990s after we arrived in Paris. One Saturday soon after our arrival, we attended a benefit at the remains of the seventeenth-century chateau near Compiegne in the north of Paris. The chateau was headquarters for Ann Morgan, J. Pierpont's daughter, in the First World War when women became the first ambulance drivers for the wounded soldiers. Ann Morgan fostered many other humanitarian causes for France, restored the chateau after the war, and then sold it to the French government in 1929. The museum now houses an ambulance from WWI and many portraits and photos from the era, including at one time our painting of the cathedral at Christmas in 1890 by Claude Beraud.

By chance we met a gentleman, Fred Bondi, who began chatting to us, making us feel quite at home. We had lunch together there. And in spite of how upbeat he was to us, he spoke often about the fact that his first wife had just died and that he was having a hard time adjusting to being alone. After that, we saw him often at the American Club, always surrounded by doting women who knew that he was alone.

Finally, we heard that he had flown to Cincinnati to attend a wedding and that he had met a beautiful lady in the reception afterward, widowed as he was and some years younger than he, and had been smitten by her. Then he had invited her to visit him. After her journey to Paris, we met her briefly at an embassy reception and noticed that she was blond and quite beautiful. They decided to marry, and when Susie became his wife, they invited us over on occasion to their apartment that had a beautiful view of Paris.

When we were slated to leave after I announced my retirement, Fred and Susie had a going-away party for us in their apartment, which was well attended. They went all out for us, and we were really taken aback by their generosity.

After Paris we did not see them until they were on a boat trip that had a stop at Fort Lauderdale. Because we lived part time in Naples on the west coast of Florida, it was an easy drive across Alligator Alley to meet them for lunch at the Ritz Hotel.

At lunch they told us that they had moved from Paris to Vienna, where Fred was born. He was forced to leave in 1938 when he was sixteen years of age because he was Jewish. His father knew the American consul, and they were given permits to escape after Hitler invaded Austria in his annexation of Austria to Germany, called Anschluss Osterreichs, backed by Wehrmacht army troops, and because the same Jewish oppression began there as in Germany, Fred and his parents had moved to New York City.

But then Austria, nearly seventy years later, far after the ending of World War II, invited him back to Vienna with full pension privileges and social security benefits, which made Fred extremely happy. Susie enjoyed living in Vienna as well. Both loved musical concerts and the opera and attended them often, and since Fred was almost ninety years of age then, he stated that Vienna had ramps everywhere, so it made it easier for him to walk. They were very happy. I recall asking him about his name. I said, "There used to be an actress years ago in the '30s and '40s whose name was Beulah Bondi. I saw her in a movie with Fredric March on TCM last night and was thinking of your name being similar. Are you related to her?"

He answered, "No, but when I was in high school in New York, some kids teased me and called me Beulah!"

It was good to see them then, but the following year, they came over from East Florida after their landing from another extensive boat trip and stayed with us in our condominium. That was when we had time to talk in more detail. I asked him about that time in Vienna in 1938. He said, "I remember vividly when the German troops marched into Vienna with boisterous music and a loud, goosestep stomp. Bands were playing, and it was almost exciting, except I knew that being Jewish, I could never be part of those rallies where people were laughing and cheering. Yet I understood the enthusiasm, even though I was soon to

EE HUNT

be an enemy, due to Hitler's failure of economic programs. He blamed it on the Jews, as always.

"Then my father had influence with the consulate, and we were able to leave. When I was in New York City on the Upper West Side, I had no friends at first. One day, it was snowing, and being used to the Austrian Alps, I took out my skis and began skiing down a small slope in Riverside Park. A schoolgirl walking by noticed me, and since no one else was skiing on such a small hill, she asked where I was from. I told her, and she understood. Then she asked if I had any friends. I replied that I didn't. Then she said, 'I will be your friend,' and she helped me join a nice gang of kids, and I felt more accepted.

"One time, our family traveled to Washington, DC, before World War II broke out, and we stayed in a hotel with a view of the German embassy. I looked out the window one day and saw the Nazi swastika flag flying, and I almost got sick. It was a damning sight. I will never forget that visual reminder of our having to leave our home, even when we were safe in the United States."

I inquired about the rest of his life in those days, and he said he went to Cornell University and majored in engineering, then joined the navy. When World War II began for the United States, he was in the army as an engineer, and then he retired after the war as a colonel. His last army job was in France, and he stayed there, working in a company he formed in Paris, married, and settled down until his first wife died. That was when we met.

This intelligent, warm, and friendly man befriended us at Blérencourt, and we thus became fast friends. With the help of his loyal and beautiful wife, he has survived prostate cancer and is still happy in Vienna. Susie wrote last year an Internet article about their going vegetarian in Vienna and how it helped reduce Fred's PSA dramatically.

> My Fred is an extraordinary guy. We were both widowed when we met and then married in Paris 17 years ago and we loved our life there. Then, in 2008 we moved to Vienna, Austria, where the healthcare is good, crime is low, and public transportation is outstanding. Fred was born in 1923 and is proud that he just turned 90.

Fred also told me a story about entering a store recently where an older woman greeted him; they had a friendly talk, and she asked, "Where are you from?"

He replied that he was born in Vienna but had to leave in 1938. She answered, "How dumb of us to have lost such nice people."

Susie's words and those of that woman in the shop define Fred Bondi. He is a true aristocrat of the spirit.

JAMES WILLIAM THOMAS

Jim introduced himself to me at the American Cathedral in Paris when he volunteered to be an usher in 1993, so after he was doing his ushering at the rear of the cathedral near the entrance door, we chatted and compared some notes as expats do about their history, and then his wife, Mary Ann, and he invited us over to their spacious apartment for dinner. We have been friends ever since. So much so that when he took time from his busy assignment in Paris as president of the Maremont division of Arvin and managing director of the TESH group, a joint venture being formed across Europe from operations in France, the UK, and Italy, he asked me to play golf with him. Usually, I played with Ed Dye, a longtime vestry member of the American Cathedral from Long Island who had lived for years in France since he married a lovely French lady, Odile. She is a talented artist. Ed knew all the places to play around Paris, from Disney World, with its four courses named after Disney characters, and nearby to Paris public course, or several places on the improved grounds of ancient chateaus that needed extra financial support.

Ed's father was Joe Dye, executive director of the USGA, but when Ed was sixteen, he told me that he believed he was so bad at golf that he threw his clubs away and did not play at Princeton or in early life. His mother was an amateur champion, and his father was an excellent player. Yet he took up golf again forty years later, and in Paris, while I was at the cathedral, we both struggled together in the game when we could. Friday was my day off, so that was when Ed and I would play.

Jim often joined in, but one time, when I was playing alone with him on some nearby course, he told me about his daughter, Susan, who died in 1978. She was two months shy of her seventeenth birthday when she died in an accident on prom night with her date. He was driving and tried to pass on a road torn up by construction work and never made it. They crashed, and he lived, but she didn't. Whatever hurt lies deep in our hearts and is shared while playing golf is usually from an unhealed scar. Jim later wrote, "Since Susan's death there has not been a day that Mary Ann or I (and usually the both of us) have not talked to Kerin (younger daughter) regardless of where we were in the world." One never forgets the loss of a child.

Susan's name is inscribed in the foyer of the American Cathedral, along with others in a commemorative memorial plaque of those donors who helped light the tower in the City of Lights.

After nearly four years, Jim planned to leave for the States after completing his managerial operations in Paris, but at the last moment, the CEO of Sogefi, located in Milan, Italy, Jim was informed that he was leaving his post for another challenge. He asked Jim to replace him, which he agreed to do. But after six months of being alone while Mary Ann had thought they were through in Paris and had returned to the States, he got tired of living in a hotel, traveling most of the time and spending all his free time alone. This was not the life he wanted, so in June 1997, after living in three foreign countries and visiting fifty-one others for business or pleasure, he returned to the United States and retired from full-time active employment. It didn't stop him, however, from traveling to four more countries but only as short-term consulting work.

In 1998, their daughter Kerin married Roderick Smith, and on December 12, 2000, they were presented with their only grandchild, Madison. Their marriage occurred at St. James Episcopal Cathedral in Chicago, and I was the officiant. I also said a prayer for Susan, who was so close to Kerin, but not in a sad way. This was a happy event, so we celebrated both their lives.

Jim and Mary Ann returned to Paris on a special occasion while I was still dean, and the baptism of Madison occurred in the cathedral.

Jim and Mary Ann live in Naperville, Chicago, and in Naples, Florida, where we see the two often, and sometimes we play golf, but he is so far ahead of me in the game that I am lucky to keep up with him at all. I always say, "I play bad golf but with good friends."

Jim is the fifth child of nine children born in Marseilles, Ohio, and of a religious Protestant family. The oldest was born in 1920 but was killed when his B-17 was shot down over Manheim, Germany, in September 1944. Jim was born on January 31, 1934, so there was a wide diversity of ages in the family. Mr. Thomas is a stalwart Christian and a man who does not forget the needs of others, nor ceases to help them. He understands that true religion is as the biblical prophet Micah has written:

> What does the Lord require of you, but to do justice, and
> to love kindness, and to walk humbly with your God.

Therefore, in my mind, Jim is an aristocrat of the spirit.

WILLIAM WALKER STEVENSON

Bill Stevenson came into our lives not because he lived in Paris, although he had visited several times in the past, but because in 1997, my son Ernest E. Hunt IV married his daughter, Holly Stevenson, who was from Charlottesville, Virginia. We were living in the deanery in Paris at the time. Earlier, Holly, Ernie's fiancée, had visited us alone in Paris, which she loved, and while staying with us at the deanery, we told her that if our son didn't marry her soon, we would adopt her! Well, Ernest did marry her shortly thereafter, and we were very happy.

In the process of the engagement and marriage, we met her father, Bill, and his wife, Carole, and they became our dear friends. Bill was an extremely interesting person. He once showed me a photo of his father taken on Hitler's own bed in his underground bunker at the end of World War II before that hidey-hole was destroyed by the Russians. Bill himself worked for the Central Intelligence Agency after law school and was stationed in Berlin and Tokyo. A photo showed him talking to the prime minister of Japan, but as one would imagine, the subject of their conversation was strictly undisclosed. He also was special assistant, United States Mission to Vietnam, in Saigon, from 1966 to1967. He also had a keen view of foreign affairs, often having lunch in Charlottesville whenever Brent Scowcroft or Lawrence Eagleburger—both foreign-service friends who served under Senior President George H. W. Bush—were in town.

For seven years, Mr. Stevenson was a columnist for the *Charlottesville Observer*, but if you don't have a wry sense of humor as he did or are not a confirmed conservative, you might be challenged by what he wrote. This is an excerpt from his public writing:

Hail Marys

> If you have tired of my recipes for French Seventy-fives (Mailbag, February 8) by now, we have a new concoction for you, the old standby known as Bloody Marys. This used to be offered at the Princeton-Harvard or the Princeton-Yale game, whichever was played at Princeton, supported by a bagpipe group from Trenton. Thompson, the sponsor, had a simple recipe requiring a 30-gallon garbage can, preferably new. Fill it half way with tomato juice, a quarter of the way with vodka, add a couple of bottles of Worcestershire sauce, and if you want to be fancy, toss in a canister of celery salt or seeds. You then dump in the ice, stir, listen to the music whether you like it or not, and enjoy."

It is obvious that Bill attended Princeton and then graduated from there in 1950, after both the Fay School and Groton earlier, and that he was a loyal alumnus. He then enrolled in the University of Virginia law school and graduated in 1959, and loving Charlottesville so much, he lived there as a prime resident until his death. He married Carole Wheeler, his wife of more than fifty years, in that town. His two children, Holly and William, were born there.

While we were living in France, Bill and Carole joined us for a trip to the Black Sea and met us after flying in from the States to Venice. We boarded a small German ship with a Russian crew, except for the cruise director who was a tall German lady who told us one day that she was also a pilot of a plane. There were about twenty-five English speakers, ten from England and fifteen from the States, along with a majority of German folk, and it was not only a scenic trip but also an interesting one because of the diversity of the passengers and crew.

Everything was going smoothly, the small ship stopping at ports for us to enter the state of Georgia, then Poland, near Gdansk, Poland,

and finally Athens, Greece. The cruise director placed the German passenger majority in three large buses so we all could tour the city and one small bus for the English for about fifteen English speakers.

We toured the Pantheon and the spot where St. Paul spoke to the Greek intellectuals, cited by the Book of Acts 17, and I was thrilled to be there. His sermon had been about their statue to the unknown god, created just in case the Epicureans and others left out one from their many gods. He of course identified the unknown one in biblical terms in the Areopagus, or on Mar's Hill, close to the tip of the Acropolis.

When it came time to leave and travel down the hill, we entered our minibus, but after rolling along nicely, we were suddenly held up by intense traffic, and we became concerned that the ship might leave without us. Yet the lady tour guide on the bus, who had explained to us what we had seen in Athens, assured us we would safely return before the ship sailed away by 5:00 PM. Actually, when we were slowly descending, we could see the ship in the distance. However, when we descended from the bus and walked through the terminal, we returned to the dock where the ship had been moored and discovered, to our horror, that the pier was empty! No ship in sight.

We all of course panicked but tried to ask some white uniformed Greek naval officers standing nearby where the ship might be and what to do, but they were not helpful at all, mainly because they knew little English, and we were certainly not fluent in the Greek language. I distinctly remember Bill, however, running down to the end of the dock, trying to hail the ship, but it had gone too far out into the Aegean to pay attention.

The leader of the people from England used his cell phone to call London, who in turn had the number of the Russian captain, who, when informed of his missing passengers, evidently cursed as one might expect but stopped the ship. What to do next? The ship could not reenter without permits, so if "Mohammed could not go to the mountain, so the mountain had to go to him." In this case, the fifteen of us, as "Mohammed," were finally placed on a small pilot boat. Thankfully, the Aegean was quite calm, and we reached the side of the ship in about twenty minutes, but the saga did not end there.

The opening in the side of the ship was about double horse hands high. So the crew threw a rope ladder down, but since some of the stranded older passengers were on canes, it was not long before that attempt was abandoned. Finally, the captain's executive officer arrived and decided the best way to lift us up was by a human ladder of strong crewmen. I jokily yelled to Bill, "Women and children first!" and he laughed in good humor. When we were finally hauled up and on board, the suave German lady cruise director denied a reduced rate for our trip by saying, "You had a more exciting journey this way."

She too chuckled, all except Bill, who thought we deserved a reduction. Later, he found an error in our general billing, and we did receive a rebate, but not for the added so-called exciting pilot trip from Athens.

Bill's expertise was in finance. He was one of the founders of the Monticello National Bank and its president. When First Virginia Bank bought this, he became chairman of the board until 1998. Then he became president of Eglinton Investments, a private company that invested in real estate. Concerning foreign affairs, he and Carole endowed the Miller Center (for foreign affairs) in Charlottesville with a biennial speaker conference. He was very active in many organizations, but his wry sense of humor prevailed when asked toward the end of his life, "What was the best thing you have done?" and he replied simply, "Buy land!"

Bill was a modest, intelligent person who served his country and who endured stoically and without complaint an aggressive prostate cancer and then acute myeloid leukemia. In my estimation, Bill was an aristocrat of the spirit, especially as he calmly approached his death at eighty years of age in 2008.

CHAPTER EIGHT

Naples, Florida and Onteora, New York

HELENE GORMAN

THE AMERICAN CATHEDRAL in Paris sponsored a trip to the Holy Land in 1993 that was led by Canon Benjamin Shambaugh, and my wife was asked by the canon if she would like to attend. This was shortly after we had arrived and I had my hands full, getting to know the congregation, learning French, and obtaining a driver's license for my car. It was not a good time to leave for three weeks, but Ben had already been on the staff about a year, preceding me by being called to his position by the former dean. I asked him to remain as canon and also continue the well-planned trip, but he told me that he needed one more person to fill the quota for the excursion, or they could not go. That left only Elsie Beard Hunt, and she consented if she had her own room like some others had requested. The group gathered and flew to Israel, toured Jerusalem, then Mount Sinai, where Ben celebrated the Eucharist, Petra, Jordan, Syria, and other locations. At that moment in time, political matters were somewhat peaceful in the areas they visited.

One of the most active couples on the trip was that of John and Helene "Leni" Gorman. Elsie got to know them well and discovered that they had a small apartment in Versailles, although they lived principally in Naples, Florida. Leni and John also attended the American Cathedral in Paris on occasion, even though Leni was Russian Orthodox in background, being from a family of white Russians who escaped after the Bolshevik Revolution and traveled first to Lebanon, where Leni was born in 1925. They became friends of President David S. Dodge at the American University, but way before he was abducted in 1992 as the first kidnapped American of note from the Middle East, but later released.

Later Leni moved to New York City, married, and had children, living part time in Paris, France—not the once known *Paris of the Middle East, Beirut.* One child lives in New York City and is married, with children, and the other lives near Washington, DC, is a well-known animal care advocate, and is married to a medical research doctor. She has two children. After a divorce, Leni met John Gorman, an executive CEO, and they lived happily for many years until he died peacefully but suddenly at home in Naples. Leni, however, continued to live in Naples where we often saw her almost weekly, inviting many friends to her Gulf Shore apartment overlooking the Bay. She is a vivacious person, with fine facial features, a broad grin and smiling eyes, not tall, diminutive in fact, but bustling with energy. Two particular friends of Mrs. Gorman have become ours as well; she is a catalyst for helping others make new friends.

Chantal Mathews was also born in Lebanon but raised in Egypt. She is of a French background. Her mother was a nun who left her order and married, having three daughters, and after coming to the States, Chantal finished her education. She held several jobs but eventually attained a high position in city government in Atlanta, Georgia. After an early retirement from that successful position, she settled in Naples and now paints and volunteers to teach English. She often drives Leni to art shows, restaurants, and museums as a friend, and the two have fun together.

After moving back to the States, *Ron Murphy* lost his wife, Kitty, and since has become a friend of Leni's. He has two children; his daughter lives in the States and is married while his son lives in Geneva. Ron spent thirty-five years in that city in Switzerland and several years before that in Zurich. He is a member of Alliance Francaise of Bonita Springs, which meets in Naples, and that is where Leni met him. Leni speaks French, Lebanese, Russian, as well as English.

The other friend whom we have gotten to know is *Dr. Driss Hassan*, who is from Algeria, but after education in Paris, France, and in the States, he has been a well-known surgeon who practiced in Plattsburg, New York, for years and retired in Naples, Florida.

Every time we have dinner with Leni, we meet new people because she is so gracious—a channel for meeting others, no matter the language spoken. Unfortunately, on her eighty-eighth birthday, while preparing for a party that evening, she drove to the local Walmart store to purchase napkins and candles, and while walking from the parking area to the store in the crosswalk, a woman in her car ran into her, knocking her down to the pavement. She remembers floating in the air for a few moments and then felt the shock of hitting the pavement hard. She was taken to the hospital, but an MRI showed nothing was broken, except she has struggled for months to regain her former ease in walking without pain. She has almost fully recovered but still has lingering physical problems.

How would you like being hit by an automobile while walking in a crosswalk in the parking lot of a Walmart store? It's the last thing one would expect, but such bad events do happen. She has sworn it will not get her down. She will have to give up going to Paris, France, as she has for years, because her studio apartment has a steep flight of stairs, but otherwise, she remains vivacious, generous, and still bustling with energy. She has a gift for bringing people together, and I consider her an aristocrat of the spirit.

DRISS HASSAM, MD and FACS

In this world today, when Sunni and Shia Muslims are fighting each other like Christians did in the Crusades when the Crusader's first conquest approved by the pope was sacking Christian Byzantium, Dr. Driss Hassam represents the majority of peace-loving Muslims. His life is extraordinary.

He was born on February 13, 1930, in Ras-Asfour, a small Algerian town on the Moroccan border, where his father, Hassam Habib, and his mother, Sebbane Chezala, lived because his father was a forest ranger. Patrolling the forest on horseback with a French colleague was an important responsibility in such an isolated area of Algeria. Poachers from both Morocco and Algeria often invaded the thickly wooded area. Driss's birth in Ras-Asfour was accomplished without aid from a doctor or a midwife, but only with the help of a neighbor, the wife of his father's, a French colleague.

The Hassams moved soon to a much more lively town, Tlemcen, where there were several schools, a university, and a military hospital, but the family lived in a small house with limited facilities. The city is located at 2,600 feet and avoids the humidity of the Mediterranean coast with fresh breezes coming from the nearby mountain chain. In any case, growing up there was still difficult for Driss, especially when he started attending a L'ecole primaire. For example, if he happened to be late, he was beaten hard ten times on the tips of his fingers of his right hand, palm up, with a two-foot long ruler. As a result of his tardiness, he was also given a note to take home from his school for his father, who exacted the customary treatment of another beating at home. A leather whip was applied to his naked legs until he screamed in pain. Yet he has commented, "In spite of that, I loved and respected my father."

Driss remembers his father quoting a General Clouzot, who was so conscientious in school that he finally reached the level of a general. This man was to be a model for young Driss.

The next big boost in his education came through attending a Catholic summer school. While there, Driss got up at 5:00 AM to do his school homework, starting at 8:00 AM, and then returning home by 5:00 PM to begin his French homework. His elder brother, Mustapha, supervised his homework, and if he made mistakes, he was punished with a slap on the face or a ruler on the palm of his hand.

Can you imagine if all this punishment Driss received in his early life has been discovered today in our American society? Such harsh treatment against children would be subject to prosecution, but Driss has shrugged it off.

What came next is almost unbelievable. Even though his family was of a nonpracticing Muslim faith, he was submitted to its protocol, and thus at seven years of age, he endured a horrific and painful circumcision by a religious leader, who, without any medical help or anesthesia, did the gruesome deed. All he said to Driss was "Be strong. Be a man. Do not cry!" Driss remembered the incident as being so painful that he never ever forgot how he was treated.

The next trial in his life was to endure undiagnosed typhoid fever, leaving him weak and emaciated, lying sick in his bed each day. He was saved by the intervention of a French female neighbor. Why? Because she told his mother in no uncertain terms that Driss needed to be in a hospital to receive immediate medical IVs or he would die. Driss believed that he survived as an ill teenager only because of her kindness, and after he became well again, he grew strong enough to enter a local college for a six-year program.

What helped him the most in his life and education personally then was reading the famous Arabian fables in the *One Thousand and One Nights*, such as the tales told by Scheherazade that deal with coincidence, reverse causation, and self-fulfilling prophesies. One story most of us are familiar with is "Sinbad the Sailor," and who has not seen recently in the States *The Thief of Bagdad* or the Disney film *Aladdin*? They inspired him deeply, as many of us have been.

Yet another sad episode of his early life was about to begin. In 1945, his father became very ill, and then dying at age sixty-one, left his mother to face many responsibilities alone.

His three brothers had moved out of town. His sister, in a prearranged marriage, did the same, leaving Driss to live alone with a mother who became involved with what Driss described as a "shady" character who had no love for Driss. This fellow sought him out to beat him whenever he could, driving Driss out of the house to sleep often at night in a tree in a local park. His older brother, Zaher, heard about his treatment and came to his rescue by inviting Driss to live with him in Oran, the second-largest city of Algeria on its northwestern Mediterranean coast. There he continued his studies in a local college and later moved to live with his other brother Mustapha in Meknes, Morocco, successfully passing his exams for a baccalaureate degree in order to attend medical school in Paris, France.

Fortunately, he was offered a scholarship based on his grades, which enabled him to train for his medical career at the Faculty of Medicine, eventually passing the *Externat des hopitaux de Paris*, which prepared him for another six years of direct experience with the sick and disabled.

However, he encountered a culture shock by witnessing in cafés, homes, even hospitals a free consumption of alcoholic beverages. In his Muslim country, this custom was totally taboo. Yet he became used to it in time, perhaps sooner than imagined. He also met his future wife, a young Dutch girl named Jacqueline, who was studying at the Sorbonne. But for reasons of his own—probably feeling not on her level in some way because he was from a colony of France—he failed to tell the truth about his origins. He tricked her into making her believe he was from Greece.

He bought a Vespa motor scooter that enabled him to see her more often, because she lived in a different arrondissement, but then after confessing that he was Algerian by birth and not a Greek at all, he was surprised that it didn't bother her. Thus encouraged, he took her, and the Vespa as well, to Algeria to visit formally his family. That was a successful trip using his scooter to get about the country, so when they returned to Paris, they were wed in 1957.

The two were soon blessed with a daughter, Soraya, a year later, and at the same time, Driss decided that his specialty in medicine would be surgery. Consequently, he was fortunate enough to become sponsored by the Unitarian Service Committee as an intern, not in Paris, but far away in the States, in particular, at St. Vincent Hospital in Worcester, Massachusetts. One of his first challenges was to learn enough English to help sick patients in the ER when on call. His second child, Karim, was born in 1958, just before he left St. Vincent's for another hospital, this time in Boston, at the Cambridge City Hospital.

A third child, a boy, was born, Khaalil, in 1960, but a difficult decision faced the family after he was accepted as a surgical resident at Columbia Presbyterian Hospital in New York City. Since he could not afford lodging in that expensive metropolis, his wife and children decided to go back to Holland until he was more established. A long wait occurred until Driss was asked to be a third-year surgical resident at St. Mary's Hospital in Rochester, New York, where he and his family were able to be together at last.

In 1963, he completed his surgical training, but because his visa was about to expire, he had to leave the country. He was offered a position at the South Hampton General Hospital in England, where his family once again spent time with his mother-in-law not too far away across the channel in Holland.

It was at this time that his conscience began to bother him about the sick that needed medical attention in his home country, so after the English residency, they all traveled to Algeria. Once there, however, he was dismayed by the recently made independent country, freed of

France's colonial presence, which now demanded pseudo-communist sessions before he could practice. He refused, believing it unethical that politics came before helping the medically in need. So once again, the family pulled up stakes, but since he still had to wait before re entering the States, he moved instead to Germany.

He became a civilian physician for the US Army in Giessen, which acquainted him more with American ways. After a third son, Merwan, was born, he had accomplished the regulations for entering America again and was offered a position in the General Hospital, Springfield, Rhode Island. He also served as a house physician at a VA Hospital, called the Soldiers Home in Holyoke, Massachusetts.

At last, a permanent position as a practicing surgeon opened up after passing the exam to be licensed in New York State, and so the Hassam family settled in Plattsburg, New York, where his fourth son, Driss, was born.

There was so much stress in all his different education sites, his many journeys, and the problem of constantly finding lodging adequate for his growing family that he developed a facial paralysis that affected permanently his left eye and his speech temporarily, but he pressed on. He took an exam to be a board-certified surgeon and was successful. His practice flourished. Because he spoke French, he also took on some French Canadian patients from across the border, but he treated all his patients, of any language and background, as his "family." As an innovator, he was the first to introduce the practice of colonoscopy and of laparoscopic cholecystectomy to Plattsburg.

Driss and Jacqueline retired in 1998, but he insists his retirement was just a new phase in his peripatetic, exciting, but stressful life.

Did he take seriously the lesson of General Clouzot? More than his father could have conceived. Just think what this serious and intelligent immigrant went through to become settled in the United States. Yet we are a nation of immigrants, past or present, and many have gone through similar trials like this native Algerian and Hollander have.

Now Driss and Jacqueline live part of the year in Naples, Florida, where Helen Gorman introduced us to them at a meeting of Alliance Francaise. We are very fortunate to know such a man of sterling character, and I consider Driss to be a special aristocrat of the spirit. Truly, the grace of God, and as he would devoutly say, of Allah, has been with the two through all their challenges but especially through their many accomplishments. They have almost lived "a thousand and one nights" themselves.

JOHN C. HARDY JR.

We became acquainted with June and Jack Hardy in Onteora, and soon we were fast friends for more than thirty-five years, but as a consequence of their being Manhattan residents, we also saw them frequently in the city when they lived on Sutton Place. Elsie became such a good friend to June that the two traveled together, and in fact, June introduced her to her mother, Mrs. Kay Manchee, who lived at the time in Naples, Florida, off Gulf Shore Boulevard. She was an attractive older woman and a very determined person, whose husband had been president of Macy's in the city. Once, when Jim and Louise Beard, Elsie's parents, were visiting her in Naples, Mr. Beard, who was a former University of Texas football player, became very nervous when Mrs. Manchee drove them around Naples. Why? Because he noticed that Kay was ignoring stop signs on residential Crayton Road. He reminded her that she had just run through one, not bothering to stop at all. But she simply replied, "Oh, don't worry. No one was coming on the adjacent street, was there?"

Jim therefore tightened his seatbelt and said no more, thinking how necessary it was in Texas, where he lived, not to ignore those large red signs for fear of an accident or an arrest by its diligent police. The first time June and Elsie flew to Naples to visit June's mother, my wife fell in love with Florida's beaches and its relaxed hospitality. Those happy experiences of my wife prompted us much later to settle in Naples part time when retired.

Jack attended McGill University in Canada for his MBA and before that was an undergraduate major in chemistry at the University of Delaware. He was born in 1927, and June, in 1929. He is a serious person who has a big laugh and is very sharp at answering questions about chemical or financial problems. He has a very sound memory of such things. June is a pretty, wide-eyed, smiling lady who loves to be helpful and is very communicative. She is also a very good artist. When we first knew Jack, he worked as an analyst for Standard and Poor's rating company in New York City. Then the Hardys soon began attending the Church of the Epiphany regularly, although Jack took seriously his previous scheduled duties as an usher at St. Thomas's Church on Fifth Avenue. Eventually, he was elected to Epiphany's vestry, and the two participated fully in our parish life.

Jack's brother, Daniel, we soon found out, was an ordained Episcopal priest and had moved to England, where he became a theological professor at the University of Birmingham and later at Cambridge. Jack's niece, Daniel's daughter, married a collaborator of Daniel Hardy at Cambridge, David F. Ford, a well-known regius professor of divinity and author of several books. Debra Ford is an ordained Church of England priest and chaplain at Cambridge Hospital's Addenbrooke section for the mentally ill.

Previously, while I was rector of the Epiphany, Marin Seeley, one of my assistants for four years, who was also from England, eventually returned to his homeland and married a female Anglican priest. The two with family moved to Cambridge, where he was at first an assistant to David Ford. Now he is the dean of the seminary at Cambridge. Sometimes when I hear of these serendipitous encounters, I truly believe it is a small world, along with Walt Disney, but Jack's family was committed to the church, as one can see, and the church, regardless of country, is much like a worldwide extended family.

Jack and June once visited us in Paris, where the four of us took a long road trip in my small car to Alsace-Lorraine because her great-grandfather came from there and was an expert crystal designer named Christian Dorflinger.

When he left Alsace for the advantages of his trade and personal skills in the States, he settled in White Mills, Pennsylvania, where he began a crystal factory. Today it is a museum with one of our country's largest collections of hand-cut crystal from the past.

After we reached the area in Alsace-Lorraine where Dorflinger learned his expertise of creating crystal, June was welcomed with open arms by the workers in the Saint Louis factory, where Christian had originated. We then had an escorted overview of the site as well as a demonstration on how to blow glass. It was truly amazing to see how it was done. I can still, in my mind, picture a local expert standing, with a long pipe, beginning to blow what looked like a shiny small bubble until it took on a predicted shape, was crafted some more and then cooled, producing a florid and artistic crystal piece. We stayed in interesting hotels en route and ate equally interesting Alsatian food before returning to Paris.

Jack and June were also very supportive of us when we were on the road, raising funds for the cathedral from the friends of the cathedral who had returned home to the States. Our budget in Paris always had a shortfall, or we were forced to make costly repairs, so we reached out for extra support in America. These were men and women who had spent time in Paris or who had lived there and appreciated the cathedral being a home away from home. We labeled them our alumni.

Our annual trips for such usually began in Dallas, then on to Nashville, next would be Florida, finally ending our soirees in Washington, DC, and New York City, where we coordinated with the biannual meeting of the Board of Foreign Parishes, which owned the cathedral property. I was obligated to give an annual report.

In Florida, Mrs. Marta Weeks, an Episcopal priest from a geologist family, hosted one session in Miami, and June and Jack hosted another in Naples in their spacious high-rise apartment. It was a lot of work for June, which included invitations for guests, hors d'oeuvres, drinks, and hospitality arrangements, but it was for a good cause, and we were longtime friends.

Most of all, June and Jack have helped us move to Naples. One delivery of furniture from Paris arrived before we did, and the two rolled up their sleeves to help van deliveries properly locate tables and chairs in the condominium we had purchased. The two had also helped us find the right spot in which to live by recommending a real estate firm, and when we stayed with them in Naples, they carted us about in their car to see everything available. Once we decided on a location, they watched over the condominium in Pelican March while we were abroad until we could arrive in person. When we finally moved for good, we attended church services with them every Sunday. They never missed.

They also allowed our daughter and her children at various times to stay with them. Both June and Jack have had the knack to know how to encourage them, and this included our grown son Ernest when he sought to earn an MBA. They have been like unrelated uncles and aunts to both our children and grandchildren. We often have lunches or dinners together because they are always stimulating and hospitable, relating to us the last speech given about domestic finances or foreign affairs, for example, at Naples' Forum Club. Elsie and I consider both to be aristocrats of the spirit, who, without children themselves, have helped others as if they were true family.

FRANK GIUNTA, MD

When we settled in Naples in the winter, we met new friends, some younger, some older. One older couple was Dr, and Mrs. Frank Giunta (Lib), who were originally from Rhode Island but lived part time then in Massachusetts. Somehow I met Frank on the Pelican Marsh golf course and club, and we began playing golf together, where I found out how old he was. I believe he was about eighty-nine when we began playing, and he continued for another two or three years until he was beginning to slow down because of aches and pains, like most of us.

We also attended the monthly socials in our Pelican Marsh subdivision, called Clermont, where we became acquainted with our new neighbors. It always is a BYO and potluck at our small clubhouse next to the common swimming pool, but somehow Frank and Lib's offering for the evening was unique. Chuckling, with a smile on his face, he claimed his meatballs that he offered were from an Italian family recipe. I took him at that time at his word because they were delicious. As we became better acquainted, he informed us that he was a retired pediatrician and that Lib, his spouse, was a retired nurse. He was almost always jovial, sharp witted, not tall, with a sly smile and a happy attitude. Colin and Marian Appleton often oversaw these group sessions with the help of all the members.

One time when we had a chance to talk longer together, jocular Frank told me that he was in World War II in 1944–1946 as a full army medical doctor, not a children's specialist, and was stationed in Okinawa after we captured the island. He said he was handed the full responsibility to take care of soldiers, and most of the time, aside from colds or pneumonia, illness was caused by syphilis contracted by the local prostitutes.

Finally, when the base received the new drug penicillin to take care of the situation, he was able to stop infections. Yet he worried about the native girls at a popular brothel that kept transmitting the disease. So he took it upon himself to go to the ladies' public house to offer each of them doses that would stop the spread of the disease, that is, until his commander heard about it, telling him that in no uncertain terms he did not have permission to minister to former enemies of the United States because it had not yet been officially approved. Well, as he told me, as one expected, that didn't stop the disease multiplying, but he just did the best he could.

On another occasion, he said that he had a full pediatric practice in a clinic for years in Rhode Island, and later in Boston, and one of the debilitating illnesses after childbirth in the earlier days was jaundice in some babes. Why? He wondered. He did intense research with others to rid the newborn afflicted with jaundice caused by a malfunctioning liver and the rises in bilirubin levels that could cause anemia, abnormal neurological findings, and death. He worked together especially with a group of physicians who cared for infants with Rh erythroblastosis to form a tedious procedure of exchange transfusion. Evidently, the jaundice was caused by genetic inheritance in some cases.

Frank was quiet about many of his achievements, but behind the modest outward appearance, he was a very caring man who had accomplished much in his professional life, ably supported by his equally intelligent wife, Lib. He began having some serious bladder problems and lived successfully off and on for several years with a catheter, even playing golf. But when he was about ninety-four, I went by to see him at home, just to chat. He was Roman Catholic, and I was Episcopalian/ Anglican, but we understood each other. He said that he thought the end was near. He didn't want to go on living like he was, causing trouble for his wife and family, and he asked for a blessing. I said our Book of Common Prayers of unction with him and encouraged him to feel better. He seemed relieved in a way I could not personally understand, but I never forgot those moments with this brave doctor. He inspired me! Along the way, we had met his daughter, wonderful grandsons, and his son. Lib has moved to an easier place without stairs in which to live nearby.

After Frank passed away on April 18, 2013, his burial office was at St. John the Evangelist Roman Catholic Church not far from us. The service was officiated by the assistant priest of that parish, and the liturgy was similar to ours, so I felt at home as a guest. I still think about this aristocrat of the spirit with deep fondness and remember him well, especially his meatballs. He confessed somewhere toward the end of his life about the recipe. Was it an old family one from Italy, or just Costco's meatballs and commercial Ragu sauce? You tell me.

GEORGE LORD SELDEN

George and Ann Selden are our friends who live in New York City and in Onteora Park of the Catskill Mountains. We have known them ever since we purchased our cottage, Crowfoot, one of the first houses we later found out that had been built in the park in 1888–1889. As a matter of fact, our home was used to board guests and visitors who would take their meals next door at the first field house, the Bear and Fox Inn. Now the Bear and Fox is a private residence. When we moved to Onteora as a retreat from the city in 1977, George and Ann lived down the street. However, the family soon left for Boston, where George was asked to assist again in his family company. Then the two returned ten years later to the city and to Onteora, where they restored another house on Cranberry Road.

Onteora contains an interesting assortment of members, some from New York City like lawyer Brooks and Kate Clark; Peter and Louise Palmer, also from New York City, both families our neighbors. Peter has had a deep interest in helping the Onteora Arboretum, begun by Dr. Edward H. Ahrens. Pete Ahrens, as we knew him, was a researchers at Rockefeller University in New York City who discovered the role of cholesterol in the cause of heart-related ailments. Sissal Cooper Boss, from Norway, and her husband, Peter Boss, a former nuclear submarine officer; Mary Gaillard, her sister Martha and brother Bill, a pediatric neurosurgeon, children of Allan and Dave Gaillard, an Onteora historian; Lou Pauly and Carole Clark, professors at Toronto University; Skip Nay, a surgeon, and children, all professional acting ladies who have acted in the Onteora Theatre; Tony Milbank and his wife from France; Pierce Sioussat, who sings in the choir, and his wife, Abby, an actress; Sebastian de le Selle, from France, and his wife, Nancy; lawyer John Reboul and his wife, Josie, also from France; Irmgard Sell, an artist from Germany; and Peter Hansen were also members.

The late Peter Rowley, a patron of old mansions and churches from land he inherited in England, and his wife, Terez, from Hungary, have been personal friends. Peter sponsored a conference on peace in New

York City before his untimely death and also provided a large donation of a million pounds for St. Neots' Lord of the Manor Rowley Arts Center in England. In fact, the Rowley Screen within is the only cinema screen across the country.

Patrick Curley, whose father was ambassador to France, and his wife, Jane, are members. My son, who works for the UN and is trying to restore and save the Catskill Railway line from Kingston to Phoenicia, is a member. His wife, Holly, who is head of All Souls vestry, and children Caroline and Louisa, are also part of the Onteora Community, along with the Raymonds, William and his wife, Gillian, who is from England. Bruce Johnson, CEO of Sears' outside divisions, and his lawyer wife, Kathryn, born in Peru, enhance the membership of the club along with Arthur Lubow, advertising specialist, and his wife, Anne.

Onteora itself was founded by writers, artists, and actors from New York City and still has many who are devoted to similar pursuits, like Mark and Elena Patterson, originally from South Africa, or Mike Magdol, a New Yorker or Piers Playfair, from England, and the most generous benefactor, Charles Royce, all who have been instrumental in refurbishing Tannersville and environs or restoring the Orpheum Theatre in town or bringing international artists to the mountaintop. The McCaffreys and the Moores, the Struthers family, Tony Milbank, who is an advocate of financial outreach to the local community through All Souls Church, or Tanner Rose. Skip Pratt, from a fellow club named Twilight, also heavily supports the local arts.

Richard Baumann, the club's able director who is a war veteran from the Bush War, as it was known with Angola (not Iraq), and his wife, Sandy, are from South Africa, and golf professional Joe Benevento, who owned his own golf course before semiretirement, and his wife, Maryann, "man" the golf shop. The membership of Onteora is diverse and very international, as I have illustrated.

Yet it is not just members of the clubs—Onteora, Twilight, or Elka—but it is also the town of Tannersville that has creative people where many have lived for generations.

Take the Thorpe family for example. There is Phil, the father, and his two sons, Eric and Brad, who sell and repair GMC cars. My son and I bought all our cars from them because they are so trustworthy, just like Ed Thorpe, whose sons are contractors under the direction of his oldest, Greg. Ed's grandfather was one of the founders of Greene County. Bruce Feml, and friends as well as family who help him, owns a horse farm and is a most competent general contractor. Tony Lucido has become the "owner" of the local US Post Office and has a masonry contracting business, and his son-in-law Bobby Hermance is a specialist in garden care. Wally Gallagher is in possession of the sole liquor store and is like a wise counselor to many, and Dr. Robert Schneider has a medical clinic that cares for everyone. Donny Van Falkenberg is at your door for foundation work when you need it. Wayne Pierce will make sure that your electrical outlets are doubly safe. Dolph Semenza owns the Village Market. When Hurricane Irene shut down local towns from intense flooding and the power was lost for days, his generator-operated store was kept open to care for everyone in need. Peggy Graham and her ninety-five-year-old mother, Mrs. Betty Meehan, know more about each member of the club than they do themselves. There are many heroes and heroines in the area, and this becomes more evident every year because the town appreciates the club, and the club needs each of them.

George's family is also interesting, at least to me it is. A cousin of his grandfather was George Baldwin Selden, who was a patent lawyer, a soldier, and an inventor. He patented in the late nineteenth century the first "road engine," that is, before it was used to power automobiles. George's father, James Kirkland Selden, was the owner of Selden Worsted Mills that soon became Methuen International Mills. George himself worked when younger as an assistant superintendent, learning the ropes, I suspect, and then switched gears and went into banking. After all, he was a graduate of Andover and Harvard with a BS degree, but then the family emergency occurred when his father planned to retire. Who will run the business? That was when George assumed the responsibility and returned to his family's company, leaving New York altogether.

As soon as George became the new president of the company, he was immediately faced with many tough decisions. The "worsted" competition had stiffened globally, and he was forced to travel often to London and Scotland, but due to the unstable economic climate, George decided to sell the company. That transaction must have been difficult because of his family connection, but George believed it was the best move. Then George wisely decided to officially retire.

Ann, who is quite beautiful, was born in California and grew up in Hillsborough, not far from San Francisco. Her father was president of a large real estate company. Ann attended Hollins College in Virginia and then graduated from the University of California. George and Ann have two children, James, named after his grandfather, and Jenny, who is married to Taylor Gray, whose grandfather was the Episcopal bishop of Connecticut. The Seldens have five grandchildren.

When the two were once again settled in Onteora, we began to see them often, and especially at Onteora's All Souls Church, where George and Ann took a strong lead. He has been a regular usher, a treasurer, and a vestry member, and he, like several others, never missed a Sunday. George and Fran Everett, another Onteorean, also discovered a vibrant Presbyterian Church in New York City and became very active; Fran did the bookkeeping, and George became a lay minister.

George is a very self-disciplined person but infinitely polite and very humorous. He seldom goes out to dinner in the evenings without a tie. I understand him, because I grew up with a father who went to his office every day wearing a tie, as I do often as well for a night out. George is no longer a youngster now, for after all, he was born in 1925, but he is still full of energy.

It is a known fact that when one plays golf, much of our inner selves rise to the surface, fortunately or not, in what has been called one of the toughest sports to play. It demands a perfection that is out of reach of most players, but then one learns to persevere. It becomes a lesson for life, as George and I have learned.

The four of us play a form of "scramble," where we compete as teams, Hunt versus Selden, but which stimulates each of us to do a little better, regardless of who wins. Sometimes we tie each other in our score, or one of the family teams wins, but the challenge is always there, lurking in the background.

Religious faith is very similar; there is so much in the world that seeks to defeat a positive take on life, whether the adversary is illness or some overwhelming humanitarian tragedy of displaced people or by just viewing images of innocents having their heads cut off by a group that wants to enflame rivalries in the Middle East. How about a compulsive Czar-like figure who pushes forcibly for freed countries to return to the fold of an enslaved past?

Faith is not based on happiness, however, but such contentment can be a byproduct. Faith is basically a result of persevering with the conviction that God is on the side of the innocent, that he wants the best for each of us, and that we have our own role to play in his long-term victory. The judgments of God in history are moral in time. I believe that George upholds this view, as I do. Is this the same as golf? No, but I draw a comparison from those who have to persevere but retain hope.

George is the first to say, "Good shot, Elsie." Ann joined him. We say the same, no matter if we lose. George compliments me even when I drive the four of us in our car somewhere in a normal fashion and return safely. He is pleasant company. That is why I consider George and Ann to be aristocrats of the spirit, religious but cheerful people to have as good friends.

POSTSCRIPT

I T IS MY belief that these aristocrats of the spirit encourage us to cope with our daily challenges. In his book *The Power and the Glory*, Graham Greene described a flawed but faithful whiskey priest, who, after he was hunted down in the Mexican Revolution when priests were persecuted, reminisced the following in his prison cell before his execution (page 251):

> It seemed to him at that moment that it would have been quite easy to have been a saint. I would only have needed a little self-restraint and a little courage.

Perhaps, but is that the question we should ask of ourselves? How much can we triumph as well with a little self-restraint and courage, even in the light of all our struggles? Is it possible to understand seriously what the priest thought in his cell about sainthood in our culture today labeled by some as an Age of Entitlement, with selfies dominating our vision? How do we replicate his insight about simple virtues and common decency? Religion at its best offers us the view that the more we give, the more we receive, which is nothing new as Harry Emerson Fosdick, famous pastor at Riverside Church in New York, once reminded us:

> The sea of Galilee and the Dead Sea are made of the same water. It flows down clean and cool from the heights of Herman and the roots of the Cedars of Lebanon, the Sea of Galilee makes beauty of it; the Sea of Galilee has an outlet. It gets to give. But the Dead Sea with the same water makes horror. For the Dead Sea has no outlet. It gets to keep.

In my opinion, not one of the men and women I have listed or mentioned thought only to get and keep, but rather to give. How much are we worth? Our true self-significance is affirmed through thinking of others, worrying about them, and then doing something for or with them. Each aristocrat may not be an actual saint in the classical case, but these aristocrats of the spirit *are, or were, saintly* and have truly inspired my life and that of others.

CPSIA information can be obtained at www.ICGtesting.com
Printed in the USA
LVOW10s0151050815

448707LV00002B/104/P